St. Augustine

St. Augustine

Being and Nothingness

Emilie Zum Brunn

Paragon House Publishers
New York

First English translation

Published by
Paragon House Publishers
90 Fifth Avenue
New York, New York 10011

Originally published as *Le Dilemme de l'Etre et du Ne'ant chez saint Augustin*, with an Appendix originally published in *Dieu et l'Etre*, by Etudes Augustiniennes (Paris), 1978.

Translation prepared by Ruth Namad

Library of Congress Cataloging-in-Publication Data

Zum Brunn, Emilie, 1922–
St. Augustine : being and nothingness in the Dialogs and Confessions.

1. Augustine, Saint, Bishop of Hippo.
2. Ontology—History. 3. Nothing (Philosophy)—
History. I. Title.
B655.Z7Z813 1986 111'.092'4 86–22642
ISBN 0–913729–17–5

Contents

Preface To The Second Edition

To follow the ontic development of the *Dialogues* and *Confessions* is to attempt to "embrace philosophy" personally as one embraces religion, for the sole purpose of such a quest, according to Augustine's intention, is salvation. It is this deep meaning of a soteriological ontology, or an ontology centered on deliverance, which Heidegger was able to formulate according to the Platonic viewpoint that belongs to the common heritage that is found in the great traditions, from India to the Far East. " 'To save' is to bring back into essence, so that the latter may appear, for the first time, as it should."[1]

This is what Augustine is trying to obtain in reflection together with prayer, tears, and supplications, to which the texts quoted here attest. But, for him, to be saved, that is to say, to be brought back into one's own essence, is to be brought back close to the first Essence that, beginning with the *De uera religione,* he identified with Moses' God: "He who is," as I have indicated in this book, *The Dilemma of Being and Nothingness.*

Since then, I have examined the numerous passages in which, all through his different writings, Augustine commented on this name "He who is," which became, thanks to him, the main divine name in the Latin West. I noticed that these texts, while forcefully expressing this ontology of the return, scarcely bring any new elements to the study of the problems of being and of growing in being, elaborated in an almost definitive way in the *Dialogues* and in the *Confessions*. Augustine henceforth was satisfied with drawing from the treasure that he had built up with the help of the "Platonists' books" during his first investigations into understanding faith. But the passages in which he quoted and commented on the Exodus 3:14 verse during the subsequent work do not indicate any less of an evolution in his way of conceiving the intelligibility of faith, for the Scriptures play a more important part there than in the *Dialogues*.

"These texts represent . . . something of a *sui generis* in the development of Augustinian thought. If the ontological themes there are not new, the way in which Augustine uses them in his interpretation of the Bible combines with the *exercitatio scripturarum* which then takes the place of the *disciplina scientiarum* or rather takes up its part." Such is the conclusion of this later study, published here as an Appendix.[2]

The author, in these passages, goes back to a patristic tradition that is already established. But he uses this verse in an unequalled way, in the abundance of these "comments" on Exodus 3:14 — about fifty of them — as much as in that of the scriptural parallels. It is thus that he succeeds in reading in the Scriptures themselves a confirmation of the Neo-Platonic metaphysics of the return, and that he gives the latter a Christian foundation by drawing a parallel between the *ego sum qui sum* revealed to Moses and the *ego sum (ἐγώ εἰμι)* of the Gospel according to Saint John: "Before Abraham was, I am" (Exod. 8:58. Cf. 8:24 and 8:28).

Just as important is the complementary quality that Augustine picks up henceforth between the Exodus verse 3:14 and that of Exodus 3:15: "I am the God of Abraham, Isaac, and Jacob," these two verses making up "a sort of manuscript containing the sum of the divine mysteries" (Sermon 7). The first, "I am who I am," says what God is in himself; the second teaches the economy of salvation. Contrary to the interpretation, which will later be that of Pascal, Augustine thus does not contrast these two verses one with the other, except if there is a denial of the Mediator. It is a question of advancing, if possible, from knowing the God of Abraham, Isaac, and Jacob to knowing the "philosophers' God," that is to say from faith to understanding faith, by leading towards the final state, which will be for everyone that of intellective intuition. By right, it is the second of these cognitions that lays the foundations for the first: "*sic sum ipsum esse ut nolim hominibus deesse*" ("I am Being itself so as not to want to be absent from men." Sermon 7). The intellect thus is not separated from salvation or deliverance, since Christ himself has come to teach the *doctrina rationis*. Therefore "the true philosopher himself is a lover of God." It is thus that Augustine adopts the Neo-Platonic ontology *in as much as it is an ontology of the soul's deliverance*, while expressing by means of it his own doctrine of salvation.

Let us point out a different interpretation in Werner Beierwaltes. According to him, Augustine ushered in a Christian theology of Exodus by his thought on "the name of mercy," while his speculation on the "name of eternity" remained determined by the thought structures that characterize Greek philosophy.[3]

The theme of the growth in being, a major theme of this book, has scarcely been discussed, as far as I know, in the rather rare texts recently published on Augustinian ontology.[4] Nothing is found there that recalls Maurice Blondel, John Burnaby, Jules Chaix-Ruy, and Ragnar Holte's thoughts on ontogenesis. This theme, however, appears at least in its counterpoint, "to lead towards nothingness," in a work by René Nelli on the dualism of the Catharists in the thirteenth century, as well as in an article by Goulven Madec, criticizing the arguments held by the author — mainly the one concerning the influence that the Augustinian conception of *nihil* would have exerted on Medieval Catharism. The major text that Nelli recalls for this subject is the verse from John 1:3: "Without him nothing was made" *(sine ipso factum est nihil), nihil* becoming in the Catharic interpretation a synonym of this bad reality that is the tangible world.[5]

Let us point out in connection with this that, without going as far as "reifying" it thus, the heavy interpretation of *nihil* met great success in the Middle Ages, in particular in Rheno-Flemish mysticism and in the theology of the Rhenish school. It is found, for example, within the *In Iohannem* of Master Eckhart, in a rather long development in which these words from John 1:3 are repeated as in a leitmotif and are the subject for appealing several times to Augustine's authority. Here are two excerpts:

> But sins and as a universal law wrong doings are not beings. From which one concludes that they are not made by (God) but without him. And it is exactly what the continuation of the text says: *without him was made naught*, that is to say sin and wrongdoing, according to Augustine. . . .
> . . .even though other realities (than the Son and the Holy Ghost) are produced or made by realities which are themselves other than God, however all things, be they produced by nature or by art, contain being or any part of being immediately from God himself, in such a way as to permit reading the text in the following order: *All things made by him are* (*omnia facta per ipsum sunt* instead of *omnia per ipsum facta sunt*, v. 3). It follows that *without him was made naught*, that is to say that anything that was made by anyone but him is nothingness. For it is certain that everything that is without being is nothingness. Indeed, how could a thing be without being? Consequently all being and the being of all things comes from God, as it was said earlier.[6]

Perhaps Nelli's work has the advantage of reminding us that it would be necessary for us to refer to the Gnostics and Catharists in order to fully examine transformations of nothingness in Western thought. A curious turn of events for the ex-Manichean! For it is evident, as Madec emphasizes, that he wanted to avoid — contrary to these Catharists who use expressions similar to his — any dualism, any reification of nothingness. It is precisely to contrast with the Manicheans on this crucial point that he borrowed from the Neo-Platonic philosophers the conception of a wrong doing that is nothingness, of an offense that is "nihilation." Concerning this, we find in Nelli and in his critic two translations competing with certain passages from the *Soliloquia animae*, a pseudo-Augustinian text of the thirteenth century. The first of these authors affirms, and the second denies, the influence of this text on Medieval Catharism. Although I am unqualified to give a judgement concerning the possible influence of the *Soliloquia animae* on the Cathars, I would like to examine some passages from this apocryphus. The reader will be able to compare them with the texts on "nihilation" quoted mostly from p. 49 to p. 55 of the *Dilemma*, as well as with those that express spiritual participation with the expression "to be with God" *(esse cum deo)*, pp. 13 to 20. We can add to this last list the reference mentioned by Madec in the *Confessions* 10, 27, 38: "You were with me and I was not with you" *(mecum eras et tecum non eram)*.

Here are the excerpts promised, in Nelli's translation, which conveys the strength of the Latin *nihil* and *annihilare*. This last expression seems to me to be faithful to Augustine's thought, even though I did not find it in him:

> Oh Lord Word, oh God Word, by whom all things were made, and without whom was made naught, woe betide me, wretched, so often reduced to nothingness *(totiens annihilato)*, since you are the Word by whom all things were made and I am without you, without whom nothing was made."
> "Yes, I have become wretched and I have been reduced to nothingness and I did not find that out, because you are the truth and I was not with you, my iniquities have

> hurt me and I did not suffer, because you are life and I was not with you, by whom all things were made, without whom was made naught: and that is why I have become nothingness, because what leads to nothingness is nothingness . . . Wrong doing, therefore, is nothingness, since surely it was made without the Word, without whom was made naught . . . to be separated from the Word, by whom all things were made is nothing other than to lose strength and to go from effect to defect *(deficere et a facto transire in defectum)*, for without him there is nothingness. Thus each time you stray from good works, you separate yourself from the Word, for it is he who is what is good; and therefore you become nothingness, because you are without the Word, without whom was made naught . . .[7]

From this Augustine-like text of the thirteenth century, let us go back to Augustine's influence, not known enough up to now, on the Cologne School, in particular on Ulrich of Strasbourg and on Master Eckhart, studied by Alain de Libera in an article on "Being and Good: Exodus 3:14 in Rhenish Theology."[8] In it, the author shows the part played by Augustinian metaphysics in the theories about the Revealed Name, "He who is," proposed by Ulrich and by Eckhart. In it, he also shows how the latter in a way goes beyond Augustine since it is a question for the Rhenish Dominican of "becoming God" by becoming being. I have also emphasized the importance of this influence in the Eckhartian doctrine of "the process of being" or of "becoming being," according to which, as in Rheno-Flemish mysticism, man must become one and the same essence with God.[9]

Let us point out in conclusion that, from a more general and speculative point of view than the *Dilemma*'s, we shall find suggestive judgements about Augustinian ontology in the critical synthesis proposed by Kurt Flasch in *Augustin: Einführung in sein Denken.*[10] In it, the author shows, and that was necessary, that one of those who spoke the best about spiritual experience, and who lived it in the most passionate way, did not escape himself the scleroses of reification by trying to enclose the life of the spirit in a dogmatic net. The effort towards liberation is then transformed into imprisonment, according to one of those inner contradictions that no one better than the author of the *Confessions* was able to describe and to deplore. It does not come to any less that it is in great part thanks to him that the Latin West was able to express in the cultural language that was familiar to it the experience of a Revelation whose language was still foreign to it — and that in this soteriological ontology, whose meaning had started to be forgotten by Christianity after the Feudal Ages, Augustine was able to promote the symbiosis of the new religion of salvation with the ancient quest for deliverance.

NOTES

1. M. Heidegger, "La Question de la technique," in *Essais et conférences*, trans. A. Préaud (Paris: Gallimard, 1958), p. 38.

2. E. Zum Brunn, "*L'Exégèse augustinienne de ego sum qui sum et la métaphysique de l'Exode*," in *Dieu et l'Etre, Exégèses d'Exode 3, 14 et de Coran 20, 11–24*, (Paris: Etudes Augustiniennes, 1978), p. 155. See appendix p. 97.

3. W. Beierwaltes, *Platonismus und Idealismus* (Frankfurt: 1972), p. 77, n. 99.

4. At least in those into which I have been able to enquire. Here are some titles that might interest the reader: A. Giovanni, "*Creazione ed essere nelle Confessioni di Sant' Agostino*," in *Revue des Etudes Augustiniennes* (1974), pp. 285–312; D. Dubarle, "*L'Ontologie théologale d'Augustin*," in *Recherches Augustiniennes*, vol. 16 (Paris: 1981), pp. 197–288; N. Nagasawa, *St. Augustine's Ontology* (in Japanese), in *Studies of Western Medieval Thought: Essays in Honour of Professor Ken Ishiharu* (Tokyo: 1965).

5. See R. Nelli, *La Philosophie du catharisme: Le Dualisme radical au XIIIe siècle* (Paris: Payot, 1975); and G. Madec, "*Nihil cathare et nihil augustinien*," in *Revue des Etudes Augustiniennes* (1977), pp. 92–112.

6. Eckhart, *Expositio s. euangelii sec. Iohannem*, chap. 1, 1–5, *Lateinische Werke*, vol. 3 (Stuttgart: Kohlhammer, 1936). See §§ 52–58, pp. 44.4–48.14. French translation to be published in *Oeuvres latines de Maître Eckhart*, vol. 6, *Commentaire de Jean, I, le Prologue*, critical text of the German edition, along with an annotated translation by A. de Libera, E. Wéber, and E. Zum Brunn (Paris: Cerf, 1987), pp. 239–335.

7. Translation by R. Nelli, *op cit.*, pp. 163–66. Cf. G. Madec's translation, *op. cit.*, pp. 98–100, as well as the Latin text (Paris: éd. des Mauristes, 1685), Appendix, cols. 83–104, and Migne's Patrology, 863–98.

8. Published in "*Celui qui est.*" *Interprétations juives et chiétiennes d'Exode 3:14* ed. by A. de Libera and E. Zum Brunn (Paris: Cerf, 1986), pp. 127–162.

9. See, among others, E. Zum Brunn, "*Dieu n'est pas être*," in *Maître Eckhart à Paris: Une critique médiévale de l'ontothéologie* (Paris: Presses Universitaires de France, 1984), p. 84 ff; ed. by E. Zum Brunn and A. de Libera, *Maître Eckhart: métaphysique du Verbe et théologie négative* (Paris: Beauchesne, 1984), chap. 1: "Etre Dieu en Dieu." ("To Be God in God").

10. See K. Flasch, *Augustin: Einführung in sein Denken* (Stuttgart: Reclam, 1980), p. 410 ff.

Abbreviations

BA	*Bibliothèque Augustinienne*, Paris
CC	*Corpus christianorum*, Turnhout
CSEL	*Corpus scriptorum ecclesiasticorum latinorum*, Vienna
PL	*Patrologia Latina*, Paris

The spelling distinction u/v has been normalized in favor of u, in accordance with the convention of the *Oxford Latin Dictionary*.

Introduction The Augustinian Semantics of "Esse"

The theme of the ontological growth and reduction of the soul *(magis esse* and *minus esse)* is deeply rooted in a metaphysics that considers in turn Being and beings, the Immutable and that which changes, the Eternal and that which passes. Such a metaphysics is dialectical even in its analysis of that which is created, the latter being constantly referred to the two antithetical terms from which it originates and between which it is situated: absolute Being and absolute nothingness. This hanging between two opposites takes on dramatic meaning when it is a question of the spiritual created being, master — often without understanding it — of its own destiny. For it is up to it to settle either in Being or in a state close to nothingness, according to whether or not it confirms the "wanting-to-be" (*esse uelle*) rooted in it, that is to say the desire of a greater participation in Being than the one which is its own from the simple fact of existing.[1] We are going to attempt to follow the development of this relatively limited theme through Augustine's early works, even if it entails, each time that it will be necessary, calling on the broader metaphysical explanation that we intend to analyze elsewhere.[2]

If it turns towards Being, the soul "is more" *(magis esse, magis magisque esse)*; it "possesses Being itself" *(obtinere ipsum esse)* in which it is "constituted" *(constitui)*, "edified" *(exstrui)*, "stabilized" *(stare)*, "solidified" *(solidificari)*, or even "restored" *(refici)*, re-formed *(reformari)*.[3] If on the contrary the soul turns away from Being, it suffers an ontological loss that makes it "be less" *(minus esse)*, "take a lesser part in Being itself" *(idipsum esse minus habere)*, "fall, suffer a deficiency" *(defici)*, "lead towards nothingness" *(tendere ad nihilum)*, "become nihilated" *(inanescere)*.[4]

This dialectic of *magis esse* and *minus esse* immediately raises a translation problem. How can one convey in English the two different, even opposite, qualities of the Augustinian *esse*, whether it means the ontological plenitude of God and that of the spiritual created being converted to him, or whether this expression designates the inferior forms of participation in Being? We have tried to remain faithful to the Augustinian meaning by using, in the first case, the expression "being" in the strong sense, in the second the expressions "existing" or "existence" with a connotation of ontological want.[5]

We shall use this antithesis to explain rather than to translate Augustine's expressions, since in his works there is no vocabulary for "existing" counterdistinguished from the language of *esse* and *essentia*.[6] That is why we shall often resort to the Latin expressions themselves, when the English translation will seem to us unable to render the exact nuance of the text being considered.

Absolute Being, to pick up again some of these expressions, is *summum esse, ipsum esse, uere esse*, or *quod est*, also expressed, with the help of the Exodus verse 3:14, by the personal forms *ego sum qui sum, qui est*, and in an abbreviated way *sum, est*.[7] In contrast, the ontological deficiency, which characterizes our existence as long as it is not regenerated by the conversion to Being, Augustine calls according to the circumstances *minus esse, non uere esse*, or still *utcumque esse*.[8]

Nevertheless, he proclaims in numerous texts that the gift of existence, as such, is good. Thus, in the first book of the *Confessions*, he sees a participation and an analogy with divine unity in this privileged form of created *esse*, which is also life and understanding.[9] But then he shows how in his case, which he considers representative of the entire human species, he has wasted this gift by sinning since early childhood.[10] His wrong doing was even more aggravated when Augustine, as an adolescent, turned away completely from God's "stability" — a characteristic attribute of Being — something which reduced him to being himself a mere "region of indigence" *(regio egestatis)*, according to the Platonic symbol which identifies the lack of being with spiritual dearth.[11]

Such is our existence in the state of fall, of *auersio*. It is distinguished by radical poverty. He who finds himself in it, or rather who is this indigence, suffers from an inner hunger, which has been rightly defined as a hunger for being.[12] It remained more or less unconscious in Augustine until the time that reading *Hortensius* transformed it into a burning desire for another life, a life of happiness, which could be attained thanks to the wisdom of Ancient Philosophy revealed to him in the works of Cicero.[13]

Augustine then tells about his quest, beginning with his first discovery of philosophy and how, for want of succeeding, he fell again in this meaningless existence, which is in fact a spiritual death. He had hoped to attain true Being *(quod uere est)* through the Manichean religion, which seemed to promise him the realization of his philosophical ideal while allowing him to find Christ once more, as he desired.[14] But it only gave him an illusive representation, because it was founded on the imaginary. That is why, after many long years, thinking, and the trials of life, he finally separated himself from this doctrine. The loss of a friend made him experience the taste of the death of everything that is not the Absolute, without leaving him the resort of turning towards God, since instead, Manicheism had only given him a "phantasm."[15]

What particularly interests us here is the way in which Augustine expressed in retrospect the meaning of this experience in philosophical language: the taste of death for the things here below means their "nonbeing" in comparison with the Absolute in which the soul alone can be founded, that is to say "be."

> Wherever man's soul may turn, it only encounters suffering if it settles anywhere but in you, even if it is to attach itself to beautiful things outside of you and of itself; for

> these would be nothing if they were not by you; they appear and disappear; their advent is like a beginning of being, they grow to perfect it and once this perfection is attained, they come apart in old age and in death and all of them do not reach old age, but all go towards death. For when they appear and lead to being, the faster they grow to get there, the faster also they rush into nothingness.[16]

By attaching itself to temporal things, which carry it along in their race towards nothingness, the soul is wrong about the true finality of its "wanting-to-be" *(esse uelle)*. It can only "be" if, converted thanks to the call of the Word, it goes back to its true abode to be edified and stabilized in him alone who is stable.

> Let my soul praise thee for all these beauties, oh God, you their creator, but let it not allow the corporeal senses to attach it to them by the trap of love. For they go where they have always gone, towards nothingness, and they tear the soul apart with poisoned regrets because it wants to be and loves to find its peace in the object of its love. But it does not find it in the created beings, for they are not stable, they slip away and who can catch them again by means of his carnal senses? Who can seize them, even when they are present? . . . Don't be vain, oh my soul, don't let yourself be deafened by the tumult of your vanity. Listen, you too. The Word himself cries for you to return. It is there that is found the resting place that nothing can disturb, the place where love is not abandoned if it does not let go itself. See how all things come to pass in order to be replaced by others and to form the universe here below in all of its parts. "I, myself, do I go somewhere?" says the Word of God. It is there that you must build your house, store all that comes to you from him, oh my soul, if you are tired of lies. Entrust Truth with all that you hold from it and you will lose nothing; on the contrary, all that had withered in you will blossom again, all your aches will be healed, all that was unsteady in you will be restored, renewed, closely unified and will no longer drag you towards the bottom but will remain stable with you next to God who always remains stable.[17]

Augustine was to grieve some more before understanding the meaning of the taste of death that he had experienced, before finding "what truly is" and discovering the "way" that would make possible for him the conversion by which our eternal abode is erected from here below.

After a period of doubt and despair, he started to hope again for truth, under the influence of Ambrose's preaching. The "Platonists' books" made him discover the meaning behind the statements of the Milan bishop concerning the spirituality of God and of the soul. Up until reading them, their meaning had remained enigmatic for Augustine, still influenced by Manichean materialism.[18] Having learned, owing to these books, to forsake the externality of the imaginary in order to "examine his conscience," he finally succeeded in discovering the true God, "He who is" because he is spirit.

This inner knowledge made him seize the reality of transcendental Being with more assurance than that of his own existence.[19] It showed him at the same time his spiritual unlikeness, that is to say his sin, which set him up in a state of ontological separation. He understood that without the preliminary transformation of his own being, conceived as a growth of this being nihilated by sin, it would be impossible for him to unite with true Being in a participation of knowledge and love.[20] Therefore, he could still only know it from afar, *de longinquo*, with an authentic knowledge, but which is powerless by itself to transform man, to deify him.

Augustine thus places this first stage in his discovery of God-Being at the level of the real, but inefficacious, knowledge, which he will attribute to the Platonic philosophers to whom he owes this discovery.[21] If he relegates to that level the thinkers whom he otherwise holds in such high esteem, it is because their books have proven to be incapable of leading him to the deifying participation to which he aspires. He will only get there thanks to the intermediary of Christ, who, by making the divine sustenance ready to be assimilated by his carnal being, will finally allow him to be constituted in God.[22] Such is the "way," which was to make possible the transformation no longer of his understanding alone but of his entire soul. It is owing to Christ that, instead of seeing and loving true Being only "from afar," he will be "constituted," "edified," and "solidified" in it. On the other hand, we shall see that, if the "Platonists' books" have not allowed him to attain this conversion, which is constitutive of being, it is they nevertheless that have allowed him to express it metaphysically.

This brief reminder is aimed at showing that Augustine interpreted in retrospect his experience of man's relation to God in the ontological language of *magis esse* and *minus esse* in order to throw light on the meaning of his life, mainly during the period which preceded his discovery of the true God, that is of God-Being. He felt the nihilating effect of the *auersio* as long as he did not know that God is true Being, and even as long as he only knew him "from afar," finally to be formed in Him thanks to his conversion to Christ.

We shall now try to follow the dialectic of *magis esse* and *minus esse* step by step through Augustine's early works. Perhaps it is fitting to warn the reader not to expect to find a systematic representation of it. It is far from that, so much so that one of the only critics who, as far as we know, was interested in this theme, lost its trace by looking for it only in the form in which it appears in certain of the early dialogues, that is, in the form closely linked to the "proof" of the soul's immortality.[23] We shall see this theme, on the contrary, appear and reappear in orchestrations that vary with the subjects treated, in order to finally take on unexpected breadth, according to the composition mode, which has been so rightly and so brilliantly compared to the development of a musical theme.[24]

If this way of composing bears the mark of Augustine's personal genius, it also proves he is the heir to ancient philosophy which through a kind of enchantment led the soul back to its true home. It is not simply a question of understanding a truth given from the point of view of pure speculation, but of acceding to it "with the entire soul."[25] Such is the goal of his personal quest and of his didactics. That is why his ontology is an "anagogy" at the same time, as in the "Platonists' books."[26] The "proofs" of "true philosophy," that is to say of Platonic thinking taken up by Christian faith, do not only satisfy the intelligence, but also help man climb up towards God. These "proofs" themselves are constituent elements of being, because the philosophical pursuit is a spiritual exercise.

NOTES

1. See further, p. 37 ff.

2. In a study of the exegesis of *Ego sum qui sum* (Exod. 3:14) in Augustine and Thomas Aquinas. See "*L'Exégèse augustinienne de ego sum qui sum et la métaphysique de l'Exode*" and "*La Métaphysique de l'Exode selon Thomas d'Aquin*" in the collective work *Dieu et l'Etre, Exégèses d'Exode 3,14 et de Coran 20, 11–24* (Paris: Etudes Augustiniennes, 1978), pp. 141–64 and 245–69. The first one is translated here and follows as an Appendix.

3. See further p. 38 ff. and p. 72 ff.

4. See further p. 49 ff.

5. We shall thus use this antithesis with a meaning similar to the one Simone de Beauvoir used in order to comment on the last words of her autobiography, the famous "I've been had": "So, why 'had'? Because the paradox of human life, when one has, as I do, an existentialist vision of the world, is that one looks for being and finally manages only to exist." This comment about the expression "I've been had," in S. de Beauvoir, *La Force des choses* (Paris: Gallimard, 1963), p. 686, was obtained in an interview by Madeleine Gobeil, published in the weekly *Le Nouvel Observateur*, Paris (8 April 1965), p. 20, under the title *Entrer en vieillesse* (Becoming Old). In it S. de Beauvoir succeeded in expressing, in all that it contains not only intellectually but also affectively, the meaning of the ὄντως ὄν, contrasted with the existence that is ours as long as it does not center on the Absolute. It is striking to see that this interpretation, even in its denial, remains faithful to the philosophical tradition originating in Plato. Indeed, we could not remain unaware of the bond that links together existentialist philosophy to Platonic thought, which it repudiates without being able to forget it. The nostalgia for eternity expressed by the last page of *La Force des choses* has been commented on by H.-I. Marrou, *Le Dogme de la résurrection des corps et la théologie des valeurs humaines selon l'enseignement de Saint Augustin*, in *Rev. Et. Augustin* 12 (1966), p. 135.

6. *Existere (ex-sistere)* in Augustine merely has the commonly accepted meaning since classical antiquity of "being born," "coming into existence." The gerund forms *existendi*, *existendo*, and the present participle *existens* are used as replacement forms for the verb *esse*, *essendi*, *essendo*, and *ens* not being in common use, or rarely used, at the time. As for the expression *existentia*, it is not found, as far as we know, in Augustine. Just as *esse* is used with the meaning we attribute to "being" and "existing," *essentia* is used with the meaning of "essence" and "existence." E. Hendrikx, *Introduction au "De Trinitate,"* BA, 15, pp. 39–40: In Saint Augustine, the expressions and the concepts do not always have the clear and definite meaning they have in our current scholastic philosophy. The word *essentia*, for example, sometimes means for him what we mean by *existentia*, sometimes what we mean by *essentia*, and sometimes both at the same time.

7. *De immort. anim.* 11, 18, BA, 5, p. 204: ". . . illa omnia quae quoquo modo sunt ab ea essentia sunt, quae summe maximeque est."; *En. in ps.* 101, S. 2 (10), CC, 39, p. 1445: "Esset tibi nomen ipsum esse, nisi quidquid aliud, tibi comparatum, inueniretur non esse uere?"; *En in ps.* 38, 7, CC, 38, p. 409: "Est illud simplex quaero, est uerum quaero, est germanum quaero, est quod est in illa Jerusamem sponsa domini mei . . ."; *Sermo* 7, 7, CC, 41, p. 76: "Sic sum quod sum, sic sum ipsum esse, sic sum cum ipso esse . . ."; *Sermo* 6, 4, CC, 41, p. 64: "Est uocor, quia maneo in aeternum . . . ." In his early works, Augustine especially uses the expressions *quod uere est* and *quod summe est*.

8. *Conf.* 13, 3, 4 and 5, 6, BA, 14, pp. 430 and 432, see further p. 89, n. 78.

9. *Conf.* 1, 6, 10, BA, 13, p. 288: "Eram enim et uiuebam etiam tunc et signa, quibus sensa mea nota aliis facerem, iam in fine infantiae quaerebam."; *Conf.* 1, 20, 31, BA, 13, p. 328: "Eram enim etiam tunc, uiuebam atque sentiebam . . . ." We notice that existence, when it is conceived to be a likeness of God, is expressed by the triadic phrase of Neo-Platonic origin "to be, to live, to know."

10. See J. J. O'Meara, *The Young Augustine: The Growth of Augustine's Mind up to his Conversion* (London: Longmans 1954), p. 13: "The story of Augustine's own conversion . . . is to some extent the story of a typical conversion . . . the story of Everyman."

11. *Conf.* 2, 10, 18, BA, 13, p. 360: "Defluxi abs te ego et erraui, deus meus, nimis deuius ab stabilitate tua in adulescentia et factus sum mihi regio egestatis." Concerning the theme of the spiritual hunger identified with indigence and lack of being, cf. further p. 11 and fn. 16. About this, see A. Solignac, Complementary Notes 10, "*regio egestatis,*" and 11, "*secretiore indigentia,*" BA, 13, p. 664 ff. and, by the same author, *Réminiscences plotiniennes et porphyriennes au début du "De ordine" de saint Augustin*, in *Archives de Philosophie*, 20, (1957): p. 460 ff., where the textual parallels of Porphyr, *Maxims* 40, Ed. Mommert, B.G. Teubner, 1907 and *De ord.* 1, 2, 3 are indicated.

12. *Conf.* 3, 1, 1, BA, 13, p. 362: ". . . quoniam famis mihi erat intus ab interiore cibo, te ipso, deus meus, et ea fame non esuriebam . . ."; see F. Körner, *Das Sein und der Mensch: Die existentielle Seinsentdeckung des jungen Augustin*, (Freiburg-München, Karl Alber: 1959), p. 105: ". . . *sein Wahrheitshunger, der im Grunde ein Seinshunger ist* . . . ." Also see pp. 52, 62, 84.

13. *Conf.* 3, 4, 7, BA, 13, p. 372 ff.

14. *Conf.* 3, 7, 12, BA, 13, p. 384 ff.: "Nesciebam enim aliud, uere quod est."

15. *Conf.* 3, 6, 10, BA, 13, p. 378 ff.: ". . . teipsam, ueritas, in qua non est commutatio nec momenti obumbratio, esuriebam et sitiebam. Et apponebantur adhuc mihi in illis ferculis phantasmata splendida . . . neque enim tu eras illa figmenta inania, nec nutriebar eis, sed exhauriebar magis." *Conf.* 4, 4, 9, BA, 13, p. 422: "phantasma, in quod sperare iubebatur." *Conf.* 4, 7, 12, BA, 13, p. 428: ". . . non mihi eras aliquid solidum et firmum, cum de te cogitabam. Non enim tu eras, sed uanum phantasmata, error meus erat deus meus."; *Conf.* 7, 17, 23, BA, 13, p. 626: "Et mirabar, quod iam te amabam, non pro te phantasmata." We can ask ourselves about the objectivity of this criticism of Manicheism. As a matter of fact, it is particularly difficult to judge it in a doctrine where myth and symbol play such a great part. However, it would seem that Alfaric's conclusions, favorable to Augustine's objectivity in this area, remain valid at the present time. See P. Alfaric, *Les Ecritures manichéennes*, vol. 1 (Paris: Emile Nourry 1918), p. 114 ff., and J. Ries, *La Bible chez saint Augustin et chez les Manichéens, 2, Les Premières Recherches du 20e siècle*, in *Rev. Et. August.*, 9 (1963), 201 ff. What comes closer to the subject discussed here is the hierarchy of the levels of reality that Augustine establishes in this connection. He puts above all imaginary, thus deceitful, representation of God the real existence, as precarious as it may be, of the most humble corporeal reality. *De uera rel.* 55, 108, BA, 8, p. 180: "Non sit nobis religio in phantasmatibus nostris. Melius est enim qualecumque uerum, quam omne quidquid pro arbitrio fingi potest . . . Melior est uera stipula, quam lux inani cogitatione pro suspicantis uoluntate formata . . ."

16. *Conf.* 4, 10, 15, BA, 13, p. 432: "Nam quoquouersum se uerterit anima hominis, ad dolores figitur alibi, praeterquam in te, tametsi figitur in pulchris extra te et extra se. Quae

tamen nulla essent, nisi essent abs te. Quae oriuntur et occidunt et oriendo quasi esse incipiunt et crescunt, ut perficiantur, et perfecta senescunt et intereunt, et non omnia senescunt et omnia intereunt. Ergo cum oriuntur et tendunt esse, quo magis celeriter cre- seunt, ut sint, eo magis festinant, ut non sint."

17. *Conf.* 4, 10, 15, BA, 13, p. 434: "Laudet te ex illis anima mea, *deus, creator omnium* (Ps. 145, 2), sed eis non infigatur glutine amore per sensus corporis. Eunt enim quo ibant, ut non sint, et conscindunt eam desideriis pestilentiosis, quoniam ipsa esse uult, et requi- escere amat in eis quae amat. In illis autem non est ubi, quia non stant: fugiunt, et quis ea sequitur sensu carnis?"; *Conf.* 4, 11, 16, BA, 13, p. 436: "Noli esse uana, anima mea, et obsurdescere in aure cordis tumultu uanitatis tuae. Audi et tu: uerbum ipsum clamat ut redeas, et ibi est locus quietis imperturbabilis, ubi non deseritur amor, si ipse non deserat. Ecce illa discedunt, ut alia succedant et omnibus suis partibus constet infima universitas. Numquid ego aliquo discedo ? ait uerbum dei. Ibi fige mansionem tuam, ibi commenda quidquid inde habes, anima mea, saltem fatigata fallaciis, ueritati commenda quidquid tibi est a ueritate, et non perdes aliquid, et reflorescent putria tua et sanabuntur omnes lan- guores tui et fluxa tua reformabuntur et renouabuntur et constringentur ad te et non te deponent, quo descendunt, sed stabunt tecum et permanebunt ad semper stantem ac per- manentem deum."

18. Cf. *De beata uita*, 1, 4, BA, 4, p. 228 and *Conf.* 7, 1, 2, BA, 13, p. 578.

19. *Conf.* 7, 10, 16, BA, 13, p. 618: " . . . et dixi: "Numquid nihil est ueritas, quoniam neque per finita neque per infinita locorum spatia diffusa est ?" Et clamasti de longinquo: " Immo uero ego sum qui sum" (Exod. 3:14). "Et audiui, sicut auditur in corde, et non erat prorsus, unde dubitarem faciliusque dubitarem uiuere me quam non esse ueritatem, quae per ea quae facta sunt intellecta conspicitur" (Rom 1:20).

20. *Conf.* 7, 10, 16, BA, 13, p. 616: "Et cum te primum cognoui, tu assumsisti me, ut uiderem esse quod uiderem, et nondum me esse qui uiderem. Et reuerberasti infirmitatem aspectus mei radians in me uehementer, et contremui amore et horrore: et inueni me longe esse a te in regione dissimilitudinis, tamquam audirem uocem tuam de excelso: Cibus sum grandium : cresce et manducabis me. Nec tu me in te mutabis sicut cibum carnis tuae, sed tu mutaberis in me."

21. *Tract in Ioh. euang.* 2, 4, CC, 36, p. 13 : "Illud potuerunt uidere quod est, sed uiderunt de longe."

22. *Conf.* 7, 18, 24, BA, 13, p. 636.

23. We are thinking of John Burnaby. See further p. 56 ff. and fn. 34.

24. See further p. 11, fn. 13.

25. Plato, *Rep.* 7, 518 c.

26. Cf. Plotinus, *Enn.* 1, 3, 1, 1–5: "Τίς τέχνη ἢ μέθοδος ἢ ἐπιτήδευσις ἡμᾶς οἷ δεῖ πορευθῆναι ἀνάγει; ὅπου μὲν οὖν δεῖ ἐλθεῖν, ὡς ἐπὶ τἀγαθὸν καὶ τὴν ἀρχὴν τὴν πρώτην, κείσθω διωμολογημένον καὶ διὰ πολλῶν δεδειγμένον· καὶ δὴ καὶ δι᾽ ὧν τοῦτο ἐδείκνυτο ἀναγωγή τις ἦν."

As G. Madec, *Note sur la vision augustinienne du monde*, in *Rev. Et. Augustin* 9, (1963), p. 141 ff., says, specifying "the basic intention of Augustinian speculation": "his thought does not travel on a purely physical level; his intention is not only to understand, but to rejoin God." About the word "anagogy" that Augustine himself did not use, but in which "the reality it designates is undeniably found," see O. Du Roy, *L'Intelligence de la foi dans la Trinité*, p. 170, fn. 6.

CHAPTER 1

The Participation of Wisdom and the Participation of Simple Existence

The Epistemological Condition of the *beata uita (Contra academicos)*

It is necessary to recall briefly the subject of the *Contra Academicos*, the first of Augustine's philosophical dialogues, before examining whether the theme of growing in being already appears there in one form or another.

The "exercises" that are described in this propaedeutic dialogue aim at making his disciples and readers "embrace philosophy," along with Augustine.[1] These exercises help them discover that the *beata uita* is connected with the knowledge of truth. For it is a question of surmounting once and for all the doubt, to which Augustine was a prey before converting, with complementary points of view, to the Christian faith as well as to the "Platonists' books." But it is also a question of going beyond the mostly rhetorical ideal that had long remained his and that he had instilled in his students.[2]

This act of "embracing philosophy" takes place under the double aegis of Christ and Plato. The latter had only been able to show the philosophers the existence of another world, that of the mind; but Christ had revealed it to all men. Augustine, not satisfied with only believing, wishes to study thoroughly, by means of the *subtilissima ratio*, the meaning of the mysteries that faith teaches him. Now it happens that the Platonic doctrine is the "only perfectly true philosophy," which can allow the close examination of these mysteries, owing to its method of spiritual internality.[3]

Thus armed, Augustine can go forward on the road to "truth itself, that can only be grasped on the condition of completely embracing philosophy."[4]

It is thus, on his own familiar grounds, that he succeeds in refuting the academic doubt, which is partially based on the errors of the senses: he shows that knowledge of sovereign goodness is not founded on them, and he establishes a number of absolute certainties concerning dialectics.[5] After having trained his disciples in the preliminaries to philosophical pursuit, he finally reaches the essential conclusion of the dialogue: "It is not impossible for man to find truth."[6]

Novice philosophers henceforth are assured of being able to examine closely the secrets of truth, the only way to arrive at the *beata uita.*[7]

But Augustine sometimes must remind his disciples, avid for discussions and reasonings, that it is not a matter of a sterile game involving the mind alone. What is in question here is "our life, our conduct, our soul."[8] Therefore, it is not surprising that the theme of the soul's growth is already present in the *Contra academicos*, even if it does not appear there yet in a very explicit form.

Indeed, Augustine intends there to "cultivate" *(colere)* his disciples' souls by means of the liberal sciences, according to the ideal of ancient philosophy, by encouraging them to practice the ascetic exercises that this ideal includes and that is expressed by the virtue of temperance *(temperantia)*. It is thus that they will succeed in acquiring "knowledge of the truly fruitful truths *(uere fructuosarum rerum)*."[9] He asserts there, through Trygetius, that the *beata uita* consists of the fruitful possession of this *ratio*, which plays in the Augustinian dialogues a role analogous to that of the *logos* in Plotinus *(sapiens. . .ratione perfruatur. . .fruaturque merito diuina beatitudine, qui humana sit ante perfructus*[10]*)*.

We notice the appearance, in this first dialogue, of the *frui* theme which will be so very important in subsequent Augustinian thought and, through him, in that of the Middle Ages. This verb and its derived meanings express here the assimilation of a spiritual sustenance and the joy that is its fruit. The expressions *colere, temperantia, frui, perfrui*, and *fructuosus*, used as if in passing, already point out in a discreet way the presence of the theme of the incorporation into being, which will be developed in a broader way beginning with the following dialogue.

Truth: The Soul's Sustenance *(De beata uita)*

The second dialogue, *De beata uita*, marks a new stage in the definition of the "blissful life." After having succeeded in establishing in the *Contra academicos* that it consists in knowing the truth, Augustine intends to show now that this knowledge is a satiating possession of God, that is to say, a sui generis participation.[11] It is a question of "possessing God" *(habere deum)*, in opposition to a type of inferior participation, expressed by the passive turn of phrase "to be possessed by God" *(haberi a deo)*. The second of these expressions conveys the relation of ontological causality that links God to any being whatsoever, even the man who turns away from him, who for this reason does not "possess" him.[12]

In order to understand what this sui generis participation consists of, Augustine resorts to the notions of food and fullness — which were used traditionally in this sense in the "Platonists' books" — accompanied by a procession of harmonics, the main one being *frui*. It is the way in which he progressively elaborates these notions — combined, especially towards the end, with that of measure *(modestia, modus)* — that confers unity and structure to this Augustinian "Banquet."

The topic discreetly touched on in the *Contra academicos* is exposed here in full light, within a series of developments in which in turn, by interpenetrating, the themes of nourishment, of "having," of fullness, and of measure dominate.[13] Even though Augustine is still largely ignorant about the soul's nature, as he confides to his friend Mallius Theodorus in the dedication of the opus, he nevertheless reaches a first certainty concerning this subject, which he tries to share with his disciples.[14]

This certainty concerns the sustenance the soul needs as much as the body, and which, for the soul, consists of the knowledge of the real. The soul attains that by means of its ideas and speculations; it must practise for it by studying the liberal sciences.[15] If it is deprived of this knowledge, which makes up its own food, it becomes overtaken by famine. Stricken with illness and sterility, it wastes away. Ignoring the truth, that is to say the real, is therefore the soul's evil, its vice, a kind of ontological failure.

In order to help his disciples understand this explanation, which is at the same time epistemological and ontological and which seems to disconcert them, Augustine resorts first to the etymology of *nequitia* (depravity, wickedness), which comes from *necquiquam* (nothing, nothingness). Virtue, as opposed to vice, is *frugalitas*, temperance that includes the notion of fecundity, for it draws its origin from *frux*, harvest. Beyond these etymological considerations, Augustine tries to help his disciples gain access to a metaphysical conception of the soul's life, by showing them that virtue partakes of being and vice of nothingness:

> "Let's see," I said, "won't you agree with me that the minds of educated people are in a way much larger and fuller than those of ignorant people?" Everybody said it was evident. "It is right then to say that the minds, which have had no teaching, which have drawn nothing from the source of virtues, are, so to speak, fasting and famished-looking." "I think," said Trygetius, "that those minds are also full, but full of vices and depravity *[nequitia]*." "Believe, me," I said, "this is very much a kind of sterility and a type of famine of the mind. The body, which lacks nourishment, is most often overcome with illnesses of all sorts, aches that reveal the hunger in it. Those minds also are full of illnesses that uncover their famine. The ancients, indeed, claimed depravity *(nequitia)* to be at the source of all vices, because it is nothing *(nequiquam)*, because it is nothingness *(nihil)*. The opposite virtue for this vice is called 'frugality' *(frugalitas)*, a word that comes from *frux* (harvest) and includes the notion of fruit *(fructus)*, for this virtue has as its effect a certain fecundity of the soul. On the other hand, depravity *(nequitia)* holds its name from the sterility it causes, that is to say, from nothingness *(a nihilo)*. For everything that passes, comes undone, dissolves, and perishes continually is nothingness *(nihil)*; therefore, we say that those who are depraved are 'lost' men. What is, on the contrary, is what stays, lasts, and always remains the same, like virtue, which, in its most important and most beautiful part, is called 'temperance' and 'frugality'."[16]

After this definition of virtue, Augustine goes to its ultimate foundation, God, that is to say, the reality that always remains, true being according to the Platonic definition. The *beata uita* or wisdom consists in possessing this wealth that alone is permanent *(habere deum)*. Therefore, indigence, *egestas*, understood in the philosophical sense, consists in lacking this wisdom, and thus the only true asset.[17] He who suffers from it has a "non-having" *(habet non habere)*.[18] It is thus that, in order to characterize the opposition between "being" and "not being," the notions of *plenitudo* and *egestas* are connected again with those of *frugalitas* and *nequitia*, vice and virtue, happiness and unhappiness, wisdom and folly, measure and lack of measure, having and not having:

> Now folly is indigence and the very name of indigence: for this word designates usually a kind of sterility and dearth. . . . I believe that you agree also that the foolish soul is depraved and that the word folly by itself designates all the soul's vices. Now the first day of our discussion we had said that depravity *(nequitia)* was thus called because it is nothing *(nec quidquam)* and that its opposite, "frugality" *(frugalitas)* receives its name from *frux* (harvest). Thus, we see the culmination in these two opposites of that which makes up "being" and "not being."[19]
>
> Therefore, plenitude and indigence are opposites and, as for depravity *(nequitia)* and temperance *(frugalitas)*, we see the manifestation there of these two opposites: "being" and "not being." Now, if folly precisely is indigence, it follows that wisdom is plenitude. It has also been repeated, and rightly so, that "frugality" is the mother of all virtues. Tullius was of the same opinion, he who had said in one of his counsel's speeches: "Think what you may; as for me, I judge that 'frugality,' that is to say moderation and temperance, is the greatest virtue." A very erudite and judicious opinion: for he has considered fruitfulness *(frux)*, that is to say what we call "being," in contrast with "not being."[20]

Having thus closed the circle, Augustine describes once more the two opposite attitudes of the soul, by using the notions acquired during these "exercises." When it turns away from temperance, a synonym of measure, the soul rushes into the excesses of the passions, which act to "confine" it *(coarctatur)*.[21] When on the contrary it attaches itself to God, no longer fearing a lack of measure, it is protected from indigence and unhappiness.

It has been claimed that Augustine has not yet succeeded in making in this work a perfectly coherent synthesis of his different philosophical sources concerning the *beata uita*.[22] Be that as it may, the ontological nature of the "blissful life" is already firmly established. We shall also notice, in the Trinitarian conclusion that ends the dialogue, the important part played by the notions of *frui* and *satietas:* it is a question of making one understand that the participation of the soul in God is beatifying participation because it is satiating, "fruitive."[23] Such is the main theme of this "Banquet,"[24] which Augustine at that time considered to be the most religious of his dialogues, and whose most apparent sources are philosophical.[25]

The Return to the "ratio" *(De ordine)*

Augustine's main preoccupation in the *De beata uita*, in which he was trying to get across the ontological and "fruitive" nature of the participation of wisdom, is going to be henceforth combined with a broader viewpoint. Far from pushing this preoccupation into the background, the pursuit undertaken in the *De ordine* will reveal a new, somewhat cosmic dimension of the participation of wisdom. As the title of the dialogue indicates, it is a question of considering order, another name for unity, such as it is in God and such as it is or should be in the world governed by him. Its flaw, which is discovered at the level of human realities, indeed leads one to question the divine omnipotence and goodness. Augustine's goal is to show that in spite of appearances the divine order is safeguarded; in other words, that the problem of evil does not remain unanswered for him who is capable of reaching a certain level of metaphysical depth.

We shall limit our analysis to the new aspects of the question that occupied Augustine in the two previous dialogues, and whose importance, moreover, could not be exaggerated in the *De ordine*. For he shows us, from the dedication on, that without wisdom it is impossible to understand the problem of order, whose aspects are all very closely connected, whether it be a question of God, the soul, the universe, or even the steps that may allow one to acquire, with wisdom, an understanding of this problem.

If the theme of nourishment and assimilation is no longer here, as in the *De beata uita*, the leitmotiv of the dialogue, nevertheless it remains present. It is recognized here and there, in the form of *uirtus*, *temperantia*,[26] and *frui*,[27] in the middle of synonymic expressions that we already partly know, but whose range is growing richer. Here we find again the theme of indigence,[28] and the notion of culture[29] and science that nourish.[30] The antithetical couple, which is added to those that we had already encountered, is that of multiplicity opposed to unity or order, the "leitmotiv" of this third dialogue.

Thus, Augustine tries to define in a more complete way than he had done till then the characteristics of wisdom, this *habere deum* as it is called henceforth, and preferably, *esse cum deo*. He tries moreover to make his disciples understand that even men who are not, as the wise man is, "with God," cannot truly be "without God." Augustine here goes back to the discussion that had been started about *habere deum* in the previous dialogue. We understand better now with what intention he was differentiating there between the men who possess God and those who without possessing him themselves are nevertheless possessed by him. It is thus that two types of participation are suggested: *esse cum deo* or the participation of wisdom, and *non esse sine deo* that could be called the participation of simple existence.[31] But this question will only be elucidated beginning with the *De immortalitate animae*.

The problem of the participation of wisdom is thus put in close connection with the problem of evil, *esse cum deo* being defined in contrast with the existence of men who turn away from God, and vice versa. Because it lacks order, such an existence lacks the consistency that is the very trademark of being and that defines virtue: it is *minime constans, minime ordinata*. The solution Augustine proposes here for the problem of evil consists in showing that in spite of their inner disorder, wicked or foolish people have their place in the divine order, an inferior place, of course, to that which would have been theirs if they had accepted to "be with God."[32]

In contrast with this life lacking consistency, because it centers on things that pass and that make it go down into the lower realms of being, the wise person, thanks to the self-knowledge he acquired by means of the liberal sciences, succeeds in contemplating God in his eternity. That means that he partakes of the main attribute of God, explicitly defined for the first time as "He who truly is" *(qui uere est).* [33] (We remember that in the previous dialogue, it is by the expedient of participation and non-participation, that is, of virtue and vice, that the notions of being and nonbeing had been broached.)

The difficulties presented by the questions concerning the soul, along with the problem of evil, are such that, according to Augustine, faith alone is not enough to elucidate them. One can only succeed in this by thoroughly studying the data given by faith in the light of true philosophy *(uera et germana philosophia).* It has to do, as in the *Contra academicos*, with Platonic philosophy, which alone allows one to understand the reality of God and the soul. But this assertion is accompanied by a warning against the pride of certain philosophers who refuse to accept the Incarnation. [34]

The access to this philosophical understanding is only considered possible, apart from exceptional cases, owing to the study of the liberal sciences. They alone permit, after long efforts, the understanding of the notions essential to the knowledge of the real. It seems typical to us that, in the enumeration he makes of them, Augustine begins with that of nothingness, *nihil.* [35] It will provide him with the key to the problem of evil, which he is trying to work out by opposing the Manichean conception of a substantial evil. This notion also allows one to understand metaphysically the problem of the soul, which determines by itself its own destiny, according to whether it chooses to "be with God," who alone "truly is," or whether it turns towards the nothingness of illusion and of vice. The conception of a soul partaking of divine Being or, at least to a certain extent, of nothingness, according to whether it turns towards one or the other, is also in itself contradictory to the Manichean conception of a soul consubstantial with God, as Augustine will frequently point out. [36]

It is only by the practise of the thorough study of these philosophical notions that it is possible to succeed in achieving self-knowledge and, inseparably, knowledge of this *ratio*, which has been compared to the Plotinian *logos.* [37] Augustine insists, on the one hand, on the immanence of this *ratio* — it is in us, perhaps it is even us[38] — but also on its transcendence. He opposes the use men make of it in the realm of illusion to that that the wise man makes of it. The former imagine doing everything by reason, but they do not know its true nature. [39] Only he who goes beyond its empirical or even artistic use knows it, in order to regulate, by means of it, the particularly important work that is his own life. [40] Augustine insists on the dual aspect of this knowledge of the *ratio*, which is at the same time speculative and practical. But it has to do with a practice that takes place at the level of being.

In fact, the nature of the *ratio* is, in itself, divine. Our own soul, that of "reasonable animals," has fallen far from it into the realm of the tangible, and must bring about its return to what is divine in us. [41] It is this return to the *ratio (regressus in rationem)* that makes up the philosophical conversion which Augustine urges on his disciples, for it is in it that resides the solution, speculative and practical at the very same time, to the problem of evil.

Thus, detached from vice and turning towards virtue, the soul rises from the lower levels of being to its highest principle. It begins by uncovering the traces of *ratio* in what is tangible, then little by little it climbs the steps of the liberal sciences, which show it, with progressive clarity as it goes up these steps, their divine origin. At the same time, as it carries out this ascent, the soul finds out the formative part played by the *ratio* in the structure of human civilization. After having gotten over the last stages i.e., the science of numbers and dialectics — which prepare it for the knowledge of wisdom, the soul will be able finally to rise to one of the summits of this ascending activity of the *ratio:* the proof of the soul's immortality. It then understands that the *ratio*, which is in it, is identical to the supreme principle, or at least that it allows one to have access to it.[42] Augustine, moreover, does not hesitate to define the transcendence of the *ratio*, based on the eternity of truth, in the way he will constantly use later on to characterize God-Being in opposition to the world here below, which changes and passes.[43]

The question that is then raised is that of the relation that connects the soul with the *ratio*. It is the difficulty peculiar to the theme of the participation of wisdom, of *esse cum deo*, that Augustine studies thoroughly in the following works. Whatever this relation may be, whether the soul itself is the *ratio* or whether the *ratio* is in it, it is the *regressus in rationem* that is the road to immortality.[44] Augustine will venture into it in the *Soliloquies*. In them he will tackle from close up the condition of the *beata uita:* the participation of wisdom and its fruit, which is immortality.

"Am I Immortal?" *(Soliloquies)*

This "immortality of wisdom" for which Augustine yearned since his first encounter with philosophy (reading *Hortensius*), is the goal at which he aimed ever since he truly "embraced philosophy." It was obvious since the dedication to the *Contra academicos*, in which, addressing his friend Romanianus, he was hoping to give him an inkling of "another life," the only truly blissful one;[45] when he was trying to stir in him this "indescribable divine thing, dormant in the lethargic sleep of this life."[46] The immortal fruit of wisdom was already being shown in this dialogue:

> Here below, the wise person finds his joy in the *ratio*, and it is of this that happiness consists, as we agreed earlier; therefore he finds himself ready, on the last day of his life, to start being in possession of that which he had desired to acquire. And after having enjoyed human happiness, he deserves to enjoy divine happiness.[47]

In the second dialogue, Augustine was especially pointing out the ontological and "fruitive" meaning of virtue, starting with the *beata uita*. Being was defined there as "that which stays, lasts and always remains the same."[48] In the *De ordine*, the identification of the *beata uita* with immortality was asserted in an even more explicit way:

> Sing with all your soul the praise of pure and true love, thanks to which the souls, enriched by science and embellished by virtue, unite with Understanding by means of philosophy and not only flee death, but even enjoy a very happy life.[49]

Augustine (in this dialogue) even went as far as to assert that immortality, the fruit of knowledge, is accessible in full from here below to the *pauci* who have practised wisdom, according to a common conception in ancient philosophy: "There are few who already attain from here below this knowledge, and even after this life it is impossible to go beyond it."[50]

But Augustine does not intend to be satisfied with simple assertions. He thirsts for the absolute evidence, which in his eyes characterizes metaphysical knowledge even more certainly than mathematical knowledge. As far as the soul is concerned, he aspires to go beyond the doubt and the hesitations of which he complains in the first two dialogues, in order to reach the certainty of proof. He wants to know "to what extent the soul dies, and how its immortality is proven."[51]

Thus we notice that the "exercises" carried out by Augustine with his disciples, during the *irregressus in rationem*, are directed, in an ever clearer way and progressively as they more "completely embrace philosophy," towards proving immortality. It, as we have seen, is considered to be like one of the summits of the ascending activity of the *ratio* in its progressive access to the One.

It is in the *Soliloquies* that Augustine tries to face this difficult question, no longer accompanied by his disciples, but in a dialogue with his *ratio* alone, for the part he attributes to himself there is that of the student and not of the master. "Am I immortal?" Such is the problem whose solution matters the most to him at this period of his thought.[52] He wants to know it in a certain way, specifying immediately after, that he does not aspire to any form of survival. To remain after death with the ignorance that is currently his would be for him a kind of misery that would be much worse than annihilation.[53] Augustine only wishes immortality to the extent to which it is synonymous with knowledge.

Before the "proof" that he is going to ask of the *ratio*, the liminal prayer gives evidence of the identification that he establishes between the notions of being and immortality. He expresses it in an admirable synthesis of the language of Plato with that of Saint Paul:

> God, thanks to whom death is absorbed in victory. God who converts us. God who strips us of that which is not in order to put on us again that which is.[54]

This prayer is inserted in a context in which we find once more the characteristics (applied in an eminent way to God-Trinity) that had been attributed to *esse* in the previous dialogues:

> . . . the only true and eternal substance, in which there is no disagreement, no confusion, no change, no indigence, no death; but a supreme harmony, supreme evidence, supreme constancy, supreme plenitude, supreme life; to which nothing is missing, in which nothing is superfluous . . . .[55]

This God, the cause of everything that "tends towards being," allows the *pauci* who take refuge in "what truly is," to grasp the secrets of being and nonbeing, especially that of evil that is nothingness.[56]

Can this refuge be found by means of faith, virtue, or science? Augustine admits his uncertainty concerning this subject. The only thing of which he is sure is that it is necessary to leave what is changing and perishable for what is eternal and certain. We can ask ourselves, however, if this question is not a subsequent addition, for it is without any hesitation that, in his dialogue with the *ratio*, Augustine begins on the "science" path and not on that of faith alone or of virtue alone.[57]

In the attempts at proof, which he practises under the guidance of the *ratio*, we see that he is trying to study thoroughly the equivalences asserted all through the previous dialogues between truth, being, and immortality.[58] The force of his proofs lie in his demonstration that truth, which is immortal, dwells in us.

These proofs, or these attempts at proof, are of a rather pronounced technical nature, which is one of the reasons that they require, as a preliminary condition, a knowledge of the liberal sciences. However, they are not proofs whose aim is to reach an object that is already entirely constituted, whose existence or truth would only have to be passively recorded by the knowing subject. On the contrary, "proving" is a spiritual exercise allowing one to have a hold over immortality, to regain it, and to turn it into a reality in oneself, thanks to the conversion to the intelligible world. It is a very Platonic type of proof; it makes the soul participate in the reality which is to be proven:

> — *(ratio):* The soul is immortal: believe finally in your own arguments, believe in truth; it proclaims that it dwells in you, that it is immortal, and that no corporeal death can take its dwelling place away from it. Turn away from your shadow, examine your conscience; there is no death for you, except if you are unaware that you cannot die.
> — (Augustine): I understand, I am examining my conscience, I am beginning to recognize myself.[59]

The *ratio* teaches Augustine that he is immortal, on the condition that he recognizes and confirms his own immortality, which is that of the truth dwelling in him. This act of becoming conscious and this confirmation characterize the conversion to the world of the mind expressed by the return to the self. They are essential in order to succeed, already from here below, at what Augustine considers to be true immortality.

But if it is on this condition that one does not die, what becomes of the soul that forgets it? If it is thanks to the *regressus in rationem* that the soul conquers immortality, what is the fate of the one that does not have access to the knowledge of wisdom? Such is the question that Augustine asks the *ratio:*

> But, I beg of you, resolve the difficulty remaining for me. How can we conceive that science and truth dwell in an ignorant soul, since it is impossible to call it a mortal soul?[60]

As one sees, the anagogical proof of immortality leads to the aporia of a certain death of the soul. It is a question Augustine had explicitly asked since the *De ordine;* but the developed account, in the *De beata uita*, of virtue as a constituent element of being and of nihilating vice already implied it. This aporia is set off by the absolute equivalence that Augustine establishes between knowledge and immortality. Since neither Christian faith nor Platonic philosophy allows the assertion that any soul can be mortal, could this mean that the soul, even if it is ignorant, possesses knowledge in an implicit way?

The answer is put off till later. For the time being, Augustine outlines an embryonic solution by calling on the theory of reminiscence.[61] But he will only be able to settle the question in a metaphysically satisfactory way by tackling it from another direction. And this is what he attempts in the *De immortalitate animae.*

The Indestructible Existence of the Soul *(De immortalitate animae)*

In this work, which is a continuation of the *Soliloquies*, the proof of immortality is not only pursued even more thoroughly, but it is set on new paths, thanks to different efforts at founding ontologically an indestructible substratum of the soul, independent of the fact that it might become converted to the truth, which is in it, or that it might turn away from it.

This rough draft allows one to grasp how thought gropes, better than a work that is entirely written. We know that Augustine complained in the *Retractationes* about the unintelligibility of this work which he had trouble understanding as he reread it.[62] It is one of the reasons why H. Dörrie has come out with the hypothesis that the work is a simple collection of notes, a summary of Porphyrian arguments.[63]

It is undeniable that at least part of the arguments that are found there are of Porphyrian origin, but we also find there the very clear sign of a personal effort at answering the aporia resulting from the *Soliloquies.*[64] It is why, if it is true that at the time when Augustine wrote the *Retractationes* he had long become uninterested in the argumentation of the *De immortalitate animae,* it does not remain any less true that this work played an important part in the elaboration of his ontology, particularly concerning the question of the soul's status.[65] We shall try to see what it contains that is essential concerning this subject.

Here are the new arguments that Augustine proposes in order to show the indissoluble union of the soul and of the Truth that dwells in it, if they are both subjects or substances (it is the solution he will keep, after the hesitations of the *Soliloquies*):

No outside force can tear the soul away from the transcendent Truth or *ratio,* which is the most powerful reality, since it is the most immutable. The *ratio* itself, not being jealous, cannot deprive the soul of the contemplation in which it finds its joy *(frui)* and which gives it an increase of being: "From the very fact that it is more, it causes what is joined to it to be, which is the exact opposite of death."[66]

On the other hand, the soul cannot voluntarily break the bond that ties it to the *ratio,* the separation of two beings that are not in space being considered a metaphysical impossibility.

It could be possible to raise as an objection the fact that, even if it is impossible to separate it from the *ratio,* the soul itself is liable to die out. It is the argument for a possible annihilation. Augustine tries to answer it by developing the theme to which he has already resorted as mentioned above: the ontological force of the *ratio* compels what is joined to it to be:

> But if this force of the *ratio* affects the soul by the very fact that the latter is linked to it, and it is impossible for it not to do so, it affects it in such a way as to give it being. For

> the *ratio*, in which we notice the greatest immutability, is to the highest degree. It is why it compels in some way the soul, which it influences, to be.[67]

In the *Retractationes*, Augustine will turn to the Scriptures to deny the statement that the soul cannot be voluntarily separated from God.[68] But this assertion from the *De immortalitate animae* shows precisely what difficulty Augustine experienced then in clearly differentiating between two levels of reality in the soul. There exists indeed a realm in which it cannot make any voluntary choice: it is that of its first incorporation into being, that of its creation. It is there that lies the impossibility for it to come to nothing, the indivisible bond that ties it to being. Augustine will show this a little later concerning suicide, in the *De libero arbitrio.*[69] Volition intervenes at another level, that of conversion, an act of knowledge and love that connects the soul with its principle in a much closer way.

By developing the evidence for immortality, Augustine has not yet given his attention to making this distinction in an explicit way, because his interest happened to be concentrated, so to say, in an exclusive way on that second level. We notice it in the arguments related above. Even though Augustine attempts to show the ontological causality of the *ratio*, his proof is not entirely convincing, since the problem is set solely in terms of a union with God. However, the fact of asserting that there exists a nonvoluntary bond between the soul and God shows that Augustine is looking for an ontological relation other than the conversion one. He notices as a matter of fact that a metaphysical explanation of the soul centering solely on conversion proves to be unable to demonstrate immortality in any case:

> But the soul cannot turn away from the *ratio* and consequently be overtaken by madness without lessening. For if it is more when it turns towards the ratio and adheres to it because it adheres to this immutable reality that is truth, and that is to the highest degree and primordial, if, on the other hand, it turns away from it, it possesses less the very Being *(idipsum esse)*: its lessening consists in this. But any lessening tends towards nothingness; and what most exactly defines death is the annihilation of something that existed. That is why to tend towards nothingness is to tend towards death. It is quite *difficult to say why the soul, being subject to lessening, is not subject to death.*[70] (Emphasis mine.)

Augustine himself points out on several occasions that it is the ontological experience of wisdom and folly that can make one fear total annihilation of the soul:

> Here is, let us take notice, the sole reason for this fear: we recognize that the foolish soul suffers a reduction whereas the wise soul has more stability and a greater plenitude of being.[71]

He considers this the only objection of any consequence that one could contrast with the assertion that the soul is immortal. It is why, after having looked for evidence other than that of unitive knowledge, he finds himself finally induced to distinguish clearly, for the first time, two levels of reality in the soul.[72]

Augustine himself emphasizes this distinction, which establishes a first participation of the soul in the divine *esse* on the level of existence, independently of the participation of wisdom:

> *Were we to look for that which is opposed to truth, not in as much as it is the truth, but in as much as it is in a supreme way and to the highest degree*, even though it may only be to the extent in which it is truth . . . For if no essence, in as much as it is an essence, has nothing that is opposed to it, with greater reason, this first essence called truth does not have, in as much as it is an essence, any opposite. Now truth, the first principle, is. . . . It is thus impossible for any reality to be in any way opposed to this substance, which is in a supreme and primordial way. If it is to it that the soul owes the very fact that it is *(idipsum quod est)* — not owing it to itself, it can only owe it to this reality, which is superior to it — nothing can make it lose it, because there exists no reality opposed to the one to which it owes that; that is why it does not cease being. As for wisdom, which it possesses because of its conversion to that to which it owes being, it can lose it by turning away from it. For turning away is the opposite of converting. But being, which it owes to the one to which nothing is opposed, it cannot be led to lose it. Thus it cannot perish.[73] (Emphasis mine.)

Augustine defines rather laboriously the soul's first level of reality, its initial metaphysical establishment, for he sees himself compelled to use for this definition the expression *esse*, which he had set aside up till now in an almost exclusive way for the participation of wisdom, as was seen earlier. Wishing to avoid any ambiguity about this, Augustine momentarily avoids using the vocabulary of being to designate it, and remains satisfied with the expression *sapientiam habere*. As for the ontological substratum whose everlastingness he is trying to establish, he designates it by the expression *idipsum quod est*, that is to say, the very fact of being, understood in the banal sense of the word: we would say, the fact of existing.

This argumentation bears the sign of a personal quest. Augustine feels the need to prove what the Neo-Platonic philosophers from whom he draws his inspiration are satisfied to assert, because their presuppositions imply it: the soul cannot die even when it leans towards nothingness.[74]

This distinction, in brief, only serves to make clear what Augustine was trying to give an inkling of to his disciples during the earlier dialogues: that there exists an ontological relation of man to God even when man does not partake of him through conversion, that is, even when he "is" not "with him." Up till then, Augustine had only characterized this relation by the rather enigmatic expression *non esse sine deo*, which he set against the impossible *esse sine deo* and which he distinguished from *esse cum deo*, defined in reference to immortality. We remember the solutions of an eschatological nature that he had outlined concerning this, and that a stricter orthodoxy will lead him to rectify on certain points.[75] But the metaphysical solution to the problem, from a point of view such as his, requires an ontological definition of the soul. What is the soul, when it is not turning towards God, since it can truly be only when it converts to him?

Augustine will work out this problem by analyzing the constituent elements of the spiritual created being, and more generally of any created being. But he will not succeed at it at one go. There will be several stages before his final solution, which is that of the last books of the *Confessions* and of the *De Genesi ad litteram*. The distinction of two levels of reality in the soul, proposed in the *De immortalitate animae*, constitutes for it somewhat of a first outline, and that is what in our opinion makes up its main interest.

We are not forgetting the other attempts made in this work in order to settle the question of the aporia of annihilation. The proof by an analogy with the body, indestructible although divisible ad infinitum aims at reaching a form of the soul that would be its *existendi species* and that it could never lose entirely.[76] Finally, the soul would be a kind of immobile motor, it would be immutable to a certain extent.[77] As interesting as this last piece of evidence might be, it brings us back to the participation of wisdom. We know moreover that Augustine's views on this will evolve: afterwards, mutability became for him the trait that differentiates in a radical way not only the corporeal created being, but the soul itself, from God who alone is immutable by essence.[78]

As for the assertion, founded on an analogy with the body, of a *species* not entirely destructible, it interests us much more for it allows one to disclose how Augustine elaborated little by little the explanation of the ontological structure of the soul, and in a more general way, that of the created being:

> That it is not the material mass of the body, but its formal principle that makes it be, this opinion is proven in a complete irrefutable way: indeed, the body is more when it is better formed and more beautiful, it is less when it is uglier and deformed. And this being less does not come from an amputation of matter (of which we have spoken enough already), but from a loss of form.
>
> We must examine and discuss this point carefully, in order to avoid having one come to assert that the soul dies from this lessening, in order not to have one induce from the fact that folly implies for the soul a certain loss of form, that this loss, by increasing, can even get to the point of stripping the soul of all form, of bringing it back to nothingness and of making it perish. Thus, if we can succeed in showing that the body itself cannot be completely deprived of the form that precisely makes it a body, we shall probably be rightly granted that the soul cannot, with greater reason, lose what makes it be a soul. For there is no one who does not admit, after a careful self-examination, that any soul is preferable to any body.[79]

Augustine attempts to establish the immortality of the soul from the point of view of creation. It is seen more clearly here than in the proof founded on the Essence without opposite. He uses, concerning the body, the verb *facere*. The force that has "made" it, *effectoria uis*, does not let it be defrauded of "the form by which it is to the extent in which it is."[80] Even though it changes form, which is characteristic of the tangible universe, the body never loses its being:

> No part of the body can return to nothingness, for this efficient force contains it completely, and without making an effort nor however remaining inactive, it gives being to all the things which are by it to the extent in which they are.[81]

Nothing goes back to nothingness, not even the slightest particle of corporeal being. This assertion can seem surprising from a man who has been able to express with so much force the inconsistency of everything that is not absolute. It is owing to the notion of mutability that Augustine makes the connection between the transience of becoming, its "non-being,"[82] and the ontological value of the slightest particle of created being.[83] Originating from Him who is Being without opposite, it partakes in its own way of his incorruptibility.

It is within the framework of this solution to the dilemma of being and nothingness, valid for all that is created, that Augustine inserted the evidence that the soul is immortal even in the case in which it would not be by itself, *per seipsum*, where it would not be its own *causa existendi.*[84] For in the *De immortalitate animae* he still envisages this Platonic explanation, which allows one to avoid the aporia of annihilation, and for which proof by immutability is an aspect. Proof by an analogy with the body happens to be from a different point of view, that of creation. Therefore, we are going to find it again, elaborated a little differently, in the work in which this creational point of view is going to assert itself in a much clearer way, the *De libero arbitrio.* On the other hand, Augustine will show in this work that the participation of simple existence, whose notion was brought out in the *De immortalitate animae,* is finalized in its entirety by the participation of wisdom, in which alone it finds its meaning.

NOTES

1. See H.-I. Marrou, *Saint Augustin et la fin de la culture antique* (Paris: 1938), p. 303 ff. on the part attributed to the liberal disciplines in the philosophical dialogues: "this study has the advantage of training the mind, of getting it used to the frequenting and handling of the pure idea, of the spiritual realities."

2. H.-I. Marrou, p. 162 ff.

3. *Contra acad.* 3, 19, 42–20, BA, 4, p. 196 ff. Concerning the *una uerissimae philosophiae disciplina* (3, 19, 42), see O. Du Roy, *L'Intelligence de la foi en la Trinité*, p. 116 ff. Contrary to R. Holte, *Béatitude et Sagesse: Saint Augustin et le problème de la fin de l'homme dans la philosophie ancienne* (Paris: 1962), p. 87 ff., who is trying to prove that this expression designates Christianity, O. Du Roy is of the opinion that in the *Contra academicos* it merely designates the thought of Plotinus, which represents for Augustine the true Platonic tradition, set down in a unified doctrine. Concerning the *ratio subtilissima (Contra acad.* 3, 19, 42 and 3, 20, 43) see O. Du Roy, op. cit., p. 117 ff. It is a question of a reality similar to the Plotinian *logos,* whose role is to be specified in the subsequent dialogues.

4. *Contra acad.* 2, 3, 8, BA, 4, p. 74: "Nam ipsum uerum non uidebis, nisi in philosophiam totum intraueris."

5. *Contra acad.* 3, 11, 24 ff., BA 4, p. 158 ff.

6. *Contra acad.* 3, 20, 43, BA, 4, p. 198: " . . . cui satis est iam non arbitrari non posse ab homine inueniri ueritatem."

7. *Contra acad.* 3, 20, 44, BA, 4, p. 202: "Habemus ducem qui nos in ipsa ueritatis arcana, deo iam monstrante, perducat."

8. Far from being presented as if it were of a purely speculative nature, knowledge of the truth, from this Neo-Platonic viewpoint, is considered to be allowing the soul to return to its origin, owing to the virtue of temperance.

   Contra acad. 2, 9, 22, BA, 4, p. 98: De uita nostra, de moribus, de animo res agitur, qui se superaturum inimicitias omnium fallaciarum, et ueritate comprehensa, quasi in regionem suae originis rediens, triumphaturum de libidinibus, atque ita temperantia uelut coniuge accepta regnaturum esse praesumit, securior rediturus in coelum. Cf. *Contra acad.* 3, 1, 1 BA, 4 p. 112: Sed antequam ad partes meas ueniam, quae ad eam pertinet explicandam, pauca, quaeso, de spe, de uita, de instituto nostro non ab re abhorrentia libenter audiatis.

9. *Contra acad.* 3, 4, 7, BA, 4, p. 125 ff.:

   . . .Si tamen aliquid iam de te *Hortensius* et philosophia meretur . . . qui te uehementius quam ista poetica incenderat ad magnarum et uere fructuosarum rerum scientiam. Sed dum ad istarum disciplinarum, quibus excoluntur animi, circum reuocare uos cupio. . . .

10. *Contra acad.* 1, 8, 23, BA, 4, p. 54 ff.

11. The words *particeps* and *participatio* will only be used a little later. It will be specified that the soul is a substance partaking of the *ratio* (*De quantitate animae* 13, 22, BA, 5, p. 272: ". . . mihi uidetur esse substantia rationis particeps.") or of wisdom (*De libero arbitrio* 2, 9, 25, BA, 6, p. 258 ff.: ". . . quid de ipsa sapientia putas existimandum? . . . an uero unam praesto esse communiter omnibus, cuius quanto quisque fit particeps, tanto est sapientior?"). It is especially in the collection *De diuersis quaestionibus* 83 that Augustine delved into this problem in a more technical way (see concerning this J.-A. Beckaert, *L'Ame et la participation platonicienne*, in *Mélanges doctrinaux*, BA, 10, complementary footnote 3, pp. 702–3). But he attempts to make his disciples understand it and live it from the early dialogues on.

12. *De beata uita* 4, 34, BA, 4, p. 282: "Quisquis igitur ad summun modum per ueritatem uenerit, beatus est. Hoc est animo deum habere, id est deo frui. Caetera enim quamuis a deo habeantur, non habent deum." Augustine differentiates between the true possession of God, which is that of the *beata uita*, and the state of the person who aspires to it without having reached it yet, which is *nondum beatus (De beata uita* 3, 21, BA, 4, p. 258 ff.*)* He contrasts with these two states the alienation of the one who makes himself foreign to God by sinning. Therefore, he establishes from the start a fundamental distinction between those who possess God or who are on their way towards him and the beings who, while belonging to him, by being possessed by him, do not possess him. The expressions *habere deum* and *haberi a deo* thus serve to distinguish two very uneven levels of participation: that of a life that comes from God but which alienates him from it by turning away from him, and that of wisdom. It has been pointed out that the connection between the word *habere* and the notion of participation is more apparent in Greek, where μέθεξις includes the root *to have:* ἔχειν. See R. Holte, *Béatitude et sagesse*, p. 57, n. 2, and pp. 217–18.

13. H.-I. Marrou, *Saint Augustin et la fin de la culture antique*, II, *Retractatio* (Paris: 1949), p. 667: "Saint Augustine proceeds like a skilful musician who makes one hear delicately, *mezza voce*, told in confidence to a secondary voice and played by a discreet instrument, the outline of a theme which is soon going to form the subject of a main development. The listener does not notice it, but when this theme reappears, bursts down-stage in the

orchestra, far from being surprised by it, we realize that we already know it, that we recognize it. . . ." The developments of the nourishment theme or the explicit references relating to it (independently of the equivalents which are the notions of having, fullness and measure) are found in the *De beata uita* 2, 6, BA, 4, p. 232 ff.; 3, 17, p. 253; 3, 20, p. 258; 3, 22, p. 260 ff.; 4, 30–31, p. 274 ff.; 5, 34–36, p. 282 ff.

14. *De beata uita* 1, 5, BA, 4, p. 230: "Quid enim solidum tenui, cui adhuc de anima quaestio nutat et fluctuat?"

15. *De beata uita*, 2, 8, BA, 4, p. 234 ff.:

> Quid ergo anima, inquam, nullane habet alimenta propria? An eius scientia uobis uidetur? Plane, inquit mater; nulla re alia credo ali animam quam intellectu rerum atque scientia . . . Inde, mihi crede, et talibus epulis animus pascitur, id est theoriis et cogitationibus suis, si per eas aliquid percipere possit. Cf. Plato, Phaedros 247 d-e: ἅτ' οὖν θεοῦ διάνοια νῷ τε καὶ ἐπιστήμῃ ἀκηράτῳ τρεφομένη καὶ ἁπάσης ψυχῆς, ὅση ἂν μέλλῃ τὸ προσῆκον δέξεσθαι, ἰδοῦσα διὰ χρόνου τὸ ὂν ἀγαπᾷ τε καὶ θεωροῦσα τἀληθῆ τρέφεται καὶ εὐπαθεῖ, ἕως ἂν κύκλῳ ἡ περιφορὰ εἰς ταὐτὸν περιενέγκῃ· ἐν δὲ τῇ περιόδῳ καθορᾷ μὲν αὐτὴν δικαιοσύνην, καθορᾷ δὲ σωφροσύνην, καθορᾷ δε ἐπιστήμην, οὐχ ᾗ γένεσις πρόσεστιν, οὐδ' ἥ ἐστίν που ἑτέρα ἐν ἑτέρῳ οὖσα ὧν ἡμεῖς νῦν ὄντων καλοῦμεν, ἀλλὰ τὴν ἐν τῷ ὅ ἐστιν ὂν ὄντως ἐπιστήμην οὖσαν· καὶ τἆλλα ὡσαύτως τὰ ὄντα ὄντως θεασμένη καὶ ἑστιαθεῖσα, δῦσα πάλιν εἰς τὸ εἴσω τοῦ οὐρανοῦ, οἴκαδε ἦλθεν, ἐλθούσης δὲ αὐτῆς ὁ ἡνίοχος πρὸς τὴν φάτνην τοὺς ἵππους στήσας παρέβαλεν ἀμβροσίαν τε καὶ ἐπ' αὐτῇ νέκταρ ἐπότισεν.

16. *De beata uita* 2, 8, BA, 4, p. 236 ff.:

> Nonne, inquam, conceditis hominum doctissimorum animos multo esse quam imperitorum quasi in suo genere pleniores atque maiores? Manifestum esse dixerunt. Recte igitur dicimus eorum animos, qui nullis disciplinis eruditi sunt, nihilque bonarum artium hauserunt, ieiunos et quasi famelicos esse. Plenos, inquit Trygetius, et illorum animos esse arbitror, sed uitiis atque nequitia. Ista ipsa est, inquam, crede mihi, quaedam sterilitas et quasi fames animorum. Nam quemadmodum corpus detracto cibo plerumque morbis atque scabie repletur, quae in eo uitia indicant famem, ita et illorum animi pleni sunt morbis quibus sua ieiuna confitentur. Etenim ipsam nequitiam matrem omnium uitiorum, ex eo quod nequicquam sit, id est ex eo quod nihil sit, ueteres dictam esse uoluerunt. Cui uitio quae contraria uirtus est, frugalitas nominatur. Ut igitur haec a fruge, id est a fructu, propter quamdam animorum fecunditatem, ita illa ab sterilitate, hoc est a nihilo, nequitia nominata est : nihil est enim omne quod fluit, quod soluitur, quod liquescit et quasi semper perit. Ideo tales homines etiam perditos dicimus. Est autem aliquid si manet, si constat, si semper tale est, ut est uirtus, quae temperantia et frugalitas dicitur.

These etymologies come from Cicero, *Tusculanes* 3, 8, 18: "Frugalitas, ut opinor, a fruge, qua nihil melius in terra, nequitia ab eo . . . quod nequicquam est in tali homine, ex quo nihili dicitur. Qui sit frugi igitur, uel, si mauis, moderatus et temperans, eum necesse est esse constantem; qui autem constans, quietem; qui quietus, perturbatione omni uacuum . . . ." Concerning this conception of *frugalitas* synonymous with temperance, Augustine quotes a little further another text by Cicero. See p. 12 and fn. 20. This etymology of *nequitia* is resumed in the *De uera religione*, in which it supports a more elaborate interpretation of sin conceived as a "nihilation" of the soul. See further p. 51, n. 12.

17. Augustine indicates the philosophical origin of these notions in a somewhat later text, written in 387: growth, wealth and freedom are the attributes of the intelligible world, lessening and indigence those of the tangible world. *Epistula* 3, CSEL, 34, p. 6 ff.:

> . . . nisi forte illud, quod aliquando Alypio dixi occultissime, habet magnam vim, ut, quoniam numerus ille intelligibilis infinite crescit, non tamen infinite minuitur — nam quid est aliud sensibilis numerus nisi corporeorum uel corporum quantitas? — minui quidem infinite, sed infinite crescere nequeat,et ideo fortasse merito philosophi in rebus intelligibilibus divitias ponunt, in sensibilibus egestatem. Quid enim aerumnosius quam minus atque minus semper posse fieri? quid ditius quam crescere, quantum uelis, ire, quo uelis, redire, cum uelis, quousque uelis, et hoc multum amare, quod minui non potest?

Cf. Porphyry, *Maxims* 37, Mommert, p. 33, 17–34, 3:

> ἐπεὶ δὲ πρὸς μὲν ὕλην ῥέπον ἴσχει ἀπορίαν πάντων καὶ τῆς οἰκέιας δυνάμεως κένωσιν, εἰς δὲ τὸν νοῦν ἀναγόμενον τὸ πλῆρες αὐτῆς καὶ τὴν δύναμιν ἔχειν τῆς πάσης εὑρίσκετο, τὴν μὲν εἰκότως Πενίαν, τὴν δὲ Κόρον οἱ τοῦτο πρῶτον γνόντες τῆς ψυχῆς τὸ πάθος ἠνίξαντο.

Maxims 40 quoted further p. 50, fn. 7. See the interpretation given by Plotinus of the Platonic myth of *Penia* and *Poros* in *Enn.* 3, 5, 5–9.

18. *De beata uita*, 4, 29, BA, 4, p. 272:

> Sic ergo dicimus aliquem habere egestatem, quasi dicamus habere nuditatem. Egestas enim uerbum est non habendi. Quamobrem, ut quod uolo explicem sicut possum, ita dicitur: "habet egestatem" quasi dicatur : "habet non habere."

19. *De beata uita* 4, 30, BA, 4, p. 274:

> Egestas autem stultitia est egestatisque nomen : hoc autem uerbum sterilitatem quamdam et inopiam solet significare . . . credo uos etiam concedere animum stultum esse uitiosum omniaque animi uitia uno stultitiae nomine includi. Primo autem die huius disputationis nostrae nequitiam dixeramus esse ab eo dictam quod nec quidquam sit, cui contrariam frugalitatem a fruge fuisse nominatam. Ergo in iis duobus contrariis, hoc est frugalitate atque nequitia, illa duo uidentur eminere, esse et non esse.

20. *De beata uita*, 4, 31, BA, 4, p. 276:

> Plenitudo igitur et egestas contraria sunt: at etiam hic similiter, ut in nequitia et frugalitate apparent illa duo, esse et non esse. Et si egestas est ipsa stultitia, plenitudo erit sapientia. Merito etiam uirtutum omnium matrem multi frugalitatem esse dixerunt. Quibus consentiens Tullius etiam in populari oratione ait: " Ut uolet quisque accipiat: ego tamen frugalitatem, id est modestiam et temperantiam, uirtutem esse maximam iudico." Prorsus doctissime ac decentissime: considerauit enim frugem, id est illud quod esse dicimus, cui est non esse contrarium.

Cicero's quotation comes from *Pro Deiotaro* 26.

21. *De beata uita* 5, 33, BA, 4, p. 280: "Coarctatur autem sordibus, timoribus, moerore, cupiditate . . . ." Thus we find again an expression similar to the one Licentius was questioning at the beginning of the dialogue, while Augustine was trying to establish an analogy with the body. *De beata uita* 1, 7, BA, 4, p. 234: "Et nemo dubitat cibis subtractis omnium animantium corpora macrescere. Macrescere, inquit Licentius, non decrescere. Satis est mihi, inquam, ad id quod uolo."

22. See R. Holte. *Béatitude et sagesse*, p. 219.

23. *De beata uita*, 5, 34, BA, 4, p. 282: "Quisquis igitur ad summum modum per ueritatem uenerit, beatus est. Hoc est animo deum habere, id est deo frui." *De beata uita* 5, 35, BA, 4, p. 284: "Illa est igitur plena satietas animorum, haec est beata uita, pie perfecteque

cognoscere a quo inducaris in ueritatem, qua ueritate perfruaris, per quid connectaris summo modo." The ontological meaning Augustine attributes to *frui* has been emphasized by R. Holte, *Béatitude et sagesse*, p. 197: "If the original meaning of *frux* is seed, everything that germinates, and thus depends on vegetative life, and if that of *frui* is to harvest, to enjoy what has grown, if moreover Augustine himself establishes an ontological comparison of *frux* with *esse* . . . the original meaning of *frui* must necessarily be very close to the notion of ontological participation. Thus the emphasis . . . must . . . be put on the ontological relation of the soul with God, whose meaning is that the soul receives divine life and receives from it a form which is moral plenitude, virtue, *frugalitas*. " As this author, *ibid*., n. 3, points out, the translation "to enjoy God" is not fully adequate. German allows a more satisfactory translation: *zur Frucht haben*, offered by E. Przywara, *Augustinus, die Gestalt als Gefüge* (Leipzig: Hegmer, 1934), p. 110, and repeated by R. Lorenz, *"Fruitio dei" bei Augustin*, in *Zeitschrift für Kirchengeschichte* 63 (1950–51), 87, n. 16. The latter also delved deeper into the ontological aspect of the *fruitio dei*, ibid., p. 92 ff. When *frui* relates to God, it seemed preferable for us to translate by "to find one's bliss in," which does not have the same Epicurean connotations as "to enjoy."

24. *De beata uita* 5, 36, BA, 4, p. 284:

> Ergo, inquam, quoniam modus ipse nos admonet conuiuium aliquo interuallo dierum distinguere, quantas pro uiribus possum gratias ago summo et uero deo patri, domino liberatori animarum, deinde uobis qui concorditer unuitati, multis etiam me cumulastis muneribus. Nam tantum in nostrum sermonem contulistis, ut me negare non possim ab inuitatis meis esse satiatum.

25. *De beata uita* 1, 5, BA, 4, p. 230: ". . .initium disputationum mearum, quod mihi uidetur religiosus euasisse . . . ."

26. *De ord.* 1, 8, 23, BA, 4, p. 338: "Aut quid est aliud conuerti, nisi ab immoderatione uitiorum uirtute ac temperantia in sese attoli?" Cf. ibid., the invocation to the God of virtues: "deus uirtutum."

27. *De ord.* 1, 8, 24, BA, 4, p. 340: ". . . uita beatissima perfruuntur . . ."; *De ord.* 2, 2, 6, BA, 4, p. 368: "Ille igitur sapiens amplectitur deum eoque perfruitur . . ."; *De ord.* 2, 7, 20, BA, 4, p. 396: "Siquidem deum habere, iam inter nos pridem in sermone illo quem die natali tuo iucundissimum habuimus, placuit nihil aliud esse quam deo perfrui."

28. *De ord.* 1, 2, 3, BA, 4, p. 306:

> Ita enim animus sibi redditus, quae sit pulchritudo uniuersitatis intelligit, quae profecto ab uno nominata est. Idcircoque illam uidere non licet animae quae in multa procedit sectaturque auiditate pauperiem, quam nescit sola segregatione multitudinis posse uitari. Multitudinem autem non hominum dico, sed omnium quae sensus attingit. Nec mirere quod eo egestatem patitur magis, quo magis appetit plura complecti. . . sic animus a seipso fusus immensitate quadam diuerberatur et uera mendicitate conteritur . . . .

Relating to this see the textual parallels established by A. Solignac between this text and Porphyry, *Maxims* 40 (Mommert) pointed out in n. 11 of the introduction.

29. *De ord.* 1, 2, 4, BA, 4, p. 308: "Assequeris ergo ista, mihi crede, cum eruditioni operam dederis, qua purgatur et excolitur animus, nullo modo ante idoneus cui diuina semina commitantur."

30. *De ord.* 2, 5, 14, BA, 4, p. 386:

> Talis enim eruditio, si quis ea moderate utatur (nam nihil ibi quam nimis formidandum est), talem philosophiae militem nutrit uel etiam ducem ut ad summum illum modum, ultra quem requirere aliquid nec possit, nec debeat, nec cupiat, qua uult euolet atque perueniat multosque perducat.

31. *De ord.* 2, 7, 20, BA, 4, p. 396:

> Sed illud uideamus, quoniam definitum sit a nobis quid sit esse cum deo, utrum scire possimus etiam quid sit esse sine deo, quamuis iam manifestum esse arbitror. Nam credo uideri tibi eos qui cum deo non sunt esse sine deo . . . Nam isti nec cum deo mihi uidentur esse et a deo tamen haberi; itaque non possumus eos sine deo esse dicere, quos deus habet. Cum deo item non dico, quia ipsi non habent deum. Siquidem deum habere iam inter nos pridem in sermone illo quem die natali tuo iucundissimum habuimus, placuit nihil aliud esse quam deo perfrui. Sed fateor me formidare ista contraria, quomodo quis nec sine deo sit nec cum deo.

See fn. 12 Supra, p. 23. CF. *De quant. an.* 34, 77, BA, 5, p. 388: "cum quo esse non omnes possunt, et sine quo esse nemo potest." Augustine in an admirable way made this theme clear in the *De trinitate,* 14, 12, 15, BA, 16, p. 388 ff.:

> Nam quid non est in ipso, de quo divine scriptum est: *Quoniam ex ipso, et per ipsum, et in ipso sunt omnia* [*Rom.* 11:36]? Proinde si in ipso sunt omnia, in quo tandem possunt uiuere quae uiuunt, et moueri quae mouentur, nisi in quo sunt? Non tamen omnes cum illo sunt eo modo quo ei dictum est: *Ego semper tecum (Ps. 72:23).* Nec ipse cum omnibus eo modo quo dicimus dominus uobiscum. Magna itaque hominis miseria est cum illo non esse, sine quo non potest esse. In quo enim est, procul dubio sine eo non est: et tamen si eius non meminit, eumque non intelligit, nec diligit, cum illo non est.

32. *De ord.* 2, 4, 11, BA, 4, p. 380:

> Namque omnis uita stultorum, quamuis per eos ipsos minime constans minimeque ordinata sit, per diuinam tamen prouidentiam necessario rerum ordine includitur et quasi quibusdam locis illa ineffabili et sempiterna lege dispositis, nullo modo esse sinitur ubi esse non debet. Cf. PLOTIN, *Enn.* 3, 2, 17.

33. *De ord.* 2, 2, 6, BA, 4, p. 368:

> Ille igitur sapiens amplectitur deum eoque perfruitur qui semper manet, nec exspectatur ut sit nec metuitur ne desit, sed eo ipso quo uere est, semper est praesens. Curat autem immobilis et in se manens serui sui quodammodo peculium, ut eo tanquam frugi et diligens famulus bene utatur parceque custodiat. *De ord.* 2, 5, 17, BA, 4, p. 392: Nam definitionem meam tu probasti, qua dictum est quid sit esse cum deo, cum quo mentem sapientis manere immobilem me, quantum assequi ualeo, docere uoluisti.

34. *De ord.* 2, 5, 16, BA, 4, p. 390.

35. *De ord.* 2, 16, 44, BA, 4, p. 436 ff.:

> . . . quid sit nihil, quid informis materia, quid formatum exanime, quid corpus, quid species in corpore, quid locus, quid tempus. . . et quid sit praeter tempus et semper, quid sit et nusquam esse et nunquam non esse: quisquis ergo ista nesciens, non dico de summo illo deo, qui scitur melius nesciendo, sed de anima ipsa sua quaerere ac disputare uoluerit, tantum errabit quantum errari plurimum potest: facilius autem cognoscet ista, qui numeros simplices atque intelligibiles comprehenderit.

36. *De ord.* 2, 17, 46, BA, 4, p. 442: ". . .cum inter eius et dei substantiam nihil uelint omnino distare."

37. About this difficult question see O. Du Roy, *L'Intelligence de la foi en la Trinité*, pp. 109–49. One of the main indications allowing the assertion that we are dealing with a reality similar to the *logos* is the definition of the *ratio* as the soul's gaze, *aspectus animi*. Cf. *Sol*. 1, 6, 13, BA, 5, p. 50; *De quant. an*. 14, 24, BA, 5, p. 276; 27, 53, p. 340. The source of this definition goes back to Plato, *Rep*. 7, 533 d. See further in our text p. 84 and n. 44.

38. *De ord*. 2, 18, 48, BA, 4, p. 444: "Hunc igitur ordinem tenens anima iam philosophiae tradita, primo seipsam inspicit, et cui iam illa eruditio persuasit, aut suam aut seipsam esse rationem . . . ." Cf. *De ord*. 2, 19, 50 quoted further n. 44, p. 29.

39. *De ord*. 2, 11, 30, BA, 4, p. 416:

> Ratio est mentis motio, ea quae discuntur distinguendi et connectendi potens, qua duce uti ad deum intelligendum, uel ipsam quae aut in nobis aut usquequaque est animam, rarissimum omnino genus hominum potest, non ob aliud, nisi quia in istorum sensuum negotia progresso redire in semetipsum cuique difficile est. Itaque cum in rebus ipsis fallacibus ratione totum agere homines moliantur, quid sit ipsa ratio et qualis sit nisi perpauci prorsus ignorant. Mirum uidetur, sed tamen se ita res habet.

40. *De ord*. 2, 19, 50, BA, 4, p. 450:

> Gradatim enim se et ad mores uitamque optimam non iam sola fide, sed certa ratione perducit. Cui numerorum uim atque potentiam diligenter intuenti nimis indignum uidebitur et nimis flendum, per suam scientiam uersum bene currere citharamque concinere et suam uitam seque ipsam quae anima est deuium iter sequi et dominante sibi libidine cum turpissimo se uitiorum strepitu dissonare. Cf. *De ord*. 2, 8, 25: Haec autem disciplina ipsa dei lex est, quae apud eum fixa et inconcussa semper manens, in sapientes animas quasi transcribitur, ut tanto se sciant uiuere melius tantoque sublimius, quanto et perfectius eam contemplantur intelligendo, et uiuendo custodiant diligentius. Haec igitur disciplina eis qui illam nosse desiderant, simul geminum ordinem sequi iubet, cuius una pars uitae, altera eruditionis est.

41. *De ord*. 2, 11, 31, BA, 4, p. 416 seq.:

> Ac primum uideamus ubi hoc uerbum, quod ratio uocatur, frequentari solet; nam illud nos mouere maxime debet, quod ipse homo a ueteribus sapientibus ita definitus est: homo est animal rationale mortale. Hic genere posito quod animal dictum est, uidemus additas duas differentias, quibus credo admonendus erat homo et quo sibi redeundum esset et unde fugiendum. Nam ut progressus animae usque ad mortalia lapsus est, ita regressus esse in rationem debet.

See Cicero, *Acad*. 2, 31.

42. *De ord*. 2, 15, 43, BA, 4, p. 436:

> Hic se multum erexit multumque praesumpsit: ausa est immortalem animam comprobare. Tractauit omnia diligenter, percepit prorsus se plurimum posse et quidquid posset, numeris posse. Mouit eam quoddam miraculum et suspicare coepit seipsam fortasse numerum esse eum ipsum quo cuncta numerarentur aut si id non esset, ibi tamen cum esse quo peruenire satageret.

43. *De ord*. 2, 19, 50, BA, 4, p. 448 ff.:

> Ista enim semper talis est, mundus autem iste nec heri habuit, nec cras habebit quod habet hodie, nec hodierno ipso die uel spatio unius horae eodem loco solem habuit: ita cum in eo nihil manet, nihil uel paruo spatio temporis habet eodem modo.

44. *Ibid.:*

> Igitur si immortalis est ratio et ego qui ista omnia uel discerno uel connecto ratio sum, illud quo mortale appellor non est meum. Aut si anima non id est quod ratio et tamen ratione utor et per rationem melior sum, a deteriore ad melius, a mortali ad immortale fugiendum est. Cf. *De ord.* 2, 11, 31, BA, 4, p. 416: Ac primum uideamus ubi hoc uerbum quod *ratio* uocatur, frequentari solet: nam illud nos mouere maxime debet, quod ipse homo a ueteribus sapientibus ita definitus est: homo est animal rationale mortale (cf. Cic. *Acad.* 2, 21). Hic genere posito quod animal dictum est, uidemus additas duas differentias, quibus credo admonendus erat homo et quo sibi redeundum esset et unde fugiendum. Nam ut progressus animae usque ad mortalia lapsus est, ita regressus esse in rationem debet. Uno uerbo a bestiis, quod rationale; et alio a diuinus separatur quod mortale dicitur. Illud igitur nisi tenuerit, bestia erit; hinc nisi se auerterit, diuina non erit.

Concerning the Plotinian and Porphyrian sources of this passage and the different hypotheses made relating to this see O. Du Roy, *L'Intelligence de la foi dans la Trinité*, p. 132, n. 3.

45. *Contra acad.* 1, 2, BA, 4, p. 18: ". . . beatae alterius uitae, quae sola beata est. . . ."

46. *Contra acad.* 1, 3, BA, 4, p. 18: ". . . illud ipsum, inquam, quod in te diuinum nescio quo uitae huius somno ueternoque sopitum est. . . ."

47. *Contra acad.* 8, 23, BA, 4, p. 56:

> . . . ut et hic, quod beatum esse supra inter nos conuenit, ratione perfruatur; et extremo die uitae ad id quod concupiuit adipiscendum reperiatur paratus, fruaturque merito diuina beatitudine, qui humana sit ante perfructus.

48. Cf. *De beata uita* 1, 8. Text quoted earlier p. 11 and n. 16.

49. *De ord.* 1, 8, 24, BA, 4, p. 340:

> . . . totus attollere in laudem puri et sinceri amoris, quo animae dotatae disciplinis et uirtute formosae copulantur, intellectui per philosophiam et non solum mortem fugiunt, uerum etiam utia beatissima perfruuntur.

50. *De ord.* 2, 9, 26, BA, 4, p. 408: "Ad quam cognitionem in hac uita peruenere pauci, ultra quam uero etiam post hanc uitam nemo progredi potest." Wise men are thus, according to this text, incorporated into immortality from here below already. Those who have not deepened their faith by means of the *ratio*, while remaining faithful to God, are the *nondum beati*, the ones mentioned in the *De beata uita* 3, 21. (See earlier n. 12). Their fate is specified in the subsequent part of the text:

> Qui autem sola auctoritate contenti bonis tantum moribus rectisque uotis constanter operam dederint, aut contemnentes, aut non ualentes disciplinis liberalibus atque optimis erudiri, beatos eos quidem, cum inter homines uiuunt, nescio quomodo appellem, tamen inconcusse credo mox ut hoc corpus reliquerint, eos quo bene magis minusue uixerunt, eo facilius aut difficilius liberari.

51. *De ord.* 2, 5, 17, BA, 4, p. 390:

> Anima uero unde originem ducat quidue hic agat, quantum distet a deo, quid habeat proprium quod alternat in utramque naturam, quatenus moriatur et quomodo immortalis probetur, quam magni putatis esse ordinis, ut ista discantur?

52. *Sol.* 2, 1, 1 BA, 5, p. 86: (ratio): "Horum omnium quae te nescire dixisti, quid scire prius mauis?" — (Aug.) "Utrum immortalis sim."

53. Ibid.: (ratio) "Quid, si ipsa uita talis esse inueniatur, ut in ea tibi nihil amplius quam nosti nosse liceat, temperabis a lacrymis?"—(Aug.) "Imo tantum flebo ut uita nulla sit." Cf. *Sol.* 2, 20, 36.

54. *Sol.* 1, 1, 3, BA, 5, p. 28 ff.:

> . . . Deus qui nos conuertis. Deus qui nos eo quod non est exuis, et eo quod est induis. . . . Cf. 1 Cor. 15:53–54: Oportet enim corruptibile hoc induere incorruptionem: et mortale hoc induere immortalitatem. Cum autem mortale hoc induerit immortalitatem, tunc fiet sermo qui scriptus est: absorpta est mors in uictoria. Cf. *De uera rel.* 12, 25: Vincit enim essentia nihilum, et sic absorbetur mors in uictoriam.

See further, p. 55 and n. 32.

In the lines that immediately precede the *Soliloquies* passage that we have just quoted, we should like to draw attention to the invocations in which the conversion theme is expressed for the first time in the triadic form that goes back to Porphyry. Here are those that relate more closely to the aspect we are studying: ". . . Deus a quo auerti, cadere; in quem conuerti, resurgere; in quo habitare, uiuere est." See O. Du Roy, *L'Intelligence de la foi en la Trinité*, p. 199 ff.; P. Hadot, *Commentaire des Traités sur la Trinité de Marius Victorinus* (Paris: Cerf, 1960), 2, p. 1070; W. Theiler, *Porphyrios und Augustin* (Halle: 1933), p. 33 ff.

55. *Sol.* 1, 1, 4, BA, 5, p. 30: ". . . una aeterna uera substantia, ubi nulla discrepantia, nulla confusio, nulla transitio, nulla indigentia, nulla mors. Ubi summa concordia, summa euidentia, summa constantia, summa plenitudo, summa uita. Ubi nihil deest, nihil redundat. . . ."

56. *Sol.* 1, 1, 2, BA, 5, p. 26:

> . . . Deus, per quem omnia, quae per se non essent tendunt esse . . . Deus qui paucis ad id quod uere est refugientibus, ostendis malum nihil esse. . . .

57. Cf. *Sol.* 1, 1, 5, BA, 5, p. 34: This remark would confirm the hypothesis that this prayer is subsequent to the rest of the work, because it gives evidence of the same thought that is found in the second part of the *De immortalitate animae* (God creator and giver of being, evil identified with nothingness). See O. Du Roy, *L'Intelligence de la foi en la Trinité*, p. 196.

58. Thus, for example, the definition of what is false as what tends to be and is not (*Sol.* 2, 9, 16–17, BA, 5, p. 116 ff.)

59. *Sol.* 2, 19, 33, BA, 5, p. 154:

> (ratio) "Immortalis est igitur anima: iamiam crede rationibus tuis, crede ueritati; clamat et in te sese habitare, et immortalem esse, nec sibi suam sedem quacumque corporis morte posse subduci. Auertere ab umbra tua, reuertere in te; nullus est interitus tuus, nisi oblitum te sese quod interire non possis."—(Aug.) "Audio, resipisco, recolere incipio."

60. Ibid. "Sed, quaeso, illa quae restant expedias, quomodo in animo imperito, non enim eum mortalem dicere possumus, disciplina et ueritas esse intelligantur." Cf. *Sol.* 2, 14, 25, BA, 5, p. 136 and *De immort. an.* 4, 5–6, BA, 5, p. 178 ff.

61. *Sol.* 2, 20, 34–35, BA, 5, p. 156.

62. *Retract.* 1, 5, 1, BA, 12, p. 294.

63. See H. Dörrie, *Porphyrios' "Symmikta Zetemata"* (Münich: Beck, 1959), p. 159. Even though H. Dörrie seems to somewhat underestimate the originality of the *De immortalitate animae*, he is perfectly right in pointing out that a careful analysis of the "material" gathered in this work would enlighten us on the work method that was then Augustine's.

64. Concerning this turning point for Augustinian thought in the *De immortalitate animae*, see O. Du Roy, *L'Intelligence de la foi dans la Trinité*, p. 185 ff. The entire chapter 6, "From anagogy to ontology," pp. 173–206 throws valuable light on the subject we are trying to elucidate. In particular it contains a very pronounced appreciation concerning the "question under discussion" of the respective influences of Plotinus and Porphyry on Augustinian metaphysics. In it, O. Du Roy questions W. Theiler's exclusively "Porphyrian" thesis. He points out the change from a conception of immortality exclusively centered on the contemplation of truth to a conception centered on the notion of creation or, at the very least, of "dependence in being." Without denying the Porphyrian influence, he considers that the Christian questioning of the creation problem suffices to explain Augustine's evolution with respect to this matter.

65. See J. Burnaby, *Amor Dei: A Study of the Religion of St. Augustine* (London: 1947), p. 152.

66. *De immort. an.* 6, 11, BA, 5, p. 190: "Deinde quo magis est, eo quidquid sibi coniungitur facit ut sit, cui rei contrarius est interitus." The source of the statement that the deity is not jealous goes back to Plato, *Timaeus* 29 e and *Phaedo* 247 a. Concerning the repetition of this theme in Plotinus, *Enn.* 5, 5, 12, and in the Neo-Platonists, as well as the other passages of Augustine's opus in which it appears, see O. Du Roy, *L'Intelligence de la foi dans la Trinité*, Appendix 3, pp. 474–75.

67. *De immort. an.* 6, 11, BA, 5, p. 190:

    At si illa rationis uis ipsa sua coniunctio afficit animum; neque enim non afficere potest; ita profecto afficit ut ei esse tribuat. Est enim maxime ipsa ratio, ubi summa etiam incommutabilitas intelligitur. Itaque eum quem ex se afficit, cogit esse quodammodo.

68. Cf.. *Retract.* 1, 5, 2, BA, 12, p. 294 ff. Augustine refers to Isaiah 59:2: "Your sins bring about a separation between God and you." See further p. 38 and n. 23.

69. See further p. 37 ff.

70. *De immort. an.* 7, 12, BA, 5, p. 190 ff.:

    At enim auersio ipsa a ratione per quam stultitia contingit animo, sine defectu eius fieri non potest: si enim magis est ad rationem conuersus eique inhaerens, ideo quod inhaeret incommutabili rei quae est ueritas, quae et maxime et primitus est; cum ab ea est auersus, idipsum esse minus habet, quod est deficere. Omnis autem defectus tendit ad nihilum; et interitum nullum magis proprie oportet accipi, quam cum id, quod aliquid erat, nihil fit. Quare tendere ad nihilum est ad interitum tendere. Qui cur non cadat in animum, uix est dicere, in quem defectus cadit.

71. *De immort. an.* 11, 18, BA, 5, p. 204:

    Tamen hoc etiam attendendum est, non esse aliam causam huius formidinis, nisi quia fatendum est in defectu quodam esse animum stultum, et in essentia certiore atque pleniore sapientem. Cf. *De immort. an.* 8, 13, BA, 5, p. 194: Quaerendum de hac re diligenter ac discutiendum est, ne quis affirmet animum tali defectu interire: ut quoniam specie aliqua sua priuatur dum stultus est, credatur in tantum augeri posse hanc priuationem, ut omni modo specie spoliet animum, et ea labe ad nihilum redigat cogatque interire.

72. J. Burnaby, *Amor Dei*, pp. 151–52; while bringing up the difficulties having to do with the Augustinian questions concerning immortality, Burnaby does not seem to have noticed that Augustine is trying to resolve the aporia of annihilation owing to the distinction of two ontological levels in the soul. On the other hand, the new aspect acquired by the proof has been emphasized by F. Cayré, *Initiation à la philosophie de Saint Augustin* (Paris; Etudes Augustiniennes — Desclee de Brouwer, 1947), pp. 113–14. "Here immortality is thus bound to the existence of a truth, prime cause of the thinking soul. This evidence is immediately confirmed by considering truth from a new point of view, no longer as intelligible but as an *essence;* for essence has no opposite and thus does not risk being destroyed in that way." O. Du Roy, *L'Intelligence de la foi en la Trinité*, pp. 182–83, mentioned a nearly contemporary text in which the attempt to "go from knowledge to being and from participation to creation" is recognized. It is a question of *De diu. quaest.* 83, q. 1, BA, 10, p. 52:

> Omne uerum a ueritate uerum est. Et omnis anima eo anima est, quo uera anima est. Omnis igitur anima a ueritate habet ut omnino anima sit. Aliud autem anima est, aliud ueritas. Nam ueritas falsitatem numquam patitur, anima uero saepe fallitur. Non enim cum a ueritate anima est, a seipsa est. Est autem ueritas deus: eum igitur habet auctorem ut sit anima.

73. *De immort an.* 12, 19, BA, 5, p. 206:

> At si ueritati contrarium ita quaeramus, non in quantum ueritas est, sed in quantum summe maximeque est, quanquam in tantum est idipsum in quantum est ueritas . . . Nam si nulla essentia in quantum essentia est aliquid habet contrarium, multo minus habet contrarium prima illa essentia quae dicitur ueritas in quantum essentia est. Primum autem uerum est . . . Nullo modo igitur res ulla esse potest contraria illi substantiae quae maxime ac primitus est. Ex qua si habet animus idipsum quod est (non enim aliunde noc habere potest qui ex se non habet, nisi ab illa re quae illo ipso est animo praestantior), nulla res est qua id amittat, quia nulla res est ei rei contraria qua id habet; et propterea esse non desinit. Sapientiam uero, quia conuersione habet ad id ex quo est, auersione illam potest amittere. Conuersioni namque auersio contraria est. Illud uero quod ex eo habet cui nulla res est contraria, non est unde possit amittere. Non igitur potest interire.

It is in this text that Augustine establishes for the first time the dual immanence pointed out by A. Solignac, *L'Existentialisme de Saint Augustin*, in *Nouvelle Revue Théologique*, 80 (1948), 10: "Man has being only through God's immanence in him and his in God, an immanence furthermore imperfectly reciprocal, and which leaves entirely safe divine transcendence: God's being conditions that of man, but not inversely. As for immanence itself, it is dual, it can and cannot be lost at the same time. . . ." The argumentation concerning Being without opposite contradicts Plotinus', *Enn.* 1, 8, 6. The probable Porphyrian sources of this new development of Augustinian ontology into a "monism of being" are pointed out by O. Du Roy, *L'Intelligence de la foi en la Trinité*, p. 193 ff.

74. Cf. Porphyry, *Maxims* 23 (Mommert), quoted later pp. 63–64 n. 25.

75. See earlier p. 13 and fns. 31 and 32; p. 16 and n. 50.

76. *De immort. an.* 7, 12–8, 15, BA, 5, pp. 190–98. It is in this passage that the notion of a form is found, of a *species* that makes the soul be — just as it is the *species* that makes the body be — and of which it can only be partially deprived. *De immort. an.* 8, 13, BA, 5, p. 194:

> Quaerendum de hac re diligenter ac discutiendum est, ne quis affirmet, animum tali defectu interire; ut quoniam specie aliqua sua priuatur dum stultus est, credatur in tantum augeri posse hanc priuationem, ut omni modo specie spoliet animum, et ea labe ad nihilum redigat cogatque interire.

The expression *existendi species* is found a little further, *De immort. an.* 11, 18, BA, 5, p. 204: ". . . id est metuendum ne deficiendo animus intereat, id est dum ipsa existendi specie priuatur."

77. *De immort an.* 3, 3–4, BA, 5, pp. 174–78.

78. For example *De lib. arb.* 3, 25, 76, BA, 6, p. 466:

> Ut autem in contemplatione summae sapientiae (quae utique animus non est, nam incommutabilis est), etiam seipsum qui est commutabilis, animus intueatur, et sibi ipse quodammodo ueniat in mentem, non fit nisi differentia qua non est quod deus, et tamen aliquid est quod possit placere post deum.

See E. Fortin, *Christianisme et culture philosophique au cinquième siècle* (Paris: Etudes Augustiniennes, 1959), p. 101 ff.

79. *De immort. an.* 8, 13, BA, 5, p. 194:

> Quod si non id quod est in mole corporis, sed id quod in specie facit corpus esse, quae sententia inuictiore ratione approbatur: tanto enim magis est corpus, quanto speciosius atque pulchrius; tantoque minus est, quanto foedius ac deformius; quae defectio non praecisione molis, de qua iam satis actum est, sed speciei priuatione contingit.
>
> Quaerendum de hac re diligenter ac discutiendum est, ne quis affirmet animum tali defectu interire; ut quoniam specie aliqua sua priuatur dum stultus est, credatur in tantum augeri posse hanc priuationem, ut omni modo specie spoliet animum, et ea labe ad nihilum redigat cogatque interire. Quamobrem si potuerimus impetrare ut ostendatur, ne corpori quidem hoc posse accidere, ut etiam ea specie priuatur qua corpus est; iure fortasse obtinebimus multo minus auferri posse animo quo animus est. Siquidem nemo se bene inspexit, qui non omni corpori qualemlibet animum praeponendum esse fateatur.

O. Du Roy, *L'Intelligence de la foi dans la Trinité*, p. 188 ff. pointed out Augustine's probable sources concerning participation in being by the *species*, beauty and form. If they go back to Plotinus, *Enn.* 5, 8, 9, 44–45, among others, it seems indeed that the participation in being by form is a theme that is more typically, or more explicitly, Porphyrian than Plotinian. Relating to this see W. Theiler, *Porphyrios und Augustin*, p. 11.

80. *De immort. an.* 8, 14, BA, 5, p. 196:

> . . . et illa effectoria uis uacare non potest, quin id quod ab ea factum est tueatur, et specie carere non sinat, qua est in quantumcumque est.

81. *De immort. an.* 8, 15, BA, 5, p. 198:

> Non enim quaepiam eius pars ad nihilum redigi sinitur, cum totum capessat uis illa effectoria nec laborante nec deside potentia, dans ut sit omne quod per illam est in quantum est.

82. See for example the definition of the "nonbeing" of the tangible universe *Epist.* 2, CSEL, 34, p. 3:

> Bene inter nos conuenit, ut opinor, omnia, quae corporeus sensus attingit, ne puncto quidem temporis eodem modo manere posse, sed labi, effluere et praesens nihil obtinere, id est, ut latine loquar, non esse. . . .

83. This first development of the notion of mutability concerns corporeal being, for Augustine does not yet settle the question about the soul. Cf. *De immort. an.* 8, 15, BA, 5, p. 196 ff.

84. *De immort. an.* 8, 15, BA, 5, p. 198:

> Atque ita de proximo immortalis probatur, si potest esse per seipsum. Quidquid enim tale est, incorruptibile sit necesse est, ac per hoc interire non possit, quia nihil se deserit. Cf. *De immort. an.* 2, 18, BA, 5, p. 204: Et illa omnia quae quoquo modo sunt ab ea essentia sunt, quae summe maximeque est: aut ab illa est animus in quantum est, aut per seipsum est. Sed si per seipsum est, quoniam ipse sibi causa existendi est et nunquam se deserit, nunquam interit. . . .

"It never lets itself go": that is Plato's expression, *Phaedros*, 245 c: "**οὐκ ἀπολεῖπον ἑαυτό**."

CHAPTER 2

Existence Finalized by Being

The *auersio* of Volition, the Cause of Evil

Augustine attempts to delve deeper, in the *De libero arbitrio*, into the answer that he had brought to the problem of evil in the *De ordine*. It is still a question of showing the integration of evil with the universal order, but the emphasis here is put on the problem set by human freedom. Can it be considered something good, while so many men only use it for their unhappiness? Whereas the wise person finds happiness in the immutable and eternal law that is the *summa ratio*, most of them turn away towards perishable possessions and suffer, due to this fact, the punishment immanent in the *auersio*.[1]

As in the *De ordine*, Augustine asserts that faith alone cannot settle this question; but henceforth he bases the legitimacy of his pursuit of the *intellectus fidei* on scriptural texts.[2] The answer is given in an anagogical proof, which, through a human *ratio* henceforth better distinguished from its divine prototype than in the earlier dialogues,[3] goes all the way up to God-Being.[4] The *ratio* can then show, from that point on, which are the assets that come from him. For it is solely from the point of view of being that it is possible to understand that free will, characterized as a *fruendi uoluntas*, is an asset even when it turns away from its true end. Evil, that is to say, sin and the punishment that is immanent in it, consists of this *auersio*, which is "the movement by which the mind on its own turns the *fruendi uoluntas* away from the Creator and toward the created being."[5] Leaving reality for its shadow, the soul no longer sees "what is in a supreme way."[6] Such is the reason for its blindness and suffering.[7]

This way of identifying evil with the failing of volition and the consequences that result from it seems to have come in great part from Porphyry's influence, recognizable as well in the "monism of being" developed here in a much more detailed way than in the *De immortalitate animae*.[8] (We remember that it was outlined there in order to demonstrate the indestructible existence of the soul, founded on its participation in the Essence without opposite.)

On the other hand, as we have already pointed out in connection with the conception of the *intellectus fidei*, the *De libero arbitrio* gives evidence of a much more thorough knowledge of Christian doctrine and of the scriptural texts than the earlier works. This is especially the case when we consider the changes contained in the second writing of *De libero arbitrio*, as regards a part of Book II and Book III, clearly characterized by a creational point of view.[9] It is necessary to mention also that, from Book III on, retributive justice is no longer asserted only by means of a general and seemingly philosophical phrase, as was still the case at the beginning of the work.[10] Revelation is henceforth offered in order to invalidate the hypothesis of the annihilation of the human being in the case of *auersio*.[11]

The Indestructible Form Element, *aliquid formae (De libero arbitrio* 2, 17, 46*)*

Such is the point of view to which belong the new aspects of the evidence of immortality, which boil down to two: proof by the constituent form of being and proof by the "wanting-to-be," *esse uelle*. Much as these types of proof may be different, they are both centered on the knowledge of supreme Being acquired through the anagogical proof. This knowledge alone allows one to respond to the problem of immortality as well as to that of evil, for they are closely connected from a wisdom point of view, which defines the latter as a "nihilating" power and immortality as a privileged form of participating in Being.

That is why Augustine feels compelled to elaborate the analysis of the constituent elements of the created being that he had undertaken in the *De immortalitate animae*. He picks up again the argument of a form that neither body nor soul can lose entirely. The *species*, which was the issue previously, is called here *forma*.[12] The form possessed by any changing (that is, created) being keeps it from falling back into nothingness. It postulates the existence of an original form, eternal and immutable, creative of the other beings through their forms. Eternity and immutability, constantly attributed to the divine *ratio* or Truth, are now no longer confirmed by philosophy alone, but also by scriptural quotes that Augustine will henceforth use in order to support the definition of God-Being.[13]

If form is considered to be a constituent element of being, a material component is not yet the issue in this analysis of the ontological structure of what is created. However, we shall notice that the created being is characterized as being shapable, *formabilis*,[14] and that the indestructible substratum of the body as much as of the soul is designated as a form element, *aliquid formae*, that is to say something that no longer possesses the integral reality of form:

> Indeed, what is there that is superior to the spiritual soul among created beings, and what can be inferior to the body? As great as their fall might be and even though both may go toward nothingness, however there remains for them a form element, that is why they still are in a certain way. But whatever form might remain for any fallen reality, comes from this form that cannot fall. Its law does not allow the very movement of things which fall or grow to go beyond the law dictated to it by their numbers.[15]

These are still only steps that blaze the trail for a solution, which will be elaborated in a more complete way in some of the later works. Meanwhile Augustine is going to give new importance to his argumentation by placing himself on the ground of spiritual experience: it is another step, which we shall discover in Book 3 of the *De libero arbitrio*.

The "Wanting-to-be," *esse uelle (De libero arbitrio* 3, 6, 18–8, 23*)*

Augustine recalls the objections based on God's prescience, which deny the goodness of his providence, and that of the free will created by him: foreseeing the bad use many men would make of their freedom, he should not have endowed them with a will susceptible of turning away from him or not have created them.[16]

To answer the first of these objections, Augustine shows the greatness that is still that of the damned soul, infinitely superior to the world of bodies in spite of the reduction from which it suffers, and the part it must play in the universal order, to whose richness it contributes even in this state.[17] But what especially interests us here is the way in which he answers the objection that existence is a burden of which certain men aspire to be freed, as is proven by the desire for nothingness, which pushes them to commit suicide. This objection seems to be inspired by a text from Plotinus.[18]

Without going back to the proofs just as they stand, which appealed to the aspirants for wisdom in the philosophical dialogues, Augustine uses a dialectic that is fundamentally the same, for it attempts to reach, even in this most fallen man who is a candidate for suicide, the intuitive meaning of being which expresses our true finality:

> If there is, in his opinion, the error that consists in believing in his complete destruction, there is in his feeling, *the natural wish for rest*. Now what is at rest is not nothingness, but is on the contrary more than what is without rest. For excitement makes our affections vary, in such a way that they destroy each other, whereas rest is characterized by constancy which, better than any other thing, makes us understand what being is. It is why the entire wish of the one who wants to die goes, not to stop being in death, but to find rest there. And while his error makes him believe that he will no longer be, *his nature makes him wish for rest, that is to say an increase in being*. It is why, since it is impossible not to love being, the fact that we are must not be a reason for us to show our ingratitude towards the goodness of the creator."[19] (Emphasis mine.)

The candidate for suicide does not make a mistake in feeling this authentic wish since it corresponds to the finality of our nature, but he does not know how to understand its true meaning, for he confuses the taste for peace, which is plenitude of being, with the aspiration for nothingness. He who, in his misfortune, hesitates to commit suicide as he obeys this wish to be, which he believes however to be illusory, does not understand either its true meaning:

I should wish not to be, rather than to be unhappy. But, I must admit, I prefer to be unhappy rather than to be nothing: an even more senseless will since I am more unhappy.[20]

Just like the apparently opposite wish of the one who chooses suicide, this fear of nothingness expresses, for the person who knows how to understand it, the "wanting-to-be" inherent to the soul, the more-or-less conscious ontological hunger that is found in every human created being:

Consider thus the greatness of this asset, which is the very Being *(ipsum esse)* longed for by the unhappy people as much as the happy ones. If you think carefully about that, you will see that you are unhappy to the extent to which you remain far from that which is in a supreme way; you will understand how you were able to believe that it is better not to be rather than to be unhappy: it is because you were not seeing what is in a supreme way; you will finally grasp the reasons for nevertheless wanting to be: it is because you are thanks to that which is in a supreme way.[21]

This *esse uelle* is the spiritual will, which, although unrecognized in the state of fall, of *auersio*, constitutes the essence of the soul or at least is inseparable from it, and whose meaning can be found again by the fallen man through conversion. Augustine translates here in ontological terms what he had expressed in the previous book by means of the *notiones impressae*, those of happiness and wisdom: *notio beatitatis, sapientiae notio.*[22]

It is convenient to ask oneself if that is what he had alluded to in the *De immortalitate animae*, when he was asserting, in a kind of phrasing that he rejected later on, that in a spiritual nature the will cannot turn away from being.[23] In the form that he attributes to it here, this "wanting-to-be" gives place to the action of the free will, which, powerless to separate us from God on the level of existence, nevertheless has the power to accept or to refuse our vocation for being. But, since we are made up of this finality, which makes us participate in the everlastingness of absolute being even before any possibility of a voluntary act on our part, refusal necessarily consists in choosing, not total annihilation, but the reduction of our being.

The Edification in Being and the Two Ontological Stages of the Soul

"To be or not to be," that is the choice for which life destines us, but with a different meaning from the generally accepted one. It is necessary to choose between the misfortune that consists in refusing the ontological finality inscribed in us and the blissful life that consists in accepting it, in order to be incorporated into what is in a supreme way:

If thus you want to escape your misery, love in yourself the very fact that you want to be. For if you want to be still more, you will come closer to what is in a supreme way. And now, give thanks to God for being. Inferior to the blessed, you are superior however to the beings who do not even have any desire for happiness. And yet the unhappy ones themselves exalt most of those beings and rightly so, for they are all good, from the very fact that they are. The more you will love being, the more you will yearn for eternal life and the more also you will wish for the transformation that will allow you not to tie yourself anymore to temporal possessions, the love of which marks you and burns you; for before existing, they are not; by existing, they pass; once they have passed, they will no longer be. Therefore, when they are to come, they are not yet; when they have passed, they no longer are. Thus, how can one make something remain, which only begins to be in order not to be? He who wishes to be finds these things good to the extent to which they are, and loves what always is. This love will make him stronger, whereas the love for the things here below made him constantly change; the love of what passes made him be scattered, whereas the love of what remains will strengthen him, will stabilize him and will make him possess the very Being: that is what he desired when he feared not to be and yet could not find stability, caught in the nets of his love for what passes. That you prefer to be, even unhappy, rather than not to be unhappy, while being nothing, this therefore must not make you sad, but on the contrary make you happy to the highest degree. *Build on this foundation in you, which is the very fact that you want to be; increase it by always being more: you will rise and you will be edified in what is in a supreme way.* Thus, you will prevent the inferior things from dragging you down in their fall toward nothingness, where they destroy the strength of those who have loved them. And so you see that he who prefers to renounce to be in order to avoid being unhappy has no other outlook than wretchedness. For whoever loves being more strongly than he hates unhappiness, let him cast out what he hates by increasing what he loves; in fact, as soon as he is in a perfect way, according to his nature, he will no longer be unhappy.[24] (Emphasis mine.)

In this text, Augustine distinguishes very clearly between several levels of being:

1. First, there is the lowest level *(quod infime est)*, consisting of all the created beings that do not have the will for happiness, the *beatitudinis uoluntas*, which determines the radical split between this level and the following ones.[25]
2. The spiritual being is found on the other side of this split. But it is necessary to distinguish in him two stages of ontological reality, arranged one in relation to the other as the bud is to the flower.
   a. The first stage is that of existence, of the fact of being *(quia es)*. But it is an existence of a specific nature, characterized by this "wanting-to-be" *(quia esse uis)*, which is nothing other than the will for happiness *(beatitudinis uoluntas)*, or just the natural desire for peace *(naturale desiderium quietis)*.

      This first level of being of the spiritual created being is thus designated as being that of nature:

      > For all beings owe God first what they are, in as much as they are natures; in the second place, they owe him this improvement of their being that, if they want it, those who have been endowed with will can acquire.[26]

If one keeps in mind the word nature, used with different meanings by Augustine according to the circumstances, it is necessary to recall that it is not a question of a reality that is completed.

b. This "nature" only finds its proper dimension thanks to the conversion of the will, in the case of the spiritual created being. It then has access to this second ontological stage, which is that of participation in true being, in which it is constituted, edified, thanks to this conversion *(in permanentis amore solidabitur, et stabit, et obtinebit ipsum esse . . . consurgis atque extrueris in id quod summe est.)* Man reaches it when he confirms by means of his free will the finality inscribed in his nature, whose completion is made up of this choice *(in suo genere perfecte esse coeperit).*

Thus we find that the distinction between the two stages of being in the soul, outlined in the *De immortalitate animae,* returns and is developed here. Above the level of simple existence *(quia es),* the participation of wisdom is defined this time in ontological terms: it is a question of an edification in being *(exstrueris in id quod summe est).* What is specified moreover — something that Augustine strongly stresses — is the extent to which the first level of being is finalized by the second, which alone gives it its entire meaning. *Esse uelle,* this notion probably borrowed from Stoic thought, is an ontological explanation of the *beatitatis notio* or *sapientiae notio,* of the *fruendi uoluntas* or *beatitudinis uoluntas,* and of the *naturale desiderium quietis.*[27]

But this desire imprinted in the soul must be confirmed by free will for it to be incorporated into being. Augustine distinguishes here two stages in the process of edification. The first is that of choice, whose voluntary, active aspect is clearly shown by him, whereas he emphasizes the passive aspect of the second stage: it is God who edifies us in being by conferring the form that is still missing from His initial outline *(teque ita formari exoptabis . . . extrueris in id quod summe est.).*

We can finally ask ourselves on what ontological level are those "who refuse the being that they could acquire if they wanted" is situated.[28] He who turns away from being retains nevertheless his spiritual nature: Augustine constantly insists on the fact that the perverse soul keeps a level of being superior to that of the body.[29] But it is lessened in the order that is its own by right, and tormented by this ontological desire, which it has chosen not to recognize. "As a matter of fact you will not be nothing, but you will be unhappy."[30] It is the reversal of the edification theme: the fall far from being without ever reaching impossible nothingness.

To our knowledge we shall not find in Augustine's subsequent work developments analogous to those we have just quoted concerning the "wanting-to-be" of the soul, by means of which he has so admirably called to mind its intrinsic ordination to being, beyond the more-or-less obscure consciousness it has of it in the state of fall. In all probability, this is because, since Book XIII of the *Confessions,* he considered the "wanting-to-be" from a different point of view, centered on the analogy with the Trinity, and for this reason emphasized only the conscious aspect of *uelle,* according to the Neo-Platonic triadic schema *esse, nosse, uelle.*[31] We must observe, however, that the *esse uelle* theme, as it was set forth in the *De libero arbitrio,* was still present in his thought when he was writing the autobiographical part of the the *Confessions,* since, in a passage that we have already quoted, he characterized, by means of this expression, the dilemma that tears the soul when it decides to choose that which is not eternal:

> For (the beauties here below) go where they have always gone, toward nothingness, and they tear the soul to pieces with poisoned regrets, because it wants to be and loves finding its peace in the object of its love.[32]

The metaphysical quality of the first stage of being characterized by *esse uelle* will be specified further in this same Book III, in the answer to the objections concerning original sin. Augustine attempts to show that divine goodness cannot be questioned, whatever may be the hypothesis one assumes concerning the origin of the soul. Faith as much as experience teaches us that, when it comes into this world, the soul finds itself in the dark about truth, *ignorantia ueri*, and finds it difficult to act in a straightforward way, *difficultas recti*, a state that has as consequence mortality, *mortalitas*. Augustine distinguishes, when he comes to this subject, between two meanings of the word nature, according to whether it is a question of the inborn, that is to say original, state of man, or of the state that is his own in fact, owing to the fall, from his birth.[33]

The answers to the objection are the same as above. The first is based on the ontological superiority of the soul in relation to the body, even when it is sinful or created in the state of sin.[34] The second answer is based on free will: the soul possesses the power of cultivating in itself what is potentially good, a beginning of aptitude for supreme goodness, *summi boni capacitas*, which allows it, if it wants to, to attain with the help of God wisdom and peace.[35]

The first ontological stage of the spiritual created being, that of simple existence *(quia es)*, is thus defined here in a more complete way, in terms of the drama to which the soul is committed by the very fact of its creation. It carries in itself the components of this drama. It is, on the one hand, the yearning to be in the absolute sense, *esse uelle* and its different synonyms. But, on the other hand, it is ignorance, difficulty, and mortality. The first ontological stage of the soul means finality in relation to true being, but it also means hindrance in relation to this end. It is characterized not only by a potentiality, but by a negativity for which all of Augustine's efforts in the *De libero arbitrio* are to show that it can be surmounted by the will turned towards God.

Creation and Conversion

If we attempt to draw up an evaluation of this analysis, we can place under three headings the elements that are new, or worked out in a new way, concerning the structure of the soul and its growth or its reduction in being. There is first the form theme, which is somewhat made to be dynamic, since we are dealing with an indestructible *aliquid formae*, which implies that something of the form can be lost; and since we are dealing, on the other hand, with a formation in being proceeding from the stage of simple existence *(teque ita formari exoptabis . . . exstrueris in id quod summe est)*. On the other hand, the *esse uelle* argument translates in ontological terms the yearning for the *beata uita*, which characterizes the spiritual created being. Finally, the full particulars about the "nature" of the soul understood in the Paulinian sense show that it is necessary to characterize the stage of simple existence, of *quia es*, not only by the positive potentiality that is that of *esse uelle*, of the *summi boni capacitas*, but also by the negative aspects of ignorance, difficulty, and mortality.

Moreover, we find that the two levels of reality that Augustine has distinguished in the soul from the *De immortalitate animae* on correspond to two metaphysical "stages," since there is progress from one to the other and since the first is finalized by the second. These two stages, that of simple existence and that of the incorporation into being, are also designated as *esse* and *beatus esse*. We shall notice that Augustine establishes a bond between them and the three stages, implicitly attributed to the three persons of the Trinity, during which God created man and led him to his end: *facere*, *reficere*, and *perficere*.[36]

Even though it is given casually, this indication, like the one that concerns the formation in being corresponding to the second ontological "stage" of the soul, shows that Augustine is in search of a solution that may allow the conciliation of the doctrine of creation with the Neo-Platonic metaphysics of conversion. Therefore, the major interest of the *De libero arbitrio*, from our point of view, consists of the synthesis that is outlined there between the theme of *magis esse* and *minus esse*, on the one hand, and, on the other, the assertion all at once of the immortality of the soul and of its creation. The aporia set by the immortality problem as long as it was considered from a point of view that somewhat absolutized the theme of *magis esse* and *minus esse*, for lack of a firm doctrine concerning the soul, led Augustine to bring out the structural elements of the latter, and in a more general way those of the created being, in their relation to *quod summe est*. It has already been seen with regard to the notion of mutability. The latter is completed, from the same creational point of view, by those of formation and of that which is susceptible to being formed.

It is thus that Augustine's anagogical point of view is rectified and at the same time expanded. He had to correct some of its aspects such as they presented themselves in the early works, by taking into account the difficulties that arise when one of them is developed in an exclusive way; by taking into account as well the data of faith. It is thus that his ontology progressively gains coherence, without our being able to contrast the latter in too absolute a way with the anagogical aim. For Augustine's central metaphysical intuition concerning spiritual life remains that of *magis esse* and *minus esse*, in which anagogy and ontology coincide. This is why A. Solignac's definition, a "spiritual ontology which is directly placed on the level of ethics,"[37] seems to perfectly fit the designation for this type of metaphysics.

After having attempted to show how the dialectic of *magis esse* and *minus esse* gave rise to a development of the ontological explanation concerning the soul and, in a more general way, the created being, in great part because of the aporia of annihilation that this dialectic brought about to Augustine's point of view then, we shall be able to examine now how this theme itself was developed in the early works. The following chapter will be dedicated especially to the negative aspect of the theme: *minus esse*, following the choice of nothingness. The last chapter will mainly deal with the positive aspect: *magis esse*, following the choice of being.

NOTES

1. *De lib. arb.* 1, 6, 15, BA, 6, p. 162:

> Quid? illa lex quae summa ratio nominatur, cui semper obtemperandum est, et per quam mali miseram, boni beatam uitam merentur, per quam denique illam quam temporalem uocandam diximus, recte fertur recteque mutatur, potestne cuipiam intelligenti non incommutabilis aeternaque uideri?: *De lib. arb.* 1, 16, 34, BA, 6, p. 204: . . . utrum sit aliud male facere, quam neglectis rebus aeternis, quibus per seipsam mens fruitur, et per seipsam percipit, et quas amans amittere non potest, temporalia et quae per corpus hominis partem uilissimam sentiuntur, et nunquam esse certa possunt, quasi magna et miranda sectari.

2. Isa. 7:9: "Nisi credideritis, non intelligetis"; John 17:3: "Haec est, inquit, uita aeterna, ut cognoscant te solum deum uerum, et quem misisti Iesum Christum"; Matt. 7:7: "Quaerite et inuenietis." Cf. *De lib. arb.* 1, 2, 4, BA, 6, p. 142 and 2, 2, 6, BA, 6, p. 216.

3. *De lib. arb.* 2, 6, 14, BA, 6, p. 238 ff.:

> Sed, quaeso te, si non inueneris esse aliquid supra nostram rationem, nisi quod aeternum atque incommutabile est, dubitabisne hunc deum dicere? Nam et corpora mutabilia esse cognoscis; et ipsam uitam qua corpus animatur, per affectus uarios mutabilitate non carere manifestum est; et ipsa ratio cum modo ad uerum peruenire nititur, et aliquando peruenit, aliquando non peruenit, mutabilis esse profecto conuincitur. Quae si nullo adhibito corporis instrumento, neque per tactum, neque per gustatum, neque per olfactum, neque per aures, neque per oculos, neque per ullum sensum se inferiorem, sed per seipsam cernit aeternum aliquid et incommutabile, simul et seipsam inferiorem, et illum oportet deum suum esse fateatur.

Thus, concerning the human *ratio*, an evolution comparable to a certain extent with the one we have mentioned earlier, p. 21 and fn. 78, is established relating to the soul. The *mutabilitas* has become the criterion that differentiates between the created being and the Creator.

4. *De lib. arb.* 2, 15, 39, BA, 6, p. 290:

> Est enim deus, et uere summeque est. Quod iam non solum indubitatum, quantum arbitror, fide retinemus, sed etiam certa, quamuis adhuc tenuissima, forma cognitionis attingimus . . . .

5. *De lib. arb.* 1, 2, BA, 6, p. 326:

> . . . eius . . . proprius iste motus, quo fruendi uoluntatem ad creaturam a creatore conuertit. *Ibid.*; . . . omnisque de hac re disciplina utilis ad id ualeat, ut eo motu improbato atque cohibito, uoluntatem nostram ad fruendum sempiterno bono a lapsu temporalium conuertamus; *De lib. arb.* 3, 1, 3, BA, 6, p. 328: . . . non enim quidquam tam firme atque intime sentio quam me habere uoluntatem, eaque me moueri ad aliquid fruendum.

6. *De lib arb*. 2, 16, 43, BA, 6, p. 300:

   Ex quo incipit non posse uidere quod summe est, et malum putare quidquid fallit improuidum . . . cum ea pro merito patiatur auersionis suae . . . .

7. *De lib. arb*. 2, 12, 34, BA, 6, p. 280:

   . . .cum illa (ueritas) in se manens nec proficiat cum plus a nobis uidetur, nec deficiat cum minus, sed integra et incorrupta, et conuersos laetificet lumine, et auersos puniat caecitate. Cf. Plotin, *Enn*. 6, 5, 12, 25–28: ὀυδ' ἦλθεν, ἵνα παρῇ. ἀλλὰ σὺ ἀπῆλθες ὅτε οὐ πάρεστιν. Εἰ δ' ἀπῆλθες οὐκ ἀπ' αὐτοῦ (αὐτὸ γὰρ πάρεστιν) οὐδέ ποι ἀπῆλθες, ἀλλὰ παρὼν ἐπὶ τὰ ἐναντία ἐστράφης.

   This text was quoted by Porphyry, *Maxims* 40 (Mommert). See further p. 59, n. 7.

8. *De immort. an*. 12, 19. See earlier p. 20 and n. 73.

9. See O. Du Roy, *L'Intelligence de la foi en la Trinité*, p. 237 ff.

10. *De lib. arb*. 1, 6, 15. Text quoted p. 43, n. 1.

11. Matt. 25:41 in *De lib. arb*. 3, 9, 28, BA, 6, p. 380: "Ite in ignem aeternum, qui praeparatus est diabolo et angelis eius." Here is the chronological list of the first quotations from this text.

De Gen. contra man. 2, 17, 26	388 or 389
De lib. arb. 3, 9, 28	394–95
Contra Adimantum 7, 1; 17, 4; 27	394
De agone christiano 2, 2	396 or 397
Contra Faustum 21, 3	398

   There are more than a hundred quotations from Matt. 25:41 in Augustine's opus. They are particularly frequent in the *Enarrationes in Psalmos*. It is A.-M. La Bonnardière who was kind enough to pass this information on to us.

   In the following passage, Augustine explains the expression *non erit* from Psalm 36 (37), v. 10, as meaning not the total annihilation of the sinner, but the end of his terrestrial part, which consisted in testing the just.

   En. in Ps. 36, S. 1, 10–11, CC, 38, p. 345: *Adhuc pusillum, et non erit peccator, et quaeres locum eius, et non inuenies. Ostendit, quid dixit: non erit*; non quia omnino non erit, sed quia ad nullos usus esse poterit. Si enim omnino non erit, nec torquebitur: iam ergo securitas data est peccatori, ut dicat: Faciani quidquid uolo quamdiu uiuo, postea non ero. Non erit qui doleat, non erit qui torqueatur? Et ubi est: *Ite in ignem aeternum, qui paratus est diabolo et angelis eius?* Sed forte missi in ignem illum non erunt, et consumentur. Non illis diceretur: *Ite in ignem aeternum*, quia non futuris non esset aeternus. Et tamen quid illic futurum sit eis, utrum omnino consumtio, an dolor et cruciatus, non tacuit dominus dicens: *Ibi erit ploratus et stridor dentium*. Quomodo ergo plorabunt et stridebunt dentibus, si non erunt? Quomodo ergo hic: *Adhuc pusillum, et non erit peccator*, nisi quomodo in sequenti uersu exposuit: *Et quaeres locum eius, et non inuenies?* Quid est: *locum eius?* Usum eius. Habet enim aliquem usum peccator? Habet. Hic utitur illo deus ad probandum iustum, quomodo usus est diabolo ad probandum Iob, quomodo usus est Iuda ad tradendum Christum. Est ergo in hac uita quod agatur de peccatore. Hic est ergo locus eius, quomodo est in fornace aurificis locus paleae. Ardet palea, ut aurum purgetur; sic saeuit impius, ut iustus probetur. Sed cum transierit tempus probationis nostrae, quando non erunt qui probentur, non erunt per quos probentur. Numquid quia diximus: Non erunt qui probentur, non erunt ipsi? Sed quia iam non opus erit peccatoribus per quos iusti probentur: *Et quaeres locum eius, et non inuenies*.

12. See earlier p. 21 and fn. 76. As O. Du Roy indicates, *L'Intelligence de la foi en la Trinité*, p. 188 n. 6, the equivalence of *species* and *forma*, already indicated *Sol*. 2, 18, 32, is explicitly asserted in *De diu. quaest*. 83, q. 46, 2, BA, 10, p. 124: "Ideas igitur latine possumus uel formas uel species dicere." Augustine seems to draw his inspiration from Cicero, *Top*. 7, 30.

13. *De lib. arb*. 2, 17, 45, BA, 6, p. 302:

> Quid autem amplius de mutabilitate corporis et animi dicamus? superius enim satis dictum est. Conficitur itaque, ut et corpus et animus forma quadam incommutabili et semper manente formentur. Cui formae dictum est: Mutabis ea et mutabuntur; tu autem idem ipse es, et anni tui non deficient. (*Ps*. 101, 27–28). Annos sine defectu, pro aeternitate posuit prophetica locutio. De hac item forma dictum est, quod in se ipsa manens innouet omnia (*Sap*. 7, 27). Hinc etiam comprehenditur omnia prouidentia gubernari. Si enim omnia quae sunt, forma penitus subtracta nulla erunt, forma ipsa incommutabilis, per quam mutabilia cuncta subsistunt, ut formarum suarum numeris impleantur et agantur, ipsa est eorum prouidentia; non enim ista essent, si illa non esset.

Concerning the scriptural justification for the attribute of immutability, cf. especially *De natura boni* 24, 24, BA, 1, p. 462 ff. See relating to this our article on *L'Immutabilité de Dieu selon Saint Augustin*, in *Nova et Vetera*, 41 (1966), 219 ff.

14. *De lib. arb*. 2, 17, 45, BA, 6, p. 300:

> Omnis enim res mutabilis, etiam formabilis sit necesse est. Sicut autem mutabile dicimus quod mutari potest, ita formabile quod formari potest appelauerim.; *De lib. arb*. 2, 17, 46, BA, 6, p. 304: . . . *istae igitur duae creaturae corpus et uita quoniam formabilia sunt, sicuti superius dicta docuerunt, amissaque omnino forma in nihilum recidunt, satis ostendunt se ex illa forma subsistere, quae semper eiusmodi est*.

15. *De lib. arb*. 2, 17, 46, BA, 6, *p*. 304:

> Quid enim maius in creaturis quam uita intelligens, aut quid minus potest esse quam corpus? Quae quantumlibet deficiant, et eo tendant ut non sint, tamen aliquid formae illis remanet, ut quoquo modo sint. Quidquid autem formae cuipiam rei deficienti remanet ex illa forma est quae nescit deficere, motusque ipsos rerum deficientium uel proficientium excedere numerorum suorum leges non sinit.

We see that corporeal being is endowed with a form, and consequently with being, because it partakes of intelligible numbers. *De lib. arb*. 2, 16, 41,BA, 6, p. 294:

> . . . ipsis exteriorum formis (sapientia) intro reuocat; ut quidquid te delectat in corpore, et per corporeos illicit sensus, uideas esse numerosum . . .; *De lib. arb*. 2, 16, 42, BA, 6, p. 296: . . . formas habent, quia numeros habent: adime illis haec, nihil erunt. A quo ergo sunt, nisi a quo numerus? quandoquidem in tantum illis est esse, in quantum numerosa esse.

16. *De lib. arb*. 3, 5, 14, BA, 6, p. 350 ff.:

> . . . intuentes peccata hominum, non ut peccare desinant, sed quia facti sunt dolent, dicentes: Tales nos faceret ut semper incommutabili eius ueritate perfrui, nunquam autem peccare uellemus.

17. *De lib arb*. 3, 5, 12, BA, 6, p. 346:

> . . . quia tales instituit, ut etiam peccatis sordidatae, nullo modo lucis corporalis dignitate superentur, de qua tamen iure laudatur. *De lib. arb*. 3, 5, 16, BA, 6, p. 354 sq.: Quia igitur omnis anima omni corpore est melior, omnisque peccatrix anima quocumque ceciderit,

nulla commutatione corpus efficitur, nec omnino illi aufertur quod anima est, et ideo nullo pacto amittit quod corpore est melior, in corporibus autem lux tenet primum locum; consequens est ut primo corpori anima extrema praeponatur . . . (anima) quae ad quantumlibet sui decoris diminutionem defectumque peruenerit, omnium corporum dignitatem sine ulla dubitatione semper superabit. *De lib. arb.* 3, 9, 26, BA, 6, p. 374: Quod autem ipsae non desunt animae, quas uel peccantes sequitur miseria, uel recte facientes beatitudo, semper naturis omnibus uniuersitas plena atque perfecta est. *De lib. arb.* 3, II, 33, BA, 6, p. 388: . . . ista, quae tantummodo si non esset, non autem si peccaret, aliquid minus habetet uniuersitas.

18. It is not from Plotinus' brief treatise on suicide (*Enn.* 1, 9), that Augustine drew his inspiration. In it only a popular moral sermon is found, similar to Epictetus', as was noted by E. Bréhier, *Plotin, Ennéades* (Paris: Les Belles Lettres, I, 1924), p. 131. Here is the text in which Plotinus gets himself made fun of by the Epicurean, in order to better delve in his answer deep into the metaphysics of being and of what is good. *Enn.* 6, 7,24, 18–30:

> ὑμεῖς, ὦ οὗτοι, τί δὴ ἀποσεμνύνετε τοῖς ὀνόμασιν ἄνω καὶ κάτω ζωὴν ἀγαθὸν λέγοντες καὶ νοῦν ἀγαθὸν λέγοντες, καίτοι ἐπέκεινα τούτων; Τί γὰρ ἂν καὶ ὁ νοῦς ἀγαθον εἴη; Ἢ τί ὁ νοῶν τὰ εἴδη αὐτὰ ἀγαθὸν ἔχοι αὐτὸ ἕκαστον θεωρῶν; Ἠπατημένος μὲν γὰρ ἂν καὶ ἡδόμενος ἐπὶ τούτοις τάχ' ἂν ἀγαθὸν λέγοι καὶ τὴν ζωὴν ἡδεῖαν οὖσαν· στὰς δ' ἐν τῷ ἀνήδονος εἶναι διὰ τί ἂν φήσειεν ἀγαθά; . . . Ἢ τί ἂν διαφέροι ἐν τῷ εἶναι ἢ ὅλως μὴ εἶναι, εἰ μή τις τὴν πρὸς αὐτὸν φιλίαν αἰτίαν τούτων θεῖτο; Ὥστε διὰ ταύτην τὴν ἀπάτην φυσικὴν οὖσαν καὶ τὸν φοβον τῆς φθορᾶς τὴν τῶν ἀγαθῶν νομισθῆναι θέσιν.

19. *De lib. arb.* 3, 8, 23, BA, 6, p. 368 ff.:

> . . . in opinione habet errorem omnimodae defectionis, in sensu autem naturale desiderium quietis. Quod autem quietum est, non est nihil; immo etiam magis est quam id quod inquietum est. Inquietudo enim uariat affectiones, ut altera alteram perimat: quies autem habet constantiam, in qua maxime intelligitur quod dicitur, est. Omnis itaque ille appetitus in uoluntate mortis, non ut qui moritur non sit, sed ut requiescat intenditur. Ita cum errore credat non se futurum, natura tamen quietus esse, hoc est magis esse desiderat. Quapropter, sicut nullo pacto fieri potest ut non esse aliquem libeat; ita nullo pacto fieri oportet ut ex eo quod est quisque, bonitati creatoris ingratus sit.

20. *De lib. arb.* 3, 7, 20, BA, 6, p. 362:

> . . . magis enim non esse, quam miser esse uelle deberem. Nunc uero fateor me quidem malle uel miserum esse quam nihil; sed tanto stultius id uolo, quanto miserius. . . .

21. *De lib. arb.* 3, 7, 20, BA, 6, p. 362:

> Considera igitur, quantum potes, quam magnum bonum sit ipsum esse, quod et beati et miseri uolunt. Nam si hoc bene consideraueris, uidebis te in tantum esse miserum, in quantum non propinquas ei quod summe est; in tantum autem putare melius esse ut quisque non sit quam ut miser sit, in quantum non uides quod summe est: et ideo tamen te esse uelle, quoniam ab illo es qui summe est. See also Appendix, p. 101.

22. *De lib. arb.* 2, 9, 26, BA, 6, p. 262:

> Ut ergo constat nos beatos esse uelle, ita nos constat uelle esse sapientes: quia nemo sine sapientia beatus est. Nemo enim beatus est nisi summo bono quod in ea ueritate quam sapientiam uocamus cernitur et tenetur. Sic ergo antequam beati simus, mentibus tamen nostris impressa est notio beatitatis; per hanc enim scimus fidenterque et sine ulla dubitatione dicimus beatos nos esse uelle: ita etiam priusquam sapientes simus sapientiae notionem in mente habemus impressam, per quam unusquisque nostrum si interrogetur uelitne esse sapiens sine ulla caligine dubitationis se uelle respondet.

23. *De immort an.* 6, 11, BA, 5, p. 190:

> Voluntate autem animum separari a ratione non nimis absurde quis diceret, si ulla ab inuicem separatio posset esse rerum quas non continet locus. Cf. *Retract.* 1, 5, 2, BA, 12, p. 294 ff. See earlier p. 19 and fn. 68.

24. *De lib. arb.* 3, 7, 21, BA, 6, p. 362 ff.:

> Si uis itaque miseriam fugere, ama in te hoc ipsum, quia esse uis. Si enim magis magisque esse uolueris, ei quod summe est appropinquabis: et gratias age nunc quia es. Quamuis enim beatis sis inferior, superior tamen es quam ea quae non habent uel beatitudinus uoluntatem; quorum tamen multa etiam a miseris laudantur. Omnia tamen eo ipso quo sunt, iure laudanda sunt; quia eo ipso quo sunt, bona sunt.
>
> Quanto enim amplius esse amaueris, tanto amplius uitam aeternam desiderabis, teque ita formari exoptabis, ut affectiones tuae non sint temporales, de temporalium rerum amoribus inustae et impressae: quae temporalia et antequam sint non sunt, et cum sunt fugiunt et cum fugerint non erunt. Itaque cum futura sunt, nondum sunt; cum autem praeterita sunt, iam non sunt. Quomodo igitur tenebuntur ut maneant, quibus hoc est incipere ut sint, quod est pergere ut non sint? Qui autem amat esse, probat ista in quantum sunt, et amat quod semper est. Et si uariabatur in amore istorum, munietur in illius; et si diffluebat in amore transeuntium, in permanentis amore solidabitur, et stabit, et obtinebit ipsum esse, quod uolebat cum timebat non esse, et stare non poterat irretitus amore fugientium.
>
> Non igitur tibi displiceat, immo maxime placeat, quod mauis esse uel miser, quam propterea miser non esse, quia nihil eris. Huic enim exordio quo esse uis, si adiicias magis magisque esse, consurgeris atque extrueris in id quod summe est; atque ita te ab omni labe cohibebis, qua transit ut non sit quod infime est, et secum amantis uires subruit. Hinc fiet ut qui mauult non esse, ne miser sit, quia non esse non potest, restat ut miser sit. Qui autem plus amat esse quam odit miser esse, adiiciendo ad id quod amat, quod odit excludat: cum enim in suo genere perfecte esse coeperit, miser non erit.

25. Augustine will later specify that, if the created beings belonging to this lowest level do not persevere in being, it is without any fault of their own, for, unlike the spiritual created beings, the former did not get the possibility to be more.
De lib. arb. 3, 15, 44, BA, 6, p. 410:

> In omnibus ergo defectibus, aut non acceperunt ultra esse quae deficiunt, et nulla culpa est: sicut etiam cum sunt, quia non acceperunt amplius esse quam sunt, nihilominus culpa est; aut nolunt esse, quod si uellent esse acceperunt; et quia bonum est, reatus est si malunt.

26. *De lib. arb.* 3, 16, 45, BA, p. 410:

> Omnia ergo illi debent, primo quidquid sunt, in quantum naturae sunt: deinde quidquid melius possunt esse si uelint quaecumque acceperunt ut uelint.

27. We presume so, unless Augustine transposed the yearning for existence which characterizes matter in Plotinus. Cf. *Enn.* 3, 6, 7, 14.

28. *De lib. arb.* 3, 15, 44, BA, 6, p. 410: "Nolunt esse, quod si uellent, esse acceperunt."

29. See earlier fn. 17, p. 67. Cf. among others *De immort. an.* 13, 20–22, BA, 5, p. 208 ff.; *De mus.* 6, 13–14, BA, 7, p. 386 ff; *De uera rel.* 41, 77, BA, 8, p. 138 ff.

30. *De lib. arb.* 3, 16, 45, BA, 6, p. 410: ". . . non quidem nihil, sed miser tamen eris."

31. Cf. *Conf.* 13, 11, 12, BA, 14, p. 442 ff.; *De ciu. dei* 11, 26–28, BA, 35, p. 112 ff. See O. Du Roy, *L'Intelligence de la foi en la Trinité*, p. 427. At the last international patristic

conference, in Oxford, Father du Roy expressed an opinion in favor of this explanation in the brief presentation that followed a paper in which we had broached this question. See our article on *"Etre" ou "ne pas être" selon Saint Augustin*, in *Revue des Etudes Augustinennes* 14 (1968), 97.

32. *Conf.* 4, 10, 15, BA, 13, p. 434: "Eunt enim quo ibant, ut non sint, et conscindunt eam desideriis pestilentiosis, quoniam ipsa esse uult, et requiescere amat in eis quae amat." See earlier pp. 4–5 and n. 17. We find however a reappearance of the *esse uelle* theme in the *City of God*, precisely in connection with the Trinitarian image. Augustine no longer studies it in the same way as in the *De libero arbitrio*, but merely shows the "natural" aspect of this desire to be. *De ciu. dei.* 11, 26–27, BA, 35, p. 114 ff.:

   > Tam porro nemo est qui esse se nolit, quam nemo est qui non esse beatus uelit. Quo modo enim potest beatus esse, si nihil sit? Ita uero ui quamdam naturali ipsum esse iucundum est, ut non ob aliud et hi qui miseri sunt nolint interire et, cum se miseros esse sentiant, non se ipsos de rebus, sed miseriam suam potius auferri uelint . . . Unde enim mori metuunt et malunt in illa aerumna uiuere, quam eam morte finire, nisi quia satis apparet quam refugiat natura non esse? . . . Quid? animalia omnia etiam irrationalia, quibus datum non est ista cogitare, ab inmensis draconibus usque ad exiguos uermiculos nonne se esse uelle atque ob hoc interitum fugere omnibus quibus possunt motibus indicant . . .

33. *De lib. arb.* 3, 18, 51 ff., BA, 6, p. 420 ff. The words *ignorantia* and *difficultas*, generally used alone, are made clear by a complement 3, 22, 64, p. 446:

   > . . . si ignorantia ueri et difficultas recti naturalis est homini, unde incipiat in sapientiae quietisque beatitudinem surgere, nullus hanc ex initio naturali recte arguerit . . . De lib. arb. 3, 19, 54, BA, 6, p. 426. Sic etiam ipsam naturam aliter dicimus, cum proprie loquimur, naturam hominis, in qua primum in suo genere inculpabilis factus est: aliter istam in qua ex illius damnati poena, et mortales et ignari et carni subditi nascimur; iuxta quem modum dicit apostolus: "Fuimus enim et nos naturaliter filii irae, sicut et coeteri." *(Ephes. 2:3).*

34. *De lib. arb.* 3, 20, 56, BA, 6, p. 428 ff.: ". . . quia ipse ortus eius et inchoatio quouis perfecto corpore est melior."

35. *De lib. arb.* 3, 20, 56, BA, p. 428 ff.:

   > . . . sed etiam quod facultatem habet, ut adiuuante creatore seipsam excolat et pio studio possit omnes acquirere et capere uirtutes, per quas et a difficultate cruciante, et ab ignorantia caecante liberetur; *De lib arb.* 3, 22, 64, BA, 6, p. 444: Ignorantia uero et difficultas, si naturalis est, inde incipit anima proficere, et ad cognitionem et requiem, donec in ea perficiatur uita beata, promoueri. Quem profectum in studiis optimis atque pietate, quorum facultas ei non negata est . . . *De lib. arb.* 3, 22, 65, BA, 6, p. 446: Creator uero eius ubique laudatur, uel quod eam ab ipsis exordiis ad summi boni capacitatem inchoauerit . . .

36. *De lib arb.* 3, 20, 56, BA, 6, p. 430:

   > . . . neque omnino potuit nisi deus omni potens esse etiam talium creator animarum, quas et non dilectus ipse faciat, et diligens eas reficiat, et dilectus ipse perficiat; qui et non existentibus praestat ut sint, et amantibus eum a quo sunt praestat ut beatae sint.

37. See A. Solignac, *L'Existentialisme de Saint Augustin*, in *Nouvelle Revue Théologique* 70 (1958), 10.

CHAPTER 3

The Fall Towards Impossible Nothingness

Spiritual and Corporeal "Nihilation" *(ad nihilum uergere)*

In this chapter, we aim at examining the way in which Augustine developed the *minus esse* theme in a number of works that are situated between those we have just studied and the *Confessions*. Our interest is mainly in the sixth book of the *De musica* and in the *De uera religione*, in passages from works, the majority of which are anti-Manichean, as well as in some later texts that attest to the permanence of this theme in Augustine's thought.

However different his aims may be — the anagogical climb from the tangible to the supreme intelligible by means of the liberal sciences, the "defense" of true religion; the criticism of Manichean metaphysics — the works we have just mentioned have one fundamental trait in common: in them Augustine studies thoroughly the philosophy he has drawn from the "Platonists' books" in order to make of it a coherent instrument of *intellectus fidei* in which ontological explanation and anagogy find a balance.

In order to avoid needless repetitions, we shall first examine the negative aspect especially of the spiritual ontology elaborated in these works, reserving the more careful study of its positive aspect for the following chapter. *Minus esse* moreover holds a privileged place in these texts that are almost all anti-Manichean, for it allows the clarification of the assertion that evil is neither a substance nor a nature, but that it consists in falling far from being and in drawing near nothingness, which is its consequence.[1]

We have already seen that this theme is contained in that of the universal mutability of the cosmos, which participates, nevertheless, in as distant a way as it may be, in the stability of immutable Being. Things are transformed there, grow and lessen without ever being completely destroyed, because their tendency toward nothingness is checked "by whatever part of form remains in them."[2] This is why death is never more than a partial victory of nothingness over being.[3]

From this point of view, the reduction of the soul is presented as a particular case of a law that rules over the entirety of the tangible universe. But its true nature consists in participating in the richness of the intelligible world, which offers it the possibility of growing in being, rather than suffering the ontological fall that is the ineluctable fate of things here below. Therefore, *minus esse*, which affects the soul, is a consequence of the free choice of its will, as we have seen it in the *De libero arbitrio*.[4] It is at least the most apparent and most frequently developed aspect of this theme, as it is found in the above-mentioned works. We shall examine within the following chapter a different aspect of it, which only appears later, beginning with the last books of the *Confessions*. There Augustine will explain the creation of matter, corporeal as well as spiritual, as a kind of fall far from Being. It is a question of a later development of *minus esse* and of the triadic schema of Neo-Platonic origin in which it is contained: *auerti, reuerti,* and *conuerti*. This particular aspect of *minus esse* cannot be separated from the edification in being, whose initial stage it constitutes.

On the other hand, the aspect that we mean to analyze now corresponds to an opposition that stands out more clearly, to a true dilemma between being and nothingness. It is a matter of showing the ontological reduction, the "nihilation" to which the man is condemned who chooses the terrestrial values, in contrast with the ontological edification, "solidification," and consistency that result from his choosing being.

The Platonic origin of this theme has already been mentioned in connection with the *De beata uita*.[5] The expression *magis esse* and *minus esse* translates the Plotinian ἧττον and μᾶλλον ἐιναι.[6] Even though this expression may not be attested in Porphyry — as far as we know anyway — a clarification of Plotinus' thought concerning this is found in the *Maxims*, and it seems very much that Augustine drew his inspiration from this commentary.[7]

The dialectic of *magis esse* and *minus esse* can only be understood in all its profoundness in relation to the fundamental theme, avered by the Judeo-Christian revelation as much as by the Platonic philosophy, of an original state of man, of an original beauty coming from his total allegiance to God (in spite of the differences separating these doctrines in the interpretation of this common theme, and notwithstanding the evolution of Augustine himself concerning this). The soul then enjoyed an integrity that was conferred on it by its absolute participation in the divine essence: it had dominion over its own body and over the material universe, both of which were by nature subordinate to it, by reason of their ontological inferiority.

The second state considering the chronological point of view is this mysterious fall in which the spiritual created being, man or angel, chooses as object something inferior to God: be it the choice of oneself out of pride, a characteristic sin of the angel,[8] or the choice of values inferior to the created spirit itself, in order to satisfy sensuality, the taste for domination, or curiosity. These are the three major concupiscences of the fallen man. They make him choose the "nonbeing" that defines the body and leads the soul toward nothingness.[9] The ambiguity of the notions of "nonbeing" and body comes from the ethical harmonic which they comprise in an ontology of the Platonic type. It is quite apparent that Augustine is constantly attempting to prevent the erroneous interpretation, which has caused so many misunderstandings, about his alleged condemnation of the body. Actually he only wants to condemn the mind's subordination to the body, its corporealization so to speak, according to the suggestive expression he used in the *Letter to Secundinus:*

> To fall is not to be nothing already but to get closer to nothingness. For when what is more leans towards what is less, it is not the second but the first of these realities that

> falls and begins to be less than before. As a matter of fact, it does not become identical to that towards which it leans, but its own nature has less being. When the soul leans toward the body, thus it does not become body, but, under the effect of this desire that lessens it, it corporealizes in some way.[10]

From the moment it turns to this "less-being" (in relation to God) that the created spirit is, or to the "nonbeing" of the temporal universe, this choice leads the created being that has moved in the direction of nothingness in a fall characterized sometimes as a forsaking of original being, sometimes as a forsaking of its own being: it is one and the same. "Here thus is what constitutes evil . . . falling away from essence and tending not to be."[11]

In this definition, which Augustine proposes to the Manicheans, evil consists in failing one's own nature. In the example that follows, it is a matter of the forsaking of divine Being:

> The soul, which, by a voluntary distancing, separates from Him who has made it, in whose essence it used to find its joy, and which wants to find its joy in bodies, contrary to God's law, which has made it superior to them: this soul turns toward nothingness. That is the sin, not that the body per se is nothingness.[12]

Sin, defined as a movement that comes from nothingness,[13] turns the soul away from true Being, the originator of the created being, as the name *essentia* means, which it alone deserves in the literal sense.[14] That is why the fact of turning away from it inevitably leads to an ontological lessening. Sin has as effect the corrosion of the soul's being, it is a "fall movement, which brings about in the soul a failing of essence."[15]

While constantly insisting on the fact that this failing is voluntary, and that the sinner consequently takes upon himself the entire responsibility for it, Augustine nevertheless asserts that the soul can only turn toward "nonbeing" by means of a mistake, thinking it will find there substantial nourishment. Without this illusion, it would be impossible for it to turn away from God, for owing to the fact that it partakes, as inchoatively as it may, of his spiritual nature, it aspires exclusively to what characterizes true being, but it looks for it where it is not. "For what the soul seeks in this world, constancy and eternity, it does not find them there."[16]

That is what makes up the punishment immanent to the *auersio*. Man remains with his ontological hunger, for he no longer receives anything but the inconsistent sustenance of the values here below, which by nature are passing, and which by his choice are made even more perishable. It is thus that the soul nihilates itself and pronounces its own body's death sentence.

Indeed, in this incarnate spirit that man is, the ontological degradation of the soul falls on the body. By turning away from God, the soul becomes unable to take up normally its role of intermediary.[17] "Because of the mistake made by its master, the body is less than before, at the time when the soul was more."[18]

Therefore, not only moral evil, but physical disorder itself is the consequence of the warped choice made by the soul. It is the explanation for illness and finally for the body's death. The soul degrades the object of its choice by the very fact that it chooses it as an end:

> Indeed, it loves what has less being than itself, since it is a body. And because of this sin, the object of its love becomes corruptible, in such a way that it escapes, by coming undone, the one who loves it, because he himself, by loving it, has abandoned God. He has neglected his command, which said to him: eat this and not that (Cf. Genesis 2:16–17). He is thus pushed towards the punishment, for by loving the inferior things, he takes his place in the lower regions where, deprived of his pleasures, he will find suffering. Indeed, what is the suffering called physical, if it isn't the sudden corruption of the health that the soul itself, by the bad service it has made of it, has exposed to this corruption? What is the suffering called moral, if it isn't the deprivation of these changing possessions which the soul enjoyed or had hoped to enjoy? Thus, this is what evil comes down to: sin and the punishment of sin.[19]

In spite of the importance he attributes to the inclination towards the body to account for the *auersio* of the soul far from the original Essence and from its own essence, Augustine, however, does not see in that the ultimate reason for man's sin. He made the synthesis of this explanation with that concerning the angel's sin: the fall of the spiritual created being is fundamentally explained by the desire to enjoy oneself, by the perverted love of one's own power, as this later text strongly indicates:

> The soul that was leaving itself is called back to itself. By leaving itself, it was also its lord it was leaving. It had contemplated itself, it had liked itself, it had fallen in love with its own power. It went far from God, without, for all that, remaining in itself. And, pushed away and outside of itself, shut out from itself and hastened to the outside, it begins to love the world, to love what is subjected to time, to love the earth. If, neglecting its creator, it would love itself, it would immediately be less, it would immediately have less being for having loved what is less: for it is less than God, and even much less, just as an object has less being than him who has made it. Thus, it is God it was supposed to love. It would be necessary to love God to the extent of forgetting ourselves if possible. And so what is this transformation? The soul forgot itself by loving the world: it can forget itself, but while loving the creator of the world. For pushed away and far from itself, it is the same as being lost; it no longer knows how to see what it is doing, it justifies its iniquities: carried away by its pride, it takes pleasure in insolence, lewdness, honors, power, riches, the kingdom of vanity. But one day it feels itself being accused, stopped, it sees itself, it is displeased with itself, it confesses its ugliness, aspires to beauty, and, whereas it was drifting away, it comes back upset.[20]

The "corporealization," the nihilating fall towards externality, are only the consequence of the choice made by the soul of its individual self, to the detriment of what in it is a participation in the divine Being's internality and constitutes its true wealth:

> When it becomes inflated with pride, [the soul] goes towards outward things, and nihilates itself *(inanescere)* so to speak, which consists in being less and less. Now going a great deal to the outside, isn't it the same as throwing overboard one's inner wealth, that is to say pushing God away from oneself not in terms of space but in terms of the heart?[21]

Such are the expressions Augustine uses to characterize the ontological lessening that affects the soul led astray from Being, and whose bodily withering is only the last consequence: *minus minusque esse*, to be less and less; *ad nihilum uergere, tendere, inclinari*, to come close to nothingness; *inanescere*, "to nihilate oneself," just barely qualified by an *ut ita dicam*.[22] Without ever being able to cross the boundary that separates it from nothingness, the soul comes close to it to the extent in which it turns away from Being:

> The soul loses strength when it consents to evil, and begins to be less, and for this reason to have less vigor than when, not consenting to any evil, it remained steadfast in virtue. It is even worse since it turns away from what is to the highest degree in order to tend towards what is less, in such a way that it itself is less. Now the less it is, the closer it comes to nothingness. For all things whose being lessens tend to absolute nothingness. And even though the soul does not succeed in being nothing and in dying entirely, it is evident, nevertheless, that any lapse whatsoever is the beginning of death.[23]

The ontological lapse susceptible to wound the soul brings out its mutability, which is the sign of its condition as a created being, coming out of nothingness. As high as the level of being that is normally its own may be, since it is defined by the internality of spiritual life, it is however destructible:

> For the soul is nothing by itself; otherwise it would not be subject to change nor open to falling from its essence. Since it is nothing by itself, the entire being it possesses must come to it from God: when it remains faithful to its nature, it lives by God's very presence in the mind as well as in the conscience. The soul thus possesses this goodness inside itself.[24]

To come close to nothingness, for the soul, thus means to participate less and less in the only true life, by leading this "other life," which is that of the world, characterized by a state of degradation, ontological and moral at the same time, that Augustine symbolizes, with the Scripture, by the decrepitude of the old man. It is the state in which we begin our existence here below. If we refuse to transform it by converting to the one who is being, we follow the fall movement initiated in us by original sin and we choose to remain in this state, which Augustine, with the Scripture and with the *platonicorum libri*, calls death.[25]

We have noticed the boldness of the ontological expressions by means of which he attempts to make one understand what the death of the soul means. He seems to use them with even more assurance since henceforth he has resolved in a definitive way the aporia of absolute annihilation. It is true that beginning with the *De libero arbitrio* he depends more and more on the revealed texts in order to prove the immortality of death — or life. It does not remain any less true that he attempted to obtain an understanding of it, as far as it was possible, by examining closely the different stages of being in which the body and the soul are found, as well as their reciprocal relations based on the hierarchy of their relations with the original Essence. Moreover, we find in much later texts an eschatological application of *minus esse*. In two passages commenting on the *Ego sum qui sum* from *Exodus:* 3, 14, the divine "I am" is called to mind as a counterpoint for the "nihilation" theme, which Augustine believes to have found also in certain scriptural texts, mainly in Psalm 38:14: "Forgive me before I depart, and I will be no more."[26] He explains at length that to "be no more," far from expressing total annihilation, means the suffering inflicted on the soul made for being, when it turns away from it, this finitude which does not finish, this perpetual alteration, of which the very punishment of damnation consists:

> Thus, what does there remain for me to ask, since, without any doubt, I am doomed to leave this world for another? "O forgive me, that I may be refreshed before I go hence." See, see, Idithun, which are the sins for which forgiveness will allow you to be refreshed before you go.[27] Caught in the fire of passions, you want to be refreshed and you say: "Forgive me, that I may be refreshed." What will he forgive you, if you do not have this anguish that makes you say: "forgive us our debts" [Matt. 6:2]? "Forgive me before I go hence, and be no more." Free me from my sins before I go, that I may not leave with my sins. Forgive me, so that my conscience may be at peace, freed from the flood of worries whose burden I carry for my sins. "Forgive me, that I may be refreshed" above all else: "before I go hence, and be no more." For, if you do not forgive me, so that I may be refreshed, I shall go hence and I will be no more. "Before I go hence," for when I shall be gone, I will be no more. "Forgive me, so that I may be refreshed." But a question is raised: how will he be no more? He has not yet gone towards rest; what turns God away from Idithun? Certainly, Idithun will go hence and he will go towards rest. But let us take someone else, not Idithun, not a man turned towards the hereafter; a miser, a usurper, unjust, proud, vain, full of haughtiness, holding in contempt the poor man sitting at his door. Can it be said about this man: he will not be? Thus, what does this mean: "I will be no more?" If the wicked rich man were not, then who was the victim of the flames? Who then desired passionately that the poor Lazarus moisten his tongue with a drop of water? Who then was saying: "Father Abraham, send me Lazarus" [Luke 16:24]? Surely he was, since he was speaking in such a way, since he was burning in order to resuscitate on the last day and to be damned and sent into the eternal fire with the devil. When then did Idithun say: "I will be no more," if it weren't because he knows what being and not being is? For he was seeing the end, as much as the forces of his heart and mind allowed him, this end that he wanted to have shown to him when he was saying: "Lord, let me know my end" [Ps. 38:5]. He was seeing the number of his days, this number that is, and he was aware that things here below are not, in comparison with this being, and he was saying that he himself was not. For being remains, things here below are changing, fragile, mortal, and the eternal torments themselves are only perpetual alteration, an infinity of finitude. He turned towards this blessed region, this blessed homeland, this blessed abode where the saints participate in eternal life and immutable truth: and he feared being excluded from it and returning to nonbeing, in his desire to be where supreme Being is. And, since, placed between the two, he was able to make the comparison, he is still under the influence of fear and he says: "Forgive me so that I may be refreshed before I go hence, and I will be no more." For if you do not forgive me, I shall go far from you for all eternity. Far from whom? From him who said: "I am who I am"; from him who said: "Tell the children of Israel: he who is sent me to you." For he who goes against what truly is goes to nonbeing.[28]

The above-mentioned text, as well as a passage from *The City of God* concerning the fall of the angels suffice to prove that Augustine did not forego translating the mystery of spiritual death by a lessening of being, even though he may scarcely resort to it in the majority of the texts in which he deals with the punishments of hell.[29]

The Victory of the Body and Soul over Nothingness *(essentia uincit nihilum)*

We are impressed by the tightness of the bond that links the body's fate to that of the soul in this dialectic. The body's "more being" and "less being" follow in a rigorous way the principles borrowed by Augustine from the Neo-Platonic philosophers. Now, whereas the theme of the ontological growth and reduction of the soul is made especially clear in Porphyry's *Maxims*, we could look in this work in vain for the assertion that the body has a parallel destiny. W. Theiler, so ingenious at proving Porphyry's influence on Augustine, does not point out anything about this, but he emphasizes on the contrary the skillfulness with which Augustine uses the Porphyrian theme on behalf of the resurrection of the body.[30]

The preoccupation with making this dogma accessible to the intellect must certainly have played a part in establishing such a strict relation of reciprocal causality between the body and the soul. But it is not a mere argument suited to the occasion, for Augustine uses the *minus esse* theme in a very synthetical way, in order to explain evil from the point of view of the punishment as much as from that of the offense, from the physical point of view as much as from the moral one, on earth as much as in the hereafter. We certainly notice an eschatological application of the theme from the time when Augustine transposes the ideal of the wisdom constitutive of immortality onto the level of the final things: henceforth he asserts that it will only be acquired in an absolute way in the hereafter.[31] The resurrection of the body will be the ultimate outcome of the spiritual battle led against evil. It will testify to the integral victory against death, which will finally be reduced to nothingness, thanks to the final annihilation of its "nihilating" power.

> Therefore, it will happen that after the body's death, a consequence of original sin, it will recover its original stability, which it will not get from itself, but from the soul made firm in God . . .. "He will also give life to your mortal bodies through the Spirit which dwells in you." (Rom 8:11)
>
> When sin is removed, the punishment for the sin will also be removed: and where then is evil? "Where is, oh death, thy victory? Where is, oh death, thy sting?" *Being has conquered nothingness*: it is thus that "death is swallowed up in victory." (1 Cor. 15:54–55)[32] (Emphasis mine.)

We can ask ourselves if the extreme coherence of Augustine's thought concerning this has been sufficiently appreciated in Christian circles, if its depth and realism have been perceived — as they should be in an age which gives such importance to psychosomatic medicine. It seems that this extreme coherence has been scarcely noticed, due to the mistrust of the Platonic aspect of Augustine's doctrine, for it has been understood as a dualism of body and soul, whereas Augustine considers them as deeply united, expressing this through an ontological monism. From his anagogical point of view, Augustine worried less about defining the body-soul relation on the anthropological level than about expressing the spiritual bond that connects them or should connect them.[33] Now it seems that such a point of view is more accessible to certain religious temperaments than an anthropological explanation, because it is based in a more immediate way on internal experience.

Coherence and Permanence of the *minus esse* Theme

By examining the way in which Augustine has worked out the "*minus esse*" theme in the works that follow the philosophical dialogues, we discover how carefully he has studied and qualified it. Are we justified, then in saying, along with J. Burnaby, that the Augustinian ontology left to its particular logic would lead, without the corrective of dogma, to asserting that the sinful soul purely and simply annihilates itself?[34] The reason he gives for this view is the radicalization that this Platonic theme undergoes when it is applied to a creational concept.

Burnaby's comment is certainly justified concerning the early dialogues. The question of annihilation, we have seen, presented for Augustine a true difficulty, when he was attempting to elaborate the *intellectus fidei* from a point of view in which the anagogical impulse prevailed over ontological coherence. Having started by defining evil in a purely negative way in contrast with Manichean dualism, and unaware, as he himself complained, of the soul's status, it was difficult for him to show why it is not annihilated when it is the victim of evil.

The soul's *minus esse* would actually constitute an unsolvable aporia if the opposition between being and nothingness that Augustine substitutes for that of a right and a wrong being both substantial, were an opposition between terms susceptible of cancelling each other because they are both on the same level. But Augustine precisely attempts to show that it is a question of an opposition of another nature. Below Being that nothing can penetrate, the spiritual created being, because it comes from nothingness, can be overtaken by this mysterious "nihilating" power that is evil. But it cannot be entirely destroyed, nor change form like solely corporeal beings, because of the privileged aspect of its participation in Being even previous to any act of *auersio* or *conuersio* on its own behalf. It is in order to define this limit to the power of *minus esse* that Augustine was led to the elaboration of the soul's ontological status, as he did beginning with the *De immortalitate animae* and especially in the *De libero arbitrio*.

It is true that in order to protect divine omnipotence and the gratuitousness of the creative act, certain Church Fathers asserted that the soul is not immortal by right.[35] But Augustine, on the contrary, attempts to demonstrate the immortality inherent in even the most depraved soul. The creational point of view will surely prevent him from asserting that the soul is "by itself," *per seipsum*, as he still does by way of a hypothesis in the *De immortalitate animae*.[36] This impossibility probably encouraged him to work out an ontological explanation of the soul's status that is compatible at the same time with the Christian doctrine of creation, with that of the immortality asserted, in spite of their differences, by the Scriptures and by the *platonicorum libri*, and finally with the dialectic of *magis* and *minus esse*, which the latter have taught him.

It is in order to maintain at the same time immortality and the lessening caused by sin that Augustine started by distinguishing in the soul two stages of being, the first being indestructible even when the soul "comes close to nothingness"; he then developed this outline with the help of the notions of form, mutability, and finally later matter. We shall see this in a more precise way when we study in the next chapter the new developments given, especially in the last books of the *Confessions*, to the positive counterpart of *minus esse:* the incorporation into being.

For want of having followed closely enough the way in which Augustine went deeply into the theme that we are studying in the works following the *De immortalitate animae*, but in a context which is no longer that of the evidence for immortality, Burnaby believed he had abandoned it, because he had felt the contradiction that this Neo-Platonic theme was introducing into a structure of Christian thought. But the fact that the evidence for immortality no longer appears in the form Augustine had given it in the *De immortalitate animae* does not mean that he had dropped the idea of explaining the soul's life and death as a *magis esse* and *minus esse*. Otherwise, it would be necessary to draw similar conclusions from the fact that suicide, whose metaphysical implications Augustine analyzed at length in the *De libero arbitrio*, is only the object of doctrinal and moral considerations in the later works. Nevertheless, he reaffirmed in a completely different context the essential conclusion of this analysis, concerning the soul's "wanting-to-be."[37] Similar comments could be made about other themes, for example, that of the lie.[38]

Thus, we must not imagine that Augustine has to explain the same subject always in the same way, on pain of being accused of having put an end to his early thought. We must take into account the context in which this explanation is found in order to know what is his main intention: if it is above all of a catechetic, pastoral, or philosophical nature.

We must also take into account the fact that after having developed, in the works called philosophical, the main themes of an ontology that brings him the *intellectus* of the revealed data, Augustine no longer needs to devote himself to these "quibbles," which he criticizes in the *Retractationes*. This does not prove in any way that he has renounced the themes he has tried to study thoroughly by their means. The excerpts from the later works quoted in this chapter have allowed us to prove this concerning *minus esse*.

If, in spite of the depth and coherence that Augustine has been able to give it, this theme has remained an aporia of his thought, it is a fertile aporia that has allowed him the close examination of the metaphysical meaning of spiritual death. By this right, it remains inseparable from the keystone of his ontology, from the *quod summe est* that the nihilating power of evil cannot reach, and whose created image itself partially holds in check this power even in the beings who have turned away from Being and from themselves.

NOTES

1. Here is a very explicit and "pedagogical" text relating to this, and concerning corruption, a synonym of evil: *Contra epist, fundam.* 40, 46, BA, 17, p. 500 ff.

> Si quis autem non credit ex nihilo esse corruptionem, proponat sibi haec duo, esse et non esse, quasi ex diuersis partibus; intelligendi gratia, ut cum tardis tardius ambulemus: deinde uelut in medio constituat aliquid, ut puta corpus animantis, et quaerat hoc secum, dum formatur illud corpus et nascitur, dum augetur eius species, nutritur, conualescit, roboratur, decoratur, firmatur, in quantum manet, et in quantum stabilitur, in quam partem tendat, utrum ad esse, an non esse: non dubitabit esse quidem aliquid in ipsis etiam primordiis; sed quanto magis forma et specie et ualentia constabilitur atque firmatur, tanto magis fieri ut sit, et in eam partem tendat qua positum est esse. Nunc ergo incipiat corrumpi . . . quaerat etiam nunc per istam corruptionem quo tendat, utrum ad esse, an non esse: non puto usque adeo caecum et tardum, ut dubitet quid sibi ipse respondeat, et non sentiat quanto magis quodque corrumpitur, tanto magis ad interitum tendere. Omne autem quod ad interitum tendit, ad non esse tendit. Cum ergo deum incommutabiliter et incorruptibiliter esse credendum sit, id autem quod dicitur nihil penitus non esse manifestum sit: et cum ista tibi proposueris esse et non esse, atque cognoueris quanto magis augetur species, tanto quidque tendere ut sit; quanto magis augetur corruptio, tanto magis tendere ut non sit: quid dubitas dicere in unaquaque natura corruptibili quid in ea sit ex deo, quid sit ex nihilo; cum species secundum naturam sit, corruptio contra naturam? Quia species aucta cogit esse, et deum fatemur summe esse: corruptio uero aucta cogit non esse, et constat quod non est nihil esse. Quid, inquam, dubitas dicere, in natura corruptibili, quam et naturam dicis et corruptibilem dicis, quid sit ex deo, quid ex nihilo? Et quid quaeris deo naturam contrariam, quem si confiteris summe esse uides ei non esse contrarium?

2. See earlier p. 36 and fn. 15. Chap. 2.

3. *De uera rel.* 11, 22, BA, 8, p. 54:

> Nam si ea quae moriuntur penitus morerentur ad nihilum sine dubio peruenirent; sed tantum moriuntur quantum minus essentiae participant, quod breuius ita dici potest: tanto magis moriuntur quanto minus sunt.

4. See earlier p. 40 and fn. 28. Chap. 2.

5. See earlier p. 11 and fn. 15. Chap. 1.

6. Plotinus, *Enn.* 6, 9, 9, 11–13. Μᾶλλον μέντοι ἐσμὲν νεύσαντες πρὸς αὐτὸ καὶ τὸ εὖ ἐνταῦθα, τὸ ‹δὲ› πόρρω εἶναι μόνον καὶ ἧττον εἶναι·

> *Enn.* 6, 6, 1, 12–14: Μᾶλλον δέ ἐστιν ἕκαστον. ὀυχ ὅταν γένηται πολὺ ἢ μέγα, ἄλλ' ὅταν ἑαυτοῦ ᾖ. ἑαυτοῦ δέ ἐστι πρὸς αὐτὸ νενευκός:
>
> *Enn.* 6, 5, 12, 13–36: ἀλλ'ἢ συνθεῖν δυνηθείς, μᾶλλον δὲ ἐν τῷ παντὶ γενόμενος, οὐδὲν ἔτι ζητήσεις, ἢ ἀπειπὼν παρεκβήσῃ εἰς ἄλλο καὶ πεσῇ παρὸν οὐκ ἰδών τῷ εἰς ἄλλο βλέπειν. 'Αλλ' εἰ οὐδὲν ἔτι ζητήσεις, πῶς ποτε τοῦτο πείσῃ; Ἢ ὅτι παντὶ προσῆλθες καὶ οὐκ ἔμεινας ἐν μέρει αὐτοῦ οὐδ'εἶπας οὐδὲ σύ « τοσοῦτός εἰμι », ἀφεὶς δὲ ⟨τὸ⟩ τοσοῦτον γέγονας πᾶς, καίτοι καὶ πρότερον ἦσθα πᾶς· ἀλλ'ὅτι καὶ ἄλλο τι προσῆν σοι μετὰ τὸ πᾶν, ἐλάττων ἐγίνου τῇ προσθήκῃ· οὐ γὰρ ἐκ τοῦ ὄντος ἦν ἡ προσθήκη (οὐδέν γὰρ ἐκείνῳ προσθήσεις) ἀλλὰ τοῦ μή ὄντος. Γενόμενος δέ τις καὶ ἐκ τοῦ μὴ ὄντος ἐστὶν οὐ πᾶς, ἀλλ'ὅταν τὸ μὴ ὂν ἀφῇ· Αὔξεις τοίνυν σεαυτὸν ἀφεὶς τὰ ἄλλα καὶ πάρεστί σοι τὸ πᾶν ἀφέντι, μετὰ δὲ ἄλλων ὄντι οὐ φαίνεται, οὐδ'ἦλθεν, ἵνα παρῇ, ἀλλὰ σὺ ἀπῆλθες ὅτε οὐ πάρεστιν. Εἰ δ'ἀπῆλθες οὐκ ἀπ'αὐτοῦ (αὐτὸ γὰρ

πάρεστιν) οὐδέ ποι ἀπῆλθες, ἀλλὰ παρὼν ἐπὶ τὰ ἐναντία ἐστράφης. Οὕτω γὰρ καὶ οἱ ἄλλοι θεοὶ πολλῶν παρόντων ἑνὶ φαίνονται πολλάκις, ὅτι ὁ εἷς ἐκεῖνος μόνος δύναται βλέπειν. Ἀλλ᾽οὗτοι μὲν οἱ θεοί, ὅτι «παντοῖοι τελέθοντες ἐπιστρωφῶσι πόληας,» εἰς ἐκεῖνον δὲ αἱ πόλεις ἐπιστρέφονται καὶ πᾶσα γῆ καὶ πᾶς οὐρανός, πανταχοῦ ἐπ᾽αὐτοῦ καὶ ἐν αὐτῷ μένοντα καὶ ἔχοντα ἐξ αὐτοῦ τὸ ὂν καὶ τὰ ἀληθῶς ὄντα μέχρι ψυχῆς καὶ ζωῆς ἀνηρτημένα καὶ εἰς ἓν ἰόντα ἀμεγέθει τῷ ἀπείρῳ.

7. *Porphyra, Maxims* 40, Mommert, p. 36, 9–38, 20:

ἢ συνθεῖν [οὐ] δυνηθεὶς καὶ τῷ παντὶ ὁμοιωθῆναι τοῦ ὄντος οὐδὲν ἐπιζητήσεις ἢ ζητῶν παρεκβήσῃ εἰς ἄλλο βλέψας. εἰ οὐδὲν ἐπιζητήσεις, στὰς ἐπὶ σαυτοῦ καὶ τῆς σαυτοῦ οὐσίας, τῷ παντὶ ὡμοιώθης καὶ οὐκ ἐνεσχέθης ἔν τινι τῶν απ᾽αὐτοῦ. οὐδ᾽ εἶπας οὐδὲ σὺ τοσοῦτός εἰμι ⟨ἀλλ⟩ ἀφεὶς ⟨τὸ⟩ τοσοῦτος γέγονας πᾶς. καίτοι καὶ πρότερον ἦσθα πᾶς, ἀλλὰ καὶ ἄλλο τι προσῆν σοι μετὰ τοῦ πᾶς καὶ ἐλάττων ἐγίγνου τῇ προσθήκῃ, ὅτι μὴ ἐκ τοῦ ὄντος ἦν ἡ προσθήκη, ὀυδὲν γὰρ ἐκείνῳ προσθήσεις. ὅταν οὖν τις καὶ ἐκ τοῦ μὴ ὄντος γένηται, κόρος τῇ πενίᾳ σύνοικος καὶ ἐνδεὴς πάντων. ἀφεὶς οὖν τὸ μὴ ὂν τότε πᾶς κόρος αὐτὸς ἑαυτοῦ. ὥστε ⟨εἴ τις γέγονε πᾶς⟩, ἀπολαμβάνει αὑτὸν ἀφεὶς τὰ ταπεινώσαντα καὶ κατασμικρύναντα, καὶ μάλιστα, ὅταν ἐκεῖνα εἶναι αὑτὸν τὰ σμικρὰ τῇ φύσει καὶ οὐχ ὅστις ἐστὶν αὐτὸς τῇ ἀληθείᾳ δοξάζῃ. ἀπέστη γὰρ ἀφ᾽ἑαυτοῦ ἅμα καὶ ἀπέστη τοῦ ὄντος. καὶ ἔστης ἐν αὐτῷ παρὼν παρόντι, τότε πάρει καὶ τῷ ὄντι πανταχοῦ ὄντι. ὅταν δὲ ἀφῇς αὑτόν, ἀπέστης κἀκείνου. τοιαύτην γὰρ ἀξίαν εἴληφε, παρεῖναι τῷ αὐτῷ παρόντι καὶ ἀπεῖναι τῷ αὑτοῦ ἐκστάντι. εἰ δὲ πάρεστιν μὲν ἡμῖν τὸ ὄν, ἄπεστι δὲ τὸ μὴ ὄν, μετὰ δὲ ἄλλων οὖσιν οὐ πάρεστιν, οὐκ ἦλθεν, ἵνα παρῇ, ἀλλ᾽ἡμεῖς ἀπήλθομεν, ὅτε οὐ πάρεστιν. καὶ τί θαυμαστόν; αὐτὸς γάρ σοι παρὼν οὐκ ἀπῇς αὑτοῦ. καὶ οὐ πάρει σαυτῷ καίπερ παρὼν καὶ αὐτὸς ὢν ὁ παρών τε καὶ ἀπών, ὅταν πρὸς ἄλλα βλέπῃς παρεὶς σαυτὸν βλέπειν. εἰ δ᾽οὕτως αὑτω παρὼν οὐ πάρει καὶ διὰ τοῦτο σαυτὸν ἀγνοεῖς καὶ πάντα μᾶλλον, οἷς πάρει, καὶ πόρρω σου ὄντα εὑρίσκεις ἢ αὑτὸν σαυτῷ φύσει παρόντα, τί θαυμάζεις, ἐι τὸ οὐ παρὸν πόρρω σοῦ ἐστι, σοῦ πόρρω αὐτοῦ διὰ τὸ καὶ σαυτοῦ πόρρω γεγονότος; ὅσῳ γὰρ ἑαυτῷ πρόσει καίτοι παρόντι καὶ ἀναποστάτῳ ὄντι [αὐτὸς γὰρ ὅσῳ πρόσεισι], τόσῳ κἀκείνῳ πρόσει, ὃ δὴ οὕτω σοῦ ἐστιν ἀναπόσπαστον κατ᾽οὐσίαν, ὡς σὺ σαυτοῦ. ὥστε καὶ πάρεστί σοι καθόλου γινώσκειν, τί τε πάρεστι τῷ ὀντι καὶ τί ἄπεστι τοῦ ὄντος παρόντος πανταχοῦ καὶ πάλιν ὄντος οὐδαμοῦ; τοῖς μὲν γὰρ δυναμένοις χωρεῖν εἰς τὴν αὑτῶν οὐσίαν νοερῶς καὶ τὴν αὑτῶν γινώσκειν οὐσίαν ⟨καὶ⟩ ἐν αὐτῇ τῇ γνώσει καὶ τῇ εἰδήσει τῆς γνώσεως αὐτοὺς ἀπολαμβάνειν καθ᾽ἑνότητα τὴν τοῦ γινώσκοντος καὶ γινωσκομένου, [καὶ] τούτοις παροῦσιν αὐτοῖς πάρεστι καὶ τὸ ὄν. ὅσοι δ᾽ἂν παρεξέλθωσιν ἀπὸ τοῦ εἶναι ἑαυτῶν πρὸς τὰ ἄλλα, ἀποῦσιν ἑαυτῶν ἄπεστι καὶ τὸ ὄν. εἰ δ᾽ἡμεῖς ἐπεφύκειμεν ἱδρῦσθαι ἐν τῇ αὐτῇ οὐσίᾳ καὶ πλουτεῖν ἀφ᾽ ἑαυτῶν καὶ μὴ ἀπέρχεσθαι πρὸς ὃ μὴ ἦμεν καὶ πένεσθαι ἑαυτῶν καὶ διὰ τοῦτο πάλιν τῇ πενίᾳ συνεῖναι καίπερ παρόντος αὐτοῦ, καὶ ἀπὸ τοῦ ὄντος οὐ τόπῳ, οὐκ οὐσίᾳ κεχωρισμένοι οὐδ᾽ ἄλλῳ τινὶ ἀποτετμημένοι τῇ πρὸς τὸ μὴ ὂν στροφῇ χωριζόμεθα, δίκην ἄρα ταύτην ἀποτίνυμεν τῇ τοῦ ὄντος ἀποστροφῇ αὑτοὺς ἀποστρεφόμενοι καὶ ἀγνοοῦντες, καὶ τῇ πάλιν αὑτῶν φιλίᾳ ἑαυτούς τε ἀπολαμβάνοντες καὶ τῇ θεῷ συναπτόμενοι.

This maxim is a commentary on *Enn.* 6, 5, 12, whose text is partly quoted in the preceding note. A translation and a comparative analysis of these two passages will be found in A. Solignac, Complementary note 23, *Présence à soi-même et présence à Dieu selon Porphyre*, BA, 13, p. 679 ff.

8. *De uera rel.* 13, 26, BA, 8, p. 58:

Ille autem angelus magis seipsum quam deum diligendo, subditus ei esse noluit, et intumuit per superbiam, et a summa essentia defecit, et lapsus est; et ob hoc minus est quam fuit, quia eo quod minus erat frui uoluit, cum magis uoluit sua potentia frui quam dei. Quanquam enim non summe, tamen amplius erat, quando eo quod summe est fruebatur, quoniam deus solus summe est. Quidquid autem minus est quam erat, non in quantum est, sed in quantum minus est malum est. Eo enim quo minus est quam erat tendit ad mortem. *Contra Secund.* 2, BA, 17, p. 576: « Ita et angelica quaedam sublimitas, cum magis delectata est suo dominatu in seipsa, ad id quod minus est inclinauit affectum, et minus esse coepit quam erat, et pro suo gradu tetendit ad nihilum. Quanto enim quaequae res minus est, tanto uicinior nihilo est. Cum autem isti defectus uoluntarie fiunt, recte reprehenduntur, et peccata nominantur.

9. *De uera rel.* 11, 22, BA, 8, p. 54:

> Corpus autem minus est quam uita quaelibet; quoniam quantulumcumque remanet in specie per uitam manet . . . Corpus ergo magis subiacet morti, et ideo uicinius est nihilo: quapropter uita, quae fructu corporis delectata negligit deum, inclinatur ad nihilum, et ista est nequitia. Cf. Plotinus, *Enn.* 3, 6, 6, 60–61: οὕτω καὶ τὸ μάλιστα σῶμα γενόμενον ὡς μάλιστα εἰς τὸ μὴ ὂν ἧκον ἀναλαβεῖν αὐτὸ ἐις τὸ ἓν ἀσθενεῖ.

Concerning the three concupiscences, cf. *De uera rel.* 38, 69–55, 107, BA, 8, p. 124 ff., Augustine seems to draw his inspiration at the same time from I John 2:16 and from Porphyry. See relating to this W. Theiler, *Porph. und Aug.*, p. 37 ff.

10. *Contra Secundinum* 11, BA, 17, pp. 574–75:

> Deficere autem non iam nihil est, sed ad nihilum tendere. Cum enim ea quae magis sunt declinant ad ea quae minus sunt, non illa in quae declinant, sed illa quae declinant deficiunt et minus esse incipiunt quam erant: non quidem ut ea sint ad quae declinauerunt, sed pro suo genere minus. Non enim cum animus ad corpus declinat corpus efficitur, sed tamen defectiuo appetitu quadam modo corporascit . . . cf. *De ciu. dei* 13, 2, BA, p. 252: Impiorum namque in corporibus uita non animarum, sed corporum uita est; quam possunt eis animas etiam mortuae, hoc est deo desertae, quantulacumque propria uita, ex qua et immortales sunt, non desistente, conferre. Cf. Plotin, *Enn.* 1, 6, 5, 47–55: αἰσχρὰν δὴ ψυχὴν λέγοντες μίξει καὶ κράσει καὶ νεύσει τῇ πρὸς τὸ σῶμα καὶ ὕλην ὀρθῶς ἂν λέγοιμεν . . . καὶ ψυχή, μονωθεῖσα μὲν ἐπιθυμιῶν, ἃς διὰ τὸ σῶμα ἔχει, ᾧ ἄγαν προσωμίλει, ἀπαλλαγεῖσα δὲ τῶν ἄλλων παθῶν καὶ καθαρθεῖσα ἃ ἔχει σωματωθεῖσα . . .

11. *De mor.* 2, 2, 2, BA, p. 258:

> Idipsum ergo malum est . . . deficere ab essentia et ad id tendere ut non sit. Cf. *De diu quaest.* 83. q. 21, BA, 10, p. 70: Omne autem quod deficit ab eo quod est esse deficit et tendit in non esse. Esse autem et in nullo deficere bonum est, et malum est deficere.

12. *De uera rel.* 11, 21, BA, p. 52:

> Vita ergo uoluntario defectu deficiens ab eo qui eam fecit, et cuius essentia fruebatur, et uolens contra dei legem frui corporibus quibus eam deus praefecit, uergit ad nihilum; et haec est nequitia, non quia corpus iam nihil est.

In the preceding lines, Augustine returns to the etymology of *nequitia*, such as he had explained it in the *De beata uita*, 2, 8. See earlier p. 11 and n. 16.

13. *De lib. arb.* 2, 20, 54, BA, p. 320:

> Motus ergo ille auersionis quod fatemur esse peccatum, quoniam defectiuus motus est, omnis autem defectus ex nihilo est. . . . *De uera rel.* 14, 27, BA, 8, p. 58: Defectus autem iste quod peccatum uocatur. . . . Cf. *Conf.* 12, 2, 2, BA, 14, p. 358: motusque uoluntatis a te, qui es, ad id quod minus est.

14. *De mor.* 2, 6, 8, BA, p. 266:

> . . . cuius defectionis auctor non est qui est auctor essentiae.; *De uera rel.* 11, 22, BA, p. 54: . . . quoniam summa essentia esse facit omne quod est, unde et essentia dicitur.

15. *De mus.* 6, 11, 33, BA, p. 430:

> . . . ab omni lasciuiente motu, in quo defectus essentiae est animae.

16. *De mus.* 6, 14, 44, BA, p. 452:

> Iugum enim meum, inquit, leue est (*Matt.* 11:30). Laboriosior est huius mundi amor. Quod enim in illo anima quaerit, constantiam scilicet aeternitatemque, non inuenit. Plotin, *Enn* 6, 9, 9, 42–45: καὶ ὅτι ταῦτα μὲν τὰ ἐρώμενα θνητὰ καὶ βλαβερὰ καὶ εἰδώλων ἔρωτες καὶ μεταπίπτει, ὅτι οὐκ ἦν τὸ ὄντως ἐρώμενον, οὐδὲ τὸ ἀγαθὸν ἡμῶν, οὐδ' ὃ ζητοῦμεν. Cf. *Enn.* 1, 4, 6.

17. *De Gen. contra Man.* 2, 12, PL, 34, c. 203:

> Lignum autem uitae plantatum in medio paradisi sapientiam illam significat, qua oportet ut intelligat anima in meditullio quodam rerum sese esse ordinatam, ut quamuis subiectam sibi habet omnen naturam corpoream, supra se tamen esse intelligat naturam dei: et neque in dexteram declinet, sibi arrogando quod non est, neque ad sinistram per negligentiam, contemnendo quod est: et hoc est lignum uitae plantatum in medio paradisi. Cf. Plotin, *Enn.* 6, 2, 1, et 4, 8, 7.

Concerning the μέση οὐσία, see W. Theiler, *Porph. und Aug.*, p. 21 ff., R. J. O'Connell, *The Plotinian Fall of the Soul in St. Augustine*, in *Traditio* 19 (1963), 11 ff. and O. Du Roy, *L'Intelligence de la foi dans la Trinité*, Appendix 4, "The Median Situation of the Soul," p. 476 ff.

18. *De mus.* 6, 5, 13, BA, 7, p. 388:

> Hoc autem delicto dominae multo minus est quam erat cum illa ante delictum magis esset. *De uera rel.* 2, 22, BA, 8, p. 54: Illa uero quae facta sunt eius bono indigent, summo scilicet bono, id est summa essentia. Minus autem sunt quam erant cum per animae peccatum minus ad illum mouentur: nec tamen penitus separantur: nam omnino nulla essent.

19. *De uera rel.* 12, 23, BA, 8, p. 54:

> Id enim amat quod et minus est quam uita, quia corpus est; et propter ipsum peccatum, quod amatur fit corruptibile, ut fluendo deserat amatorem suum quia et ille hoc amando deseruit deum. Praecepta enim eius neglexit dicentis: Hoc manduca, et hoc noli. Trahitur ergo ad poenas: quia diligendo inferiora in egestate uoluptatum suarum et in doloribus apud inferos ordinatur. Quid est enim dolor qui dicitur corporis, nisi corruptio repentina salutis eius rei quam male utendo anima corruptioni obnoxiauit? Quid autem dolor qui dicitur animi, nisi carere mutabilibus rebus, quibus fruebatur, aut frui se posse sperauerat? Et hoc est totum quod dicitur malum, id est peccatum et poena peccati.

20. *Sermo* 142, 3, 3, PL, 38, c. 779:

> Reuocatur ad se anima, quae ibat a se. Sicut a se ierat, sic a domino suo ibat. Se enim respexerat, sibique placuerat, suaeque potestatis amatrix facta fuerat. Recessit ab illo, et non remansit in se; et a se repellitur, et a se excluditur, et in exteriora prolabitur. Amat mundum, amat temporalia, amat terrena; quae si se ipsam amaret, neglecto a quo facta est, iam minus esset, iam deficeret amando quod minus est. Minus est enim ipsa quam deus; et longe minus, tantoque minus, quanto minus est res facta quam factor. Ergo amandus erat

deus, et amandus est deus ita, ut si fieri potest, nos ipsos obliuiscamus. Quis ergo est iste transitus? Oblita est anima seipsam, sed amando mundum; obliuiscatur, sed amando artificem mundi. Pulsa ergo a se, quodam modo perdidit se, nec facta sua nouit uidere, iustificat iniquitates suas: effertur et superbit in petulantia, in luxuria, in honoribus, in potestatibus, in diutiis, in potentia uanitatis. Arguitur, corripitur, ostenditur sibi, diplicet sibi, confitetur foeditatem, desiderat pulchritudinem, et quae ibat effusa, redit confusa.

See the translation and the commentary on this text by A. Solignac, *L'Existentialisme de Saint Augustin*, in *Nouvelle Revue Théologique* 70 (1948), 5 ff. Cf. *De ciu. dei* 14, 13 and *De trin.* 10, 5, 7, passages quoted footnote 22, p. 62, and *De trin.* 13, 12, 17, BA, 16, p. 244:

Cum ergo huic intentioni mentis . . . carnalis iste sensus uel animalis ingerit quamdam illecebram fruendi se, id est tanquam bono quodam priuato et proprio, non tanquam publico atque communi quod est incommutabile bonum, tunc uelut serpens alloquitur feminam. Cf. Plotinus, *Enn.* 4, 8, 4, 11–28.

See relating to this R. J. O'Connell, *The Plotinian Fall of the Soul*, in *Traditio* 19 (1963), 15 ff.

21. *De mus.* 6, 13, 40, BA, 7, p. 446:

Quare superbia intumescere, hoc illi est in extima progredi et, ut ita dicam, inanescere, quod est minus minusque esse. Progredi autem in extima, quid est aliud quam intima proiicere; id est, longe a se facere deum, non locorum spatio, sed mentis affectu?

22. Augustine even uses the expression *nihil fieri* in a later text: *Tract. in Ioh. eu.* 1, 13, CC, 36, p. 7: "Peccatum quidem non per ipsum factum est; et manifestum est quia peccatum nihil est, et nihil fiunt homines cum peccant." Without claiming to give an exhaustive list, we shall add below a few examples of expressions meaning the ontological lessening of the soul to those that we have already found. *Contra Secundinum* 8, BA, 17, p. 560 ff.

Quapropter cum abs te quaero, unde sit facta uniuersa creatura, quamuis in suo genere bona . . . non inuenies quid respondeas, nisi de nihilo factam esse fatearis. Et ideo potest uergere ad nihilum, quando peccat illa creatura, et portio quae potest peccare, non ut nihil sit, sed ut minus uigeat, minusque firma sit. *Conf.* 12, 2, 2, BA, 14, p. 358: et hoc solum a te non est, quod non est, motusque uoluntatis a te, qui es, ad id quod minus est. . . . *De ciu. dei* 14, 13, BA, 35, p. 412: Sed uitio deprauari nisi ex nihilo facta natura non posset. Ac per hoc ut natura sit, ex eo habet quod a deo facta est; ut autem ab eo quod est deficiat, ex hoc quod de nihilo facta est. Nec sic defecit homo, ut omnino nihil esset, sed ut inclinatus ad seipsum minus esset quam erat cum ei qui summe est inhaerebat. Relicto itaque deo, esse in semetipso, hoc est sibi placere non iam nihil esse est, sed nihilo propinquare. *De trin.* 10, 5, 7, BA, 16, p. 134: Multa enim per cupiditatem prauam, tanquam sui sit oblita, sic agit. Videt enim quaedam intrinsecus pulchra in praestantiore natura quae deus est: et cum stare debeat ut eis fruatur, uolens ea sibi tribuere, et non ex illo similis illius, sed ex se ipsa esse quod ille est, auertitur ab eo, moueturque et labitur in minus et minus, quod putat amplius et amplius; quia nec ipsa sibi, nec ei quidquam sufficit recedenti ab illo qui solus sufficit: ideoque per egestatem ac difficultatem fit nimis intenta in actiones suas et inquietas delectationes quas per eam colligit; atque . . . perdit securitatem . . . *Epist.* 118, 3, 15, CSEL, 34, p. 679 sq.: Itaque tanto minus se esse stabilem sentit, quanto minus haeret deo qui summe est, et illum ideo summe esse quia nulla mutabilitate proficit seu deficit; sibi autem illam commutationem expedire qua proficit ut perfecte illi cohaereat, eam uero commutationem quae in defectu est esse uitiosam; omnem autem defectum ad interitum uergere, quo utrum res aliqua res perueniat tametsi non apparet, tamen apparere omnibus eo ducere interitum, ut non sit quod erat.

Concerning the expression *omnem defectum ad interitum uergere* understood in a completely general sense, see J. H. Koopmans, *Augustinus' Briefwisseling met Dioscorus* (Amsterdam: Jasonpers, Universiteits Pers. 1949), p. 163. Cf. *De lib. arb.* 2, 17, 46: "Quae quantumlibet deficiant, et eo tendant ut non sint, tamen aliquid formae illis remanet, ut quoquo modo sint.", a passage already quoted p. 36 and fn. 15. *De diu. quaest.* 83, q. 21, BA, 10, p. 70: "Omne autem quod deficit ab eo quod est esse deficit et tendit in non esse." *Contra epist. fundam.* 40, 46: "Omne autem quod ad interitum tendit, ad non esse tendit.", quoted n. 1, p. 58. Augustine recalls again the aporia of annihilation, understood in this general sense, in a very late text. *Contra adu. leg. et proph.* 1, 6, 8, PL, 42, c. 607: "Utrum autem aliqua natura, hoc est, substantia, prorsus ad nihilum redigatur, disputatio subtilissima est."

23. *Contra Secundinum*, 15, BA, 17, p. 586:

> Deficit quippe cum consentit malo, minusque iam esse, ac propterea minus ualere incipit quam ualebat dum nulli consentiens in uirtute consisteret; tanto utique deterior quanto ab eo quod summe est ad id quod minus est uergit, ut ipsa etiam minus sit. Quanto autem minus est, tanto utique fit propinquior nihilo. Quod enim minus quoque fit. eo tendit ut non sit omnino: quo quamuis non perueniat ut penitus pereundo nihil sit, manifestum est tamen quemlibet defectum exordium esse pereundi.

24. De mus. 6, 13, 40, BA, 7, p. 446:

> Cum enim anima per seipsam nihil sit; non enim aliter esset commutabilis, et pateretur defectum ab essentia: cum ergo ipsa per se nihil sit, quidquid autem illi esse est, a deo sit: in ordine suo manens, ipsius dei praesentia uegetatur in mente atque conscientia. Itaque hoc bonum habet intimum.

Further on, Augustine specifies the kind of mutability which is peculiar to the soul. *De Mus.* 6, 14, 44, BA, 7, p. 452: ". . . prior est species tantummodo tempore commutabilis quam ea quae et tempore et locis."

25. *De lib. arb.* 2, 19, 53, BA, p. 316: "atque ita homo superbus, et curiosus, et lasciuus effectus, excipitur ab alia uita, quae in comparatione superioris uitae mors est." We could multiply the quotes relating to this, the most famous being without any doubt that of *Conf.* 1, 6, 7, BA, 13, p. 284: ". . . unde uenerim huc, in istam dico uitam mortalem an mortem uitalem?" The expression "another life" means the same antithesis, although it designates its other term, "the true life," in Plotinus, *Enn.* 6, 9, 9, 48–51. R. J. O'Connell, *The Plotinian Fall of the Soul*, p. 15, thinks that it is *Enn.* 1, 4, 7, and 4, 7, 9, which have led Augustine to designate the characteristics peculiar to the state of fall under the general word death: in them Plotinus opposes the true life of spiritual being to the "death" of that which is not it, or which does not partake of this life, like the stone or wood. But it seems to us that in Porphyry a more direct source is found for the Augustinian opposition between the soul's true life and its "death," which is "a life of a certain kind," that of its passions. Porphyry, *Maxims* 23, Mommert, p. 10, 10–13:

> Τῆς οὐσίας, ἧς ἐν ζωῇ τὸ εἶναι καὶ ἧς τὰ πάθη ζωαί, ταύτης καὶ ὁ θάνατος ἐν ποιᾷ ζωῇ κεῖται, οὐκ ἐν ζωῆς καθάπαξ στερήσει, ὅτι μηδὲ τὸ πάθος ἦν ὁδὸς εἰς τὴν παντελῆ ἀζωίαν ἐπ' αὐτῆς.

See Hierocles, *Comment, in aureum carmen*, 1, 1, in *Mullach*, *Fragmenta philosophorum graecorum*, 1, (Paris: Firmin-Didot 1860), p. 418:

> καὶ μήποτε πρὸς ἀντιδιαστολὴν τῶν ἀνθρωπίνων ψυχῶν ἀθάνατοι θεοὶ οὗτοι ἐκλήθησαν, ὡς μὴ ἀποθνήσκοντες τὴν θείαν εὐζωίαν, μηδὲ ἐν λήθῃ ποτὲ

> γιγνόμενοι μήτε τῆς ἑαυτῶν οὐσίας μήτε τῆς τοῦ πατρὸς ἀγαθότητος. Τούτοις δὲ ἡ ἀνθρωπίνη ψυχὴ τοῖς πάθεσιν ὑπόκειται, ποτὲ μὲν νοοῦσα τὸν θεὸν καὶ τὴν ἑαυτῆς ἀξίαν ἀπολαμβ άνουσα, ποτὲ δὲ τούτων ἀποπίπτουσα. Διὸ καὶ εἰκοτως θεοὶ θνητοὶ λέγοιντο ἂν αἱ ἀνθρώπιναι ψυχαί, ὡς ἀποθνησκουσαί ποτε τὴν θείαν εὐζωίαν τῇ ἀπὸ θεοῦ φυνῇ, καὶ ἀναβιωσκόμεναι αὐτὴν πάλιν τῇ πρὸς θεὸν ἐπιστροφῇ, καὶ οὕτω μὲν ζῶσαι τὸν θεῖον βίον, ἐκείνως δὲ ἀποθνήσκουσαι, (ὡς οἷόν τε ἀθανάτῳ οὐσίᾳ θανάτου μοίρας μεταλαχεῖν,) οὐ τῇ εἰς τὸ μὴ εἶναι ἐκβάσει, ἀλλὰ τῇ τοῦ εὐ εἶναι ἀποπτώσει. θάνατος γὰρ λογικῆς οὐσίας ἀθέια καὶ ἄνοια, οἷς ἕπεται καὶ ἡ περὶ τὸν βίον ἄμετρος τῶν παθῶν ἐπανάστασις.

26. Here is the translation that the Jerusalem Bible gives for this verse: "Look away from me, that I may breathe before I depart, and nothing more of me." The other text understood in the sense of *non esse* is that of Psalm 1, verse 6: ". . . *iter autem impiorum peribit*": "but the way of the ungodly shall perish." (same translation) *En. in Ps.* 1, 6, CC, 38, p. 3:

> *Iter* autem *impiorum peribit* pro eo positum est, ac si diceretur: iter autem impiorum non nouit dominus. Sed planius dictum est, ut hoc sit sciri a domino, quod est manere, ut ad scientiam dei esse pertineat, ad ignorantiam uero non esse. Quia dominus dicit: *Ego sum qui sum;* and: *Qui est misit me ad uos* (Exod. 3:14).

27. *Yedouthoun* is a proper name: it is that of one of the three Levites whom David was supposed to have entrusted with the organizing of the sacred music and the transmission of its art to their descendants. Psalms 39 (38), 62 (61) and 77 (76) are dedicated to him. According to I. Koeler, *Lexikon in Veteris Testamneti libros* (Leiden: 1953), p. 364, the word remains unexplained. Augustine translated it according to an etymology of the time. The same interpretation, *transiliens eos, siue saliens eos,* is found in Jerome, *Liber interpretationis hebraicorum nominum,* CC, 72, p. 119. *Idithun* would derive from the verb *iâdâh:* to throw, to pull, a very unlikely etymology.

28. *En. in Ps.* 38, 22, CC, 38, p. 421 ff.:

> Quid ergo restat ut petam, quia hinc sine dubio migraturus sum? *Remitte mihi ut refrigerer priusquam eam.* Vide, uide, Idithun, quos nodos habeas remittendos tibi, quibus remissis refrigerari uis priusquam eas. Habes enim aliquos aestus, a quibus uis refrigerari, et dicis: *Refrigerer;* et dicis: *Remitte mihi.* Quid remittet tibi, nisi forte illum scrupulum ubi dicis et unde dicis: *Dimitte nobis debita nostra? Remitte mihi priusquam eam, et amplius iam non ero.* Immunem me fac a peccatis priusquam eam, ne cum peccatis eam. Remitte mihi, ut requiescam in conscientia mea, ut exonerata sit aestu sollicitudinis; qua sollicitudine curam gero pro peccato meo. *Remitte mihi ut refrigerer,* ante omnia, *priusquam eam, et amplius iam non ero.* Si enim mihi non remiseris ut refrigerer, ibo et non ero. *Priusquam eam;* quo si iero, iam non ero. *Remitte mihi ut refrigerer.* Est quaestio oborta, quomodo iam non erit. Ecce iam non iit ad requiem? Quod auertat deus ab Idithun? Ibit enim plane Idithun, ad requiem ibit. Sed fac aliquem iniquum, non Idithun, non transilientem, hic thesaurizantem, incubatorem, iniquum, superbum, iactantem, elatum, pauperis ante ianuam iacentis contemtorem; nonne et ipse erit? Quid est ergo: *non ero?* Si enim diues ille non erat, quis est qui ardebat? Quis est qui guttam aquae de digito Lazari stillari in linguam suam desiderabat? Quis est qui dicebat: *Pater Abraham, mitte Lazarum?* Utique qui loqueretur erat, et qui arderet erat, et qui resurgat in finem et qui cum diabolo aeterno igne damnetur. Quid est ergo: *non ero,* nisi respiciat iste Idithun, quid est esse, et non esse? Videbat enim illum finem, quo corde poterat, qua mentis acie ualebat, quem sibi ostendi desiderauerat dicens: *Notum fac mihi, domine, finem meum.* Videbat numerum dierum suorum qui est; adtendebat infra omnia quae sunt, in comparatione illius esse, non esse; et se non esse dicebat. Illa enim permanent; ista mutabilia sunt, mortalia, fragilia; et dolor ipse aeternus, plenus corruptionis, ad hoc non finitur, ut sine fine finiatur. Respexit ergo beatam

> illam regionem, beatam patriam, beatam domum, ubi participes sunt sancti uitae sempiternae atque incommutabilis ueritatis; et timuit extra ire, ubi non est esse; ibi desiderans esse, ubi est summum esse. Propter hanc ergo comparationem inter utrumque constitutus, adhuc timens dicit: *Remitte mihi, ut refrigerer priusquam eam, et amplius iam non ero*. Si enim mihi non remiseris peccata, ibo in aeternum abs te. Et a quo ibo in aeternum? Ab illo qui dixit: *Ego sum qui sum*; ab illo qui dixit: *Dic filiis Israel: Qui est misit me ad uos*. Ab eo ergo qui uere est qui in contrarium pergit, ad non esse pergit.

29. *De ciu. dei* 12, 6, BA, 35, pp. 162–64:

> Cum uero causa miseriae malorum angelorum quaeritur, ea merito occurrit, quod ab illo, qui summe est, auersi ad se ipsos conuersi sunt, qui non summe sunt . . . et qui magis essent, si ei qui summe est adhaererent, se illi praeferendo quod minus est praetulerunt. Hic primus defectus et prima inopia primumque uitium eius naturae, quae ita creata est, ut nec summe esset, et tamen ad beatitudinem habendam eo, qui summe est, frui posset, a quo auersa non quidem nulla, sed tamen minus esset atque ob hoc misera fieret.

30. W. Theiler, *Porphyrios und Augustin*, p. 32.

31. The passing from one level to another is quite unmistakable in the subsequent text: the dialectic of *magis* and *minus esse* governs the fate of the soul here below, and brings it to its end in the hereafter. *De mus*. 6, 5, 13, BA, 7, p. 386 ff.:

> Conuersa ergo a domino suo ad seruum suum necessario deficit: conuersa item a seruo suo ad dominum suum, necessario proficit, et praebet eidem seruo facillimam uitam, et propterea minime operosam et negotiosam, ad quam propter summam quietem nulla detorqueatur attentio; sicut est affectio corporis quae sanitas dicitur . . . Haec autem sanitas tunc firmissima erit atque certissima, cum pristinae stabilitati, certo suo tempore atque ordine, hoc corpus fuerit restitutum, quae resurrectio eius antequam plenissime intelligatur, salubriter crediditur. Oportet enim animam et regi a superiore, et regere inferiorem. Superior illa solus deus est, inferius illa solum corpus, si ad omnem et totam animam intendas. Ut ergo tota esse sine domino, sic excellere sine seruo non potest. Ut autem dominus eius magis est quam ipsa, ita seruus minus. Quare intenta in dominum intelligit aeterna eius, et magis est, magisque est etiam ipse seruus in suo genere per illam. Neglecto autem domino intenta in seruum carnali qua ducitur concupiscentia, sentit motus suos quos illi exhibet, et minus est: nec tamen tantum minus, quantum ipse seruus, etiam cum maxime est in natura propria. Hoc autem delicto dominae multo minus est quam erat, cum illa ante delictum magis esset.

Augustine specified the meaning that must be attributed to the *pristina stabilitas* in *Retract*. 1, 11, 3, BA, 12, p. 336.

32. *De uera rel*. 12, 25, BA, 8, p. 56 ff.:

> Inde iam erit consequens ut post mortem corporalem, quam debemus primo peccato, tempore suo atque ordine suo hoc corpus restituatur pristinae stabilitati, quam non per se habebit, se per animam stabilitam in deo . . . Dicit et apostolus: *Vivificabit et mortalia corpora uestra propter spiritum manentem in uobis*. Ablato ergo peccato, auferetur et poena peccati: et ubi est malum? *Ubi est, mors, contentio tua? ubi est, mors, aculeus tuus?* Vincit enim essentia nihilum, et sic *absorbetur mors in uictoriam*.

33. We clearly see it for example in *De mor*. 1, 5, 7–8, BA, 1, p. 146 ff. Without stopping at different possible definitions of the compound body-soul, Augustine shows — and that is what matters to him before all else — that in each one of these hypotheses the true asset of the body is the soul itself. Relating to this see R. Holte, *Béatitude et sagesse: Saint Augustin et le problème de la fin de l'homme dans la philosophie ancienne* (Paris: 1962), p. 200, and

especially G. Madec, *Critical Note* n. 284 of the *Bulletin Augustinien* for 1964, in *Revue des Etudes Augustiniennes* 12 (1966), p. 341: "But truly, was Augustine's question about man ever asked from a purely anthropological viewpoint? I do not have the feeling it was so, for I think that shortly after his discovery of spiritual internality, owing to the *libri platonicorum*, Augustine questions himself about the soul and God, not only in order to resolve the theoretical difficulties against which he comes up, but especially to train the soul for the ascent to God: if it is true that Augustine had the intention of writing a *De anima*, it is significant that this project led to the *De quantitate animae* and to the description of the seven levels of the soul that culminate in the "contemplation of Truth" (33, 76). Little by little he will doubtless move away from certain arguments of Neo-Platonic spiritualism, but he will not feel the need to disjoin dialectic from anagogy." This critical note concerns G. Mathon's typed thesis, *L'Anthropologie chrétienne en Occident, de Saint Augustin à Jean Scot Erigène* (Lille: Ed. Universitaires, 1964).

34. Owing to the fact that Augustine, while admitting with the Apologists that the soul does not have life in itself, asserts nevertheless that its life consists of justice, Burnaby is of the opinion that he does not succeed in setting up in a coherent way the immortality of the soul, even if it is sinful, from a creational point of view. J. Burnaby, *Amor Dei*, pp. 151–53:

> Augustine is at one with the Apologists and at variance with Platonism in denying that the soul has life "in itself." There is no divine *Seelengrund* which cannot die: eternal life is the gift of God. But he does hold that the life of the soul is righteousness; and the difficulty for him is to find any room within his Christian Neo-Platonism for the Catholic dogma, which he accepted for his own part, like Justin and Irenaeus, as a postulate of belief in God's justice . . . He sees, in fact, that the soul's "real immortality" can be nothing but a participation in the eternal life of God, that there can be no such thing as an eternity of evil; and it follows that the soul *potest mori, potest occidi*: there may be a "dead soul" in a living body. But he was obliged to maintain an inherent incorruptibility even of the most depraved soul; and for that he had recourse, in the early *De immortalitate animae*, to the Platonic argument which deduces the soul's immortality from its character as the perceiving subject of an eternal object, of Truth itself . . . There is indeed a remarkable contrast between the later argument for immortality in the *De trinitate*, where the whole burden of the proof rests on the risen Christ, and the dialectics of the early treatise, in which, as the *Retractations* show plainly enough, Augustine had come to lose all interest. But the breach in his theology which Scripture or tradition required is scarcely disguised. It was dogma that the soul is created immortal, and he did not see that on his own principles this is a contradiction in terms more ultimate than the idea of a "dead soul." Platonism could assert the soul's immortality without such a contradiction, for Platonism did not know what creation means.

As we have pointed out earlier, in footnote 72, page 48, Burnaby did not see that there is in the *De immortalitate animae*, other than the "Platonic" arguments, an ontological explanation of the soul's structure, by means of which Augustine attempts to work out the contradiction to which we have called attention in the early dialogues. Just as he has defined two levels of being in the soul, Augustine will define in it, in a very clear way, two levels of life: that of the *qualiscumque uita*, of the *utcumque uiuere* considered to be a *quantulacumque uita*, and that of true life, which is a participation in God's justice. *Epist.* 120, 18, CSEL, 4, p. 720:

> . . . recole, obsecro, quas dicat scriptura diuina animas mortuas; profecto inuenies iniustas, impias, infideles. Nam licet per illas uiuant corpora impiorum, de quibus dictum est *quod mortui sepeliant mortuos suos (Matt. 8:22)*, et ibi intellegantur etiam iniquae animae non esse sine aliqua uita — neque enim aliter ex eis possent corpora uiuere nisi qualicumque uita, qua omnino animae carere non possunt, unde inmortales merito nocantur — non

> tamen ob aliud amissa iustitia dicuntur mortuae, nisi quia et animarum licet inmortaliter uita qualicumque uiuentium uerior et maior uita iustitia est tamquam uita uitarum, quae cum sunt in corporibus, etiam ipsa corpora uiua sunt, quae per se ipsa uiuere nequeunt. Quapropter si animae non possunt nisi etiam in se ipsis utcumque uiuere, quia ex eis uiuunt et corpora, a quibus deserta moriuntur, quanto magis uera iustitia etiam in se ipsa uiuere intelligenda est, ex qua sic uiuunt animae, ut hac amissa mortuae nuncupentur, quamuis quantulacumque uita non desinant uiuere!

Also see *De ciu. dei* 13, 24, BA, 35, p. 340, and the definition of the soul, partly mortal, and partly immortal, *Epist.* 202, CSEL, 57, p. 313.

35. Other than Justin, *Dial.* 5 and Irenaeus, *Adu. Haeres.* 4, 4, 3 mentioned by Burnaby, we can point out Tatius, *Disc.* 15, 2–16, 6 and Theophile of Antioch, *To Autol.* 2, 27.

36. See earlier p. 22 and n. 84.

37. See earlier p. 40.

38. Cf. the metaphysical explanation of the lie in *En. in Ps.* 5, 7, CC, 38, p. 22: "Sed ne quis putet aliquam substantiam uel naturam ueritati esse contrariam, intellegat ad id quod non est pertinere mendacium, non ad id quod est. Si enim hoc dicitur quod est, uerum dicitur; si autem hoc dicitur quod non est, mendacium est. Ideo, inquit, *perdes omnes qui loquuntur mendacium*, quia recedentes ab eo quod est, ad id quod non est declinantur." On the other hand this theme is the object of doctrinal and moral considerations only, in the two short treatises that Augustine has dedicated to it: *De mendacio* and *Contra mendacium.*

CHAPTER 4

Conversion Constitutive of Being

Mediation and Meditation

If man makes his way towards nothingness as a consequence of his free choice (even though it may be based on a mistake), all the more does it seem that it must be the case of the one who turns towards Being. But his freedom is still weak and impeded when, waking from the sleep of a nonregenerated life, he discovers what is his misery, due to the attachment to the values here below.[1]

The possibility of regaining his essence by converting to "what truly is" is not implied ipso facto in the discovery man makes, owing to his inner look, of this uniquely true Being and in the complementary one of his own nothingness. As ardent as his desire to satisfy his "wanting-to-be," whose meaning he finally grasps, may be then, this desire is ineffectual by itself. After the failure of the Manichean attempts, the "Neo-Platonic" attempt made by Augustine to come closer to God, finally known in His truth, and to settle in Him did not lead to anything. This attempt to return to God is only an unfinished conversion, whose movement is interrupted on Augustine recognizing his powerlessness.[2]

Finding out that there is "a Being he should see," "a Being in whom he should settle," Augustine finds out at the same time that he himself is not yet "in such a way that he could see Him" nor "in such a way that he could settle in Him."[3] The ontological gap that separates him from that point is too wide. In these lines, Augustine does not mainly have in view the "nonbeing" that characterizes the created being, as such, in contrast with the creator. By defining as a *regio dissimilitudinis* his own state, which is that of the fallen man, Augustine wants to show especially the effect of sin, which nihilates the human *essentia* in what it has that is specific. For the latter, as such, is a structure of participation in divine life, that is to say a condition of likeness.[4]

How can the *essentia* be regained?[5] How can one pass from the level of sinful and thereby nihilated existence to that of participation?[6] If the "Platonists' books" show Augustine where he must go, they do not show him the way; if they indicate "into what it is necessary to be incorporated," they do not give him the power to do it.[7]

It is because he has painfully lived this failure that Augustine established the opposition between the vision and the way, which governs his entire viewpoint of salvation.[8] The way that is finally found is Jesus Christ, the embodiment of the Word.[9] It is by investing himself with Him that Augustine finally obtains this conversion of the entire soul that allows him to dominate the flesh and its passions[10] and that pulls him away from the "region of unlikeness" because it transforms him into God.[11]

Augustine's uncompromising Christianity is based not only on the Church doctrine but on this personal experience as well: true conversion, that which is constitutive of being because it allows man to participate in divine life, is only possible because of the one mediator.[12] This has been proven for Augustine because he only came to really know Christ after having read the "Platonists' books," and after having looked in vain for the union with God following this reading.[13] Although these books contain, according to him, almost the entire truth concerning God and the soul, in them the mediator is missing.[14] This attitude radically distinguished Augustine's "Neo-Platonizing Christianity" from all doctrine that is exclusively or mainly philosophical.

But, while asserting the absolutely necessary role of the mediator, Augustine is not afraid to keep the main part of the Neo-Platonic philosophy, beginning with this philosophy's objective, which is the wisdom constitutive of immortality. For man's odyssey is not finished once he has found the way to salvation. While relying on the temporal means that are combined with Christ's mediation, the Scripture and the sacraments, he must transcend them with the help of inner meditation in order to attain the Word, which is nothing but the eternal *ratio:*[15]

> . . . for everything that begins and everything that ends being only finds its beginning or its end when the necessity for this beginning or this end is known in the eternal *ratio* in which nothing begins nor ends. [The *ratio*] is your very Word, who is also the "principle," for He "speaks to us" [John 8:25]. Here is what he said in the Scripture through his being of flesh, and he made it be heard from the outside to men's ears so that they may believe Him, so they may look for Him inside themselves and find Him in eternal truth, where, as a good and sole master, He instructs all his disciples . . . Now who teaches us if it isn't the truth that remains? Even when it is a created being bound by change that instructs us, it leads us to the truth that remains, and there we truly learn when, dwelling in it, we listen to it and "exult from joy at the voice of the spouse" [John 3:20], which gives us back to the one from whom we come. It is why He is the principle, for if He did not remain as long as we wander, there would be no place to which we could return. But when we realize our mistake, it is precisely owing to knowledge that we realize it. He teaches us so that we may have knowledge, since He is the "principle and He speaks to us."[16]

If faith in the sole mediator is essential in order to accomplish man's return to God, the *intellectus fidei* acquired through Platonic wisdom is not any less so in this christianized conception of the *regressus in rationem*. Faith and philosophy mutually imply each other, for one without the other cannot answer the quest of immortality. Otherwise man is in danger of dissolving in the illusion of the imaginary or in a denying skepticism, in the powerlessness of a philosophy without mediator or in the contradictions of a faith without understanding. Penetrating the data of faith by means of a "human wisdom" borrowed from the Platonists, which Augustine defines in the *Contra academicos* as "the only perfectly true philosophy,"[17] will allow him to work out what he will later call "our Christian philosophy,"[18] like certain Greek Fathers.[19]

It is thus that the treasure of the Egyptians reverts to its legitimate owner and makes possible what has justly been defined as a "Christian Gnosis."[20] Owing to the intelligible wealth found there by meditation, the "true religion" reveals itself to contain also the "true philosophy":[21] it is thus that Augustine accepts the finality of ancient philosophy by showing that only Christianity is capable of accomplishing it.

It is necessary to examine, in connection with this, one of the main conclusions that Augustine has drawn from the comparison between the truths of faith and the contents of the *platonicorum libri*. It concerns the metaphysical condition of the *beata uita*, obtained through the participation of wisdom in the eternal Word:

> Here is what is found there: that before all times and above all times your only son, coeternal to you, remains immutably; and that the souls, in order to be happy, receive "from his fullness" [John 1:16], that in order to be wise they are renewed thanks to their participation in the wisdom which dwells in itself.[22]
>
> And I had come to you from the Gentiles, and I paid attention to the gold that you had ordered your people to carry out of Egypt, because, wherever it was, it was yours. And you told the Athenians through your apostle that in you "we have life, movement and being [Acts 17:28], as some of their own also said. It is indeed from there that these books came . . . .[23]

But although these philosophers know what this participation of wisdom consists of, their knowledge paradoxically becomes folly because they are unaware of, or refuse, the temporal condition that alone makes this participation accessible to man: the mediation of Christ. That is why the gold of truth is mixed in them with the matrix of pride, which turns into idolatry. It will thus be necessary to pull it away from them in order to have it be useful for the worship of the true God and to restore its purity by combining with philosophy, so that it may be "perfectly true," the recognition of Christ as the universal way to salvation.[24]

Characteristics of *magis esse*

The gold that Augustine found in the Platonists and that he considered belonged by right to the Christians is the knowledge that God is immutable Being and that the soul turned towards him partakes of his beatitude. The complete realization of this knowledge, contained in its essential part in the *platonicorum libri*, for the person who acquires it, consists of a transformation of his own being, this however being considered possible only because of his faith in the mediation of Christ. The philosophy of internality, therefore, allows one to grasp the spiritual meaning of the Christian religion — in contrast to the material meaning that the Manicheans gave it, which distorts it — in order to perfect in oneself one's involvement in the divine life, begun because of faith. This is why *magis esse* is basic to Augustinian wisdom: it defines metaphysically its objective, the *beata uita*, as an "ascending participation" towards "what truly is."[25]

After having started by showing the viewpoint of "Christian philosophy," which stemmed from his experience of conversion, and in which Augustine right away placed *magis esse*, we shall next attempt in this chapter to gather the new developments of this theme that we have encountered since the early dialogues and that we have partially examined in the previous chapters. Without lingering on certain aspects already sufficiently cleared up for our purpose, such as the progressive transposition of the *beata uita*, in its completed form, on the eschatological level, it could be of some use to briefly summarize the most characteristic points of this "ascending participation," as they are found in the early works, in order to examine then the way in which Augustine delved more deeply into the *magis esse* theme, mainly in the *Confessions*.[26]

What allows man to have access to a higher level of being and of life is a sui generis knowledge that exercises man's spiritual understanding.[27] Only this knowledge of the divine, acquired with the help of the inner look makes man truly good, in opposition to purely human knowledge, of a purely social and cultural nature.[28] This knowledge is a type of nourishment, a *fruitio*,[29] which allows man to grow ontologically and to regain his original essence[30] in the "adherence" and union of a loving knowledge.[31] It is thus that he becomes close to God, similar to Him and, according to Saint Paul's expression, "conformed" to him.[32] Such is the fruit of the *auersio* far from the world here below, far from the ties with the body,[33] and of the *conuersio* to the *ratio*, to "what truly is."[34]

Thus the soul is constituted in being thanks to a *formatio* that is also a *reformatio*,[35] thanks to a completion *(perfici)* that is also a "rebuilding" *(refici)*, a re-creation or still, according to this other Paulinian expression, a renewal *(renouare)*[36] of the fallen *(deficere)* soul. Then, turned away from the nonbeing and from the dispersion that characterize the *regio dissimilitudinus*, collected and coming together in the oneness *(colligi)*,[37] it participates in its measure of immutability, which defines absolute Being in contrast with contingent being. From the early dialogues on, it is "immobility," "constancy," and "peace," which characterize the state of the wise person,[38] as well as their equivalents *stare*, *manere*, and *requiescere*.[39] Such is the state towards which man leans at the end of this acquisition of being whose dynamic and yet passive aspect with respect to God is expressed by the verbs *solidari* and *stabiliri* which are synonymous with *formari* and *perfici*.[40] This synonymy follows from the way in which Augustine modified the equivalence relation that he had first established between form and soul. This modification had been reached when he started to delve into the ontological status of the soul.[41] It is by acquiring form, another expression for essence, that the soul "is edified in what is in a supreme way,"[42] and that it is "endowed with eternity"[43] in the full sense of the word.

We recognize in the points that we have just enumerated the main characteristics of the *regressus in rationem*. Progressively, as we move forward in the Augustinian opus, this conversion is described in a more elaborate and explicitly Christian way. It is thus that we find in the third book of the *De libero arbitrio* the assertion that Christ is the spiritual sustenance, *cibus rationalis*, essential to man on his way back, whereas, in the *Confessions*, the Word, considered as the principle of beings, is identified with the *aeterna ratio*, just as, in the early dialogues, the *ratio* was characterized as immutable Being.[44] Moreover, even though *ipsum esse* designates the entire Trinity, this name will often be attributed in its own right to the Word.[45] That is why we cannot insist enough on the importance of *magis esse* in this anagogical ontology, for it expresses the metaphysical achievement that is the true purpose of man and the end *of the regressus in rationem.*

Indeed, we recognize from the beginning of the *Confessions* the distinction between the two levels of participation that Augustine had elaborated in the early dialogues. It is used as the ontological basis of the narration of man's return to God, and it plays a part in emphasizing the privileged situation of the spiritual created being. Its specific finality is asserted from the first lines, for it is the theme that gives unity to this complex opus: "You have made us for you, and our heart is without peace until it rests in you."[46]

From this Augustine immediately proceeds by searching for the connection between everything that exists and God, in such a way as to place man in the ensemble of created beings. They are not "without God," according to a terminology familiar since the philosophical dialogues, but they are devoid of the internality that allows the presence of inhabitation. Augustine emphasizes the difference between these levels of ontological participation by calling attention to the ambiguity of the expression *esse in:*

> Since without you nothing would be of that which is, does it follow that everything that is contains you? Since I am, I also, why do I ask you to come in me, when I would not be if you were not in me?[47]

The last book picks up again and develops in a grandiose finale the *fecisti nos ad te*, which asserts from the first lines of the *Confessions* the finality of the spiritual created being, in whose achievement it will find the peace to which it aspires:

> I invoke you, "God, my mercy" [Ps. 58:18] you who *have made* me . . . you who called me in so many ways so that I may hear you from far, that I may turn towards you and answer your call by my call. Lord, you have erased all the evil from my blameworthy actions, not in order to punish my hands by which I have failed you, but you foresaw all my merits in order to reward your own hands which made me. For you were before I was, and thus I was not a being for which you were bound to grant existence. But however I am, thanks to your goodness, which anticipated the form you gave me and the substance from which you extracted me.[48] (Emphasis mine.)

If God has neither the duty nor the need to create, no more does he need man's worship, but he uses it in order to give man access to the higher level of being, a requirement he has inscribed in him:

> . . . that I may serve you and that I may offer you worship, so that thanks to you I may receive the possession of my being, you to whom I owe having a being, which allows me to receive such a possession."[49]

It is thus that the spiritual created being is called to confirm by itself its finality in order to find its joy in eternal peace, which is the consummation of this act of knowledge and love. This is why Augustine constantly recalls in this last book the distinction between the two ontological elements that make up this created being and the ordination of the first to the second. The conversion allows it to participate in the simplicity and immutability of God, in whom these two levels of the created being are but one: in Him, life is not different from wisdom, bliss, or peace, for He is life, wisdom, bliss, and peace.[50]

The soul that converts to him thus leaves the level of *utcumque esse*, of the *qualiscumque uita*, that is, of an ordinary, indefinite existence, in order to live on the level of beauty and wisdom: *sapienter uiuere, speciosa uita.*[51] For the *magis magisque esse* theme is also that of *magis magisque uiuere.*[52] The "living soul" of Genesis represents the spiritual man having reached the fullness of his growth. He understands the divine law expressed by the Scripture, owing to the force of his mind: *per mentis intellectum.*[53] So he is truly created in the image of God, an image that consists of the force of understanding and of the *ratio.*[54] He only needs from now on the inner light of the Word. Thus "renewed, he contemplates the truth he has understood."[55] He succeeds because of the perfect domination of the inferior powers, of a temporal and tangible nature, symbolized by animals and woman.[56] The very forces of the three concupiscences, once subdued, are useful for man in his voyage towards eternity, whereas their rebellion revealed the curse of temporality marked by sin.[57] Man's condition in time is reestablished: the latter no longer pulls him away from himself, scattering his energies, but leads him, owing to their tension and concentration, towards the peace of the eternal sabbath.[58]

The "Metaphysics of Conversion"

If man's odyssey and his return to God constitute the central theme of the *Confessions*, this work of Augustine's nonetheless fits within the wider framework of a cosmogony which is also a theogony.[59] That is why the schema of the *auersio* and *conuersio* in the *Confessions* takes on such breadth that it becomes the substratum of a true "metaphysics of conversion," providing that this apt expression is understood in a sense that is remarkably more comprehensive than its author did.[60] For everything, in this metaphysics, must in a certain way be converted to being. It is especially true as regards the spiritual created being, but also, analogically, as regards the human body, and as regards the entire temporal universe.[61] Augustine uses the Neo-Platonic schema of emanation and return in a constantly more synthetic way, in order to examine closely and at the same time the mystery of creation and that of the final aims, as they are symbolically expressed in the first verses of Genesis.[62] His philosophical pursuit moves in this direction from the early dialogues on; this is why it is anagogical and metaphysical in an undissociable way, "leading forward," in the Paulinian expression that resounds in Book XI of the *Confessions.*[63] The *regressus in rationem* and the definition of the ontological status of the soul get their meaning from this viewpoint, which reveals its entire dimension in this work and in the subsequent developments of the *De Genesi ad litteram.*[64]

In principio fecit deus caelum et terram (Gen. 1:1) according to Augustine, means the first metaphysical stage of creation, the sky symbolizing the spiritual created being and the earth the corporeal created being. They are both created "in the Principle," which still does not make them anything more than formless matter.[65]

They are formed according to the Word in a second metaphysical stage, during which the spiritual created beings are invited to answer freely the call *(uocatio)* of the one who then constitutes them in the perfection of their being. In the case of the angel, these two stages are simultaneous, but with regard to man they are inscribed in time. Such is the interpretation given by Augustine for the verse *Dixit dominus fiat lux et facta est lux* (Gen. 1:3).[66]

Thus he uses the same schema — the forming by the Word — in order to explain the second stage of creation and the conversion of the soul to God, owing to which it is incorporated into being. On the other hand, he also identifies, to a certain extent, the first stage of creation — the existential production, "in the beginning," of formless matter — with the fall of sin. All along Book XIII, the cosmological explanation of creation is deliberately compared with that that it symbolizes: the fall and man's return to God, whether it is a question of mankind in general or of Augustine who represents it.

> And (my soul) is still sad, because it falls again and becomes the deep, or rather because it feels it is still the deep . . . Hope . . . until the Lord's wrath passes, the wrath whose sons we too were "once" when we were "darkness" [Eph. 5: 8] . . . . "By day, I shall be up and I shall see the salvation of my face" [Ps. 42:7]. My God, "who will give back life itself to our mortal bodies because of the Spirit that dwells in us [Rom. 8:11], because in his mercy he *moved upon* the tenebrous waters of our souls. [Cf. Gen. 1:2].[67]
>
> . . . until you gather together all that I am outside this scattering and deformity in order that I may conform to your eternity and confirm myself in it forever.[68]

The intentional alternation and parallelism of the theme of the fall and of the conversion of Augustine-Everyman with the two metaphysical stages of creation indicate the meaning that must be attributed to this departure from God that takes place *in principio*, on the level of pure existential causality, and to this return to being that takes place through the formative Word, and under the power of the Holy Ghost.

Augustine insists on the close, if not fatal, connection that ties the first stage of spiritual creation, symbolized by "the damp and dark deep" of *Genesis* 1:2, to the fact of the fall. He constantly uses this symbol in order to mean the evil of sin (we shall notice that in this context *deficere* is replaced by *defluere*):

> The angel sank, man's soul sank: thus they showed that every spiritual created being would be the deep and the gulf of darkness, if you had not said from the beginning: "let there be light." (Gen. 1:3)[69]

In this first "stage," it is still only the material element of spiritual beings that is created, while the *fiat lux* designates the second "stage," that of the forming. Augustine characterizes this material element by formlessness, itself defined as an absolute mutability, meaning that it can take on any form: *capax formarum omnium.*[70] He especially insists on the negative aspect of this potentiality, on its unlikeness to God, due to the nothingness from which it is drawn.[71] This is why he attributes the first "stage" of creation to the Word considered as principle, that is to say, in his exclusively causal part in the line of existence, as far as it is possible to imagine causality without taking into account the formal and formative aspect. Augustine does not push to its extreme limit this analysis of a kind of original matter, on which existence rests, since he accepts two different kinds of matter for the corporeal created being and for the spiritual created being. But in reality he only distinguishes between them through the different formation they receive from the Word.[72] The second "stage" of creation is attributed to the Word considered as wisdom, since from this point of view He is the supreme Form, and, consequently, the formative principle of all beings in what specifically qualifies them.

We find again in this analysis of the creative act the distinction, even the dissociation, which Augustine discovered when he tried for the first time to establish the ontological status of the human soul in the *De immortalitate animae.*[73] This subject had been developed in the following works, in particular in the *De libero arbitrio,* where it was considered from a broader viewpoint that focused on the entirety of created beings, without yet finding there its final form.[74] Augustine gives it at last in the *Confessions,* where he delves deeper into the Neo-Platonic schema of the conversion thanks to a definition of matter drawn as well from the *platonicorum libri.* This definition permits him to show that there is in every created being a first ontological stage characterized by formlessness, incompletion, unlikeness to God. Augustine especially insists, it is true, on what constitutes the unlikeness peculiar to the spiritual created being, represented by the deep to which Genesis refers. If it is not bad in itself, at least it is potentially evil, to the extent to which it tends to nothingness.

Although he mainly brings out the negative aspect that characterizes this first stage of creation, Augustine nevertheless insists on the fact that the created being had not in any way deserved to be, even in this formless and, one might dare to say, bad existence.[75] He asserts, on the other hand, that God was not bound to call it back to himself during this second metaphysical stage, which is the forming by the Word. If He had not done so, He would have remained perfectly happy and perfectly good.[76] Augustine wants to make us understand that God does not need this completion, in opposition to what the Manicheans asserted. One recognizes the kind of reasoning used in the *De libero arbitrio* to relieve divine providence of the responsibility for evil.[77] But there it was a question of an already consummated sin, whereas Augustine asserts it here concerning a state of unlikeness and, so to speak, of fall, which does not imply any willful act, good or bad, coming from the spiritual created being. Once more he comes up against the mystery of the origin of evil, and it is necessary to recognize after all that in this synthesis of conversion with creation, matter, although created by God, plays a part similar to the one attributed to it by the Neo-Platonic philosophers from whom he draws his inspiration. It is like the root of this inclination towards nothingness, which is found in the very constitution of the spiritual created being, like a slope prepared, as it were, for its fall.

It is thus that *utcumque esse,*[78] which characterizes at the same time matter and the original state of the spiritual created being — the latter also being defined as a *qualiscumque uita* — reveals itself to be very close to *minus esse* and *non esse,* which characterize the consequence of the *auersio.* It becomes clearer and clearer that the *auersio* consists for the created being in remaining in this state of original imperfection, in choosing it somewhat as an end by refusing to turn towards its creator.[79]

But Augustine insists, in another connection, on the ordination of the first stage of creation, "abyss," unlikeness, lack of form, to the second stage that consists in the formation by the Word. Due to Him, the converted spiritual created being becomes "conformed to the Form that is equal" to the Father.[80] The consequence of a free choice, *magis esse* has been characterized as a "self-creation" in which are combined the freedom of this created being and the passive part which is its own in relation to the divine act that constitutes it into being.[81] Such is the true "good action," which constantly remains under the guidance of God.[82]

It is thus that the *magis esse* of the spiritual created being, while being contained in the return movement to God of the entire cosmos, gives this return its full meaning.[83] The creation is completed and perfected due to the confirmation of the divine plan by the created being, which is capable of answering consciously the call of the formative Word. By imitating it and by somewhat collaborating with it, it finds itself incorporated, through participation, into the stability signifying autonomy, which is the characteristic sign of the uncreated mind, and pulled away from the inclination towards nothingness, which is the characteristic sign of what is created.

NOTES

1. *Conf.* 4, 6, 11, BA, 13, p. 424:

   Miser eram, et miser est omnis animus uinctus amicitia rerum temporalium et dialaniatur cum eas amittit, et tunc sentit miseriam qua miser est antequam amittat eas.

2. *Conf.* 7, 17, 23, BA, 13, p. 626:

   Et mirabar quod iam te amabam, non pro te phantasmata, et non stabam frui deo meo, sed rapiebar ad te decore tuo moxque diripiebar abs te pondere meo et ruebam in ista cum gemitu; et pondus hoc consuetudo carnalis. *Conf.* 7, 17, 23–18, 24, BA, 13, p. 628 sq.: sed aciem figere non eualui et repercussa infirmitate redditus solitis non mecum ferebam nisi amantem memoriam et quasi olefacta desiderantem quae comedere nondum possem. Et quaerebam uiam conparandi roboris quod esset idoneum ad fruendum te, nec inueniebam . . .

3. *Conf.* 7, 10, 16, BA, 13, p. 616: "Et cum te primum cognoui, tu assumsisti me, ut uiderem esse quod uiderem, et nondum me esse qui uiderem." E. Tréhorel and G. Bouissou have emphasized in their translation, p. 617, the opposition certainly planned between *esse — quod uiderem* and *nondum . . . esse — qui uiderem:* "You have lifted me up to let me see that there was Being for me to see and that I was not yet a being to see it." See relating to this A. Solignac's annotation, p. 616 ff., and R. J. O'Connell, *The Riddle of Augustine's Confessions*, in *International Philosophical Quarterly* 4, (1964), 327 ff. Cf. *Conf.* 7, 17, 23, BA, 13, p. 626: "Sed mecum erat memoria tui, neque ullo modo dubitabam esse cui cohaererem, sed nondum me esse qui cohaererem . . . et inueni longe me esse a te in regione dissimilitudinis."

4. See the text quoted at the end of the preceding note. The expression *regio dissimilitudinis*, which goes back to Plato, *Polit.* 273 d, is borrowed from Plotinus, *Enn.* 1, 8, 13, 17. See relating to this A. Solignac, Complementary Footnote 26, "*Regio dissimilitudinis*," BA, 13, p. 689 ff. We do not subscribe completely to the interpretation that the author gives of it on p. 691: The "unlikeness" caused by sin is quite real; but the human subject only

discerns it, Augustine seems to say, in light of the ontological unlikeness." The close connection that Augustine establishes between the ontological reality of the human being and his moral life is better analyzed, in our opinion, by A. Solignac, in *L'Existentialisme de Saint Augustin*, p. 10 ff. In the lines from the *Confessions* quoted above, it is the ontological separation due to sin that Augustine emphasizes, in contrast with the partaking of being due to conversion, as in the above-mentioned text by Plotinus. Cf. *De ciu. dei* 9, 17, BA, 34, p. 398: "Ubi est illud Plotini, ubi ait: Fugiendum est igitur ad carissimam patriam, et ibi pater, et ibi omnia. Quae igitur, inquit, classis aut fuga? Similem deo fieri." (Cf. *Enn.* 1, 6, 8, 16 ff. and 1, 2, 3, 10 ff.). "Si ergo deo quanto similior, tanto fit quisque propinquior: nulla est ab illo alia longinquitas quam eius dissimilitudo. Incorporali uero illi aeterno et incommutabili tanto est anima hominis dissimilior, quanto rerum temporalium mutabiliumque cupidior." The unlikeness caused by sin reaches the spiritual created being in its ontological structure: therein lies the entire *minus esse* theme, and correlatively, that of *magis esse*, that is to say of the conversion constitutive of being.

5. *De uera rel.* 17, 34, BA, 8, p. 68:

> ita diuina prouidentia, cum sit ipsa omnino incommutabilis, mutabili tamen creaturae uarie subuenit, et pro diuersitate morborum alias alia iubet aut uetat; ut a uitio unde mors incipit et ab ipsa morte ad naturam suam et essentiam ea quae deficiunt, id est ad nihilum tendunt, reducat et firmet.

6. Cf. *En. in Ps.* 118, S. 16, 11, CC, 40, p. 1716: "Non enim exsistendo sunt homines dii, sed participando illius qui uerus est deus."

7. *De mus.* 6, 13, 42, BA, 7, p. 448: "Ex quo fit ut non simul habeat animus nosse in quibus consistendum sit et posse consistere."

8. *Conf.* 7, 21, 27, BA, 13, p. 640 ff.: "Et aliud est de siluestri cacumine uidere patriam pacis et iter ad eam non inuenire . . . et aliud tenere uiam illuc ducentem"; *Conf.* 7, 20, 26, BA, 13, p. 636; *De ciu. dei* 11, 2, BA, 35, p. 36; *De trin.* 4, 15, 20, BA, 15, p. 390; *In Ioh. Euang. Tract.* 2, 4, CC, 36, p. 13. See G. Madec, *Connaissance de Dieu et action de grâces*, in *Recherches Augustiniennes*, 2, 288 ff. and O. Du Roy, *L'Intelligence de la foi en la Trinité*, p. 96 ff.

9. *Conf.* 7, 17, 23, BA, 13, p. 630:

> Et quaerebam uiam conparandi roboris, quod esset idoneum ad fruendum te, nec inueniebam donec amplecterer *mediatorem dei et hominum (1 Tim. 2:5), hominem Iesum Christum, qui est super omnia deus benedictus in saecula (Rom* 9:5*)*, uocantem et dicentem: *ego sum uia et ueritas et uita (John* 14:5).

10. *Conf.* 8, 12, 29–30, BA, 14, p. 66 ff.:

> Arripui, aperui et legi in silentio capitulum, quo primum coniecti sunt oculi mei: *non in comisationibus et ebrietatibus, non in contentione et aemulatione, sed induite dominum Iesum Christum et carnis prouidentiam ne feceritis in concupiscentiis* (*Rom.* 13:13–14). Nec ultra uolui legere nec opus erat. Statim quippe cum fine huiusce sententiae quasi luce securitatis infusa cordi meo omnes dubitationis tenebrae diffugerunt . . . conuertisti enim me ad te ut nec uxorem quaererem nec aliquam spem saeculi huius . . .

11. *Conf.* 7, 10, 16, BA, 13, p. 616:

> Cibus sum grandium: cresce et manducabis me. Nec tu me in te mutabis sicut cibum carnis tuae, sed tu mutaberis in me.

12. G. Madec, *Connaissance de Dieu et action de grâces*, in *Rech. Aug.* 2, p. 291:

> From this point of view the Augustinian "apologetics" certainly does not allow any compromising; it even appears strict and abrupt in the global charge of pride which it brings against Ancient philosophy. It is that "Platonism," to the extent to which it did not accept to go beyond itself by recognizing Christianity, appears to be the story of a success that failed. Augustine himself felt its hopes and disillusions, he learned how God resists the proud ones and gives his grace to the humble, to those who recognize in Christ the sole mediator.

See the discussion of G. Madec's opinion in A. Mandouze, *Saint Augustin: l'aventure de la raison et de la grâce*, p. 504, n. 3.

13. *Conf.* 7, 20, 26, BA, 13, p. 634 ff.

14. *Conf.* 7, 9, 13 ff., BA, 13, p. 609 ff. Cf. *De trin.* 13, 19, 24, BA, 16, p. 336:

> Illi autem praecipui gentium philosophi, qui *inuisibilia* dei, *per ea quae facta sunt, intellecta* conspicere potuerunt (*Rom.* 11:20), tamen quia sine mediatore, id est sine homine Christo philosophati sunt, quem nec uenturum prophetis nec uenisse apostolis crediderunt, ueritatem detinuerunt, sicut de illis dictum est, in iniquitate.

15. *Conf.* 13, 20, 28, BA, 14, p. 476: "homines corporalibus sacramentis subditi non ultra proficerent nisi spiritaliter uiuesceret anima gradu alio et post initii uerbum in consummationem respiceret." Augustine already emphasizes, concerning the receiving of the consecrated species, the importance of inner thinking and the assimilatory function that is his own. *Conf.* 10, 43, 70, BA, 14, p. 268: "Cogito *pretium meum* [*Ps.* 61:5] et manduco et erogo et pauper cupio saturari ex eo inter illos qui edunt et saturantur." This theme of inner meditation based on faith but going beyond it, a more explicitly Christian form of the *regressus in rationem* than that of the early dialogues, is developed in the *De uera religione* 24, 45 and 50, 98 ff., BA, 8, pp. 85 ff. and 168 ff.

16. *Conf.* 11, 8, 10, BA, 14, p. 287 ff.:

> quia omne quod esse icipit et esse desirit, tunc esse incipit et tunc desinit quando debuisse incipere uel desinere in aeterna ratione cognoscitur, ubi nec incipit aliquid nec desinit. Ipsum est uerbum tuum, quod et principium est, quia et loquitur nobis. Sic in euangelio per carnem ait, et hoc insonuit foris auribus hominum ut crederetur et intus quaereretur et inueniretur in aeterna ueritate, ubi omnes discipulos bonus et solus magister docet . . . Quis porro nos docet nisi stabilis ueritas? Quia et per creaturam mutabilem cum admonemur, ad ueritatem stabilem ducimur ubi uere discimus, cum stamus et audimus eum et *gaudio gaudemus propter uocem sponsi.* reddentes nos unde sumus. Et ideo principium, quia, nisi maneret, cum nos erraremus, non esset quo rediremus ab errore, cognoscendo utique redimus; ut autem cognoscamus docet nos, quia *principium* est. *et loquitur nobis.*

Concerning the way in which Augustine uses the Latin translation of John 8:25: *Ego sum principium et loquor uobis*, see earlier p. 106 ff.

17. *Contra acad.* 3, 19, 42–20, 43, BA, 4, p. 196 ff.:

> Quod autem ad eruditionem doctrinamque attinet et mores quibus consulitur animae, quia non defuerunt acutissimi et solertissimi uiri, qui docerent disputationibus suis Aristotelem ac Platonem ita sibi concinere, ut imperitis minusque attentis dissentire uideantur, multis quidem saeculis multisque contentionibus, sed tamen eliquata est, ut opinor, una uerissimae philosophiae disciplina. Non enim est ista huius mundi philosophia, quam sacra nostra meritissime detestantur, sed alterius intelligibilis, cui animas multiformibus erroris tenebris caecatas, et altissimis a corpore sordibus oblitas, nunquam ista ratio subtilissima reuocaret,

> nisi summus deus populari quadam clementia diuini intellectus auctoritatem usque ad ipsum corpus humanum declinaret, atque submitteret, cuius non solum praeceptis, sed etiam factis excitatae animae redire in semetipsas et respicere patriam etiam sine diputationum concertatione potuissent. Hoc mihi de academicis interim probabiliter, ut potui, persuasi . . . Ait enim (Cicero) illus morem fuisse occultandi sententiam suam . . . Quae sit autem ista, deus uiderit; eam tamen arbitror Platonis fuisse. Sed ut breuiter accipiatis omne propositum meum, quoquo modo se habeat humana sapientia, eam me uideo nondum percepisse. Sed cum trigesimum et tertium aetatis annum agam, non me arbitror desperare debere eam me quandoque adepturum. Contemptis tamen caeteris omnibus quae bona mortales putant, huic inuestigandae inseruire proposui . . . Nulli enim dubium est gemino pondere nos impelli ad discendum, auctoritatis atque rationis. Mihi autem certum est nunquam prorsus a Christi auctoritate discedere: non emin reperio ualentiorem. Quod autem subtilissima ratione persequendum est (ita enim iam sum affectus, ut quid sit uerum, non credendo solum, sed etiam intelligendo apprehendere impatienter desiderem) apud platonicos me interim quod sacris nostris non repugnet reperturum esse confido.

Concerning the different interpretations given of this text by R. Holte and O. Du Roy, see p. 36, n. 3. The fact that Augustine calls "human wisdom" this *una uerissimae philosophiae disciplina* that he wants to strive to acquire in order to obtain an understanding of his faith influences us in favor of thinking with O. Du Roy that it is a question of the Platonic tradition, set down in a unified doctrine. Augustine will later consider the Christian wisdom, constituted by means of this human wisdom, but carried out owing to the mediation of Christ, to be *the uerissima philosophia*.

18. *Contra Iulian. pelag.* 4, 14, 72, PL, 44, c. 774:

> Obsecro te, non sit honestior philosophia gentium, quam nostra christiana, quae una est uera philosophia, quandoquidem studium uel amor sapientiae significatur hoc nomine . . . Erubescamus interim uariis disputationibus impiorum, qui didicimus in uera uerae pietatis sanctaque philosophia, et *contra spiritum carnem. et contra carnem concupiscere spiritum (Galat. 5:17).*

19. See A-M. Malingrey, *"Philosophia," étude d'un groupe de mots de la littérature grecque, des Présocratiques au IVe siècle après J.-C.* (Paris: Klincksieck, 1961).

20. R. Holte, in *Béatitude et sagesse*, p. 187 ff., after having analyzed the structure of this Christian gnosis from *Contra academicos*, and p. 362 ff., the way Augustine transforms it, so that it should not be the exclusive privilege of the *pauci*, shows (p. 379 ff.) that this Gnosis fully develops in the *Confessions:*

> Where then can one find this wisdom? To this question only one answer can be given, if indeed it is on a Christian path that one attempts to attain the "Gnosis": in the Scripture, of which it is the most hidden intelligible content, that one extracts with the help of an allegorical interpretation . . . By going back to God through the work of creation, just as the Scripture presents it, and just as an allegorical interpretation puts it in a position to manifest with a growing transparence God's eternal being, Augustine discovers the meaning of his life. Here is where the *telos* is found. When book 13 leads to the interpretation of the sabbatic rest as an expression of God's immutable being and of the perfect sabbatic rest of the soul through the eternal vision of God's being, it is then, and only then, that the famous words which begin the *Confessions* receive their full meaning: "Oh God, You have made us for You and our heart remains restless until it rests in You." (*Conf.* 1, 1, 1, text quoted further p. 85 n. 46).

21. *De uera rel.* 5, 8, BA, 8, p. 36: "Sic enim creditur et docetur, quod est humanae salutis caput, non aliam esse philosophiam, id est sapientiae studium, et aliam religionem. . . ." E. Gilson, *Introduction à l'étude de Saint Augustin*, p. 46:

> A philosophy that means to be a true love of wisdom must proceed from the faith whose understanding it will give. A religion that means to be as perfect as possible must lead towards an understanding stemming from faith. Thus perceived, the true religion goes hand in hand with the true philosophy and in turn, the true philosophy goes hand in hand with the true religion.

A. Mandouze, *Saint Augustin, l'aventure de la raison et de la grâce*, p. 500 ff.:

> Therefore it is no longer sufficient to characterize the relationship between the *true philosophy* and the *true religion* by words such as *coexistence, convergence* or even *concordance*. At the very most . . . it seems that one is justified in speaking, if not of *identity*, at least of progressive *identification*. . . .

G. Madec, *Connaissance de Dieu et action de grâces*, in *Rech. Augustin.* 2, 309:

> Adherence to the Word made flesh *in whom are hid all the treasures of wisdom and knowledge* (*Col.* 2, 3) brings about the joining of wisdom and devoutness, the identification of philosophy with religion, of knowledge of God with worship.

22. *Conf.* 7, 9, 14, BA, 13, p. 610:

> Quod enim ante omnia tempora et supra omnia tempora inconmutabiliter manet unigenitus filius tuus coaeternus tibi et quia *de plenitudine eius* accipiunt animae, ut beatae sint, et quia participatione manentis in se sapientiae renouantur, ut sapientes sint, est ibi.

23. *Conf.* 7, 9, 15, BA, 13, p. 614:

> Et ego ad te ueneram ex gentibus et intendi in aurum, quod ab Aegypto uoluisti ut auferret populus tuus, quoniam tuum erat, ubicumque erat. Et *dixisti* Atheniensibus per apostolum tuum, quod in te *uiuimus* et *mouemur* et *sumus*, sicut et quidam secudum eos dixerunt, et utique inde erant illi libri. (Cf. Plotin, *Enn.* 6, 9, 9, 6–11).

Augustine did not notice that the *sicut* of the Paulinian text bears on the subsequent sentence: "ipsius enim et genus sumus." See relating to this P. Henry, *Plotin et l'Occident* (Louvain: Spicilegium Sacrum Lovaniense, 1934), p. 97, n. 1; A. Solignac, BA, 13, n. 1 p. 614 ff.; P. Courcelle, *Un vers d'Epiménide dans la "Discours sur l'Aéropage,"* in *Revue des Etudes Grecques*, 76 (1963), 404 ff; G. Folliet, *Les Citations des Actes 17, 28 et Tite 1, 12 chez Augustin*, in *Rev. Et. Augustin.* 11 (1965), 293 ff.

24. *De ciu. dei* 10, 32, 1–2, BA, 34, p. 546 ff.:

> Haec est religio, qua uniuersalem continet uiam animae liberandae, quoniam nulla nisi hac liberari potest. Haec est enim quodammodo regalis uia, quae una ducit ad regnum, non temporali fastigio nutabundum, sed aeternitatis firmitate securum. Cum autem dicit Porphyrius in primo iuxta finem de regressu animae libro nondum receptum in unam quandam sectam, quod uniuersalem contineat uiam animae liberandae, uel a philosophia uerissima aliqua uel ab Indorum moribus ac disciplina, aut inductione Chaldaeorum aut alia qualibet uia, nondumque in suam notitiam eandem uiam historiali cognitione perlatam: procul dubio confitetur esse aliquam, sed nondum in suam uenisse notitiam. Ita ei non sufficiebat quidquid de anima liberanda studiosissime didicerat sibique uel potius aliis nosse atque tenere uidebatur. Sentiebat enim adhuc sibi deesse aliquam praestantissimam auctoritatem, quam de re tanta sequi oporteret. Cum autem dicit uel a

philosophia uera aliqua nondum in suam notitiam peruenisse sectam, quae uniuersalem contineat uiam animae liberandae: satis, quantum arbitror, ostendit uel eam philosophiam in qua ipse philosophatus est non esse uerissimam, uel ea non contineri talem uiam. Et quo modo potest esse uerissima, qua non continetur hac uia?. . . Praeter hanc uiam, quae, partim cum haec futura praenuntiantur, partim cum facta nuntiantur, numquam generi humano defuit, nemo liberatus est, nemo liberatur, nemo liberabitur.

25. According to the excellent expression used by A. Forest, *L'Augustinisme de Blondel*, in the collection *Le Centenaire de Maurice Blondel* (Aix-en-Provence: *Publication des Annales de la Faculté des Lettres* 35, 1963), p. 44: "They (Saint Augustine and Blondel) pursue the same effort so as to give a metaphysical meaning to the idea of elevation, to establish the principles of what can be called an ascending participation."

26. See earlier, p. 16 and n. 50, and p. 55 and fns. 31 and 32.

27. *De lib. arb.* 1, 7, 17, BA, 6, p. 168:

an forte intelligis superiorem quamdam et sinceriorem uitam esse scientiam, quam scire nemo potest, nisi qui intelligit? Intelligere autem quid est, nisi ipsa luce mentis illustrius perfectiusque uiuere? *De quant. an.* 33, 75, BA, 5, p. 382: Sed haec actio, id est appetitio intelligendi ea quae uere summeque sunt, summus aspectus est animae, quo perfectiorem, meliorem rectioremque non habet. *De mus.* 6, 5, 13; BA, 7, p. 386: Quare intenta in dominum intelligit aeterna eius, et magis est. . . .

It is a question of a spiritual use of understanding—at the same time speculative and practical, since this knowledge is also a virtue — which transcends its use at the level of the purely human activities, as has already been pointed out earlier, p. 14 and fn. 40, about the *De ordine*. Also see fn. 28 of the present chapter.

28. *De quant. an.* 33, 72–73, BA, 5, p. 378:

Magna haec et omnino humana. Sed est adhuc ista partim doctis atque indoctis, partim bonis ac malis animis copia communis. Suspice igitur atque insili quarto gradui, ex quo bonitas incipit atque omnis uera laudatio. Hinc enim anima se non solum suo, si quam uniuersi partem agit, sed ipsi etiam uniuerso corpori audet praeponere, bonaque eius bona sua non putare, atque potentiae pulchritudinique suae comparate discernere atque contemnere. . . .

29. *De quant. an.* 33, 76, BA, 5, p. 384:

quae perfructio summi et ueri boni"; ibid. 36, 80, BA, 5, p. 394: pascit in septimo; *De lib arb.*, 3, 10, 30, BA, 6, p. 382 sq.: Quia enim rationalis creatura uerbo illo tanquam optimo cibo suo pascitur; humana autem anima rationalis est, quae mortalibus uinculis peccati poena tenebatur, ad hoc diminutionis redacta, ut per coniecturas rerum uisibilium ad intelligenda inuisibilia niteretur, cibus rationalis creaturae factus est uisibilis, non commutatione naturae suae, sed habitu nostrae, ut uisibilia sectantes, ad se inuisibilem reuocaret. *De mus.* 6, 13, 40, BA, 7, p. 446: ipsius dei praesentia uegetatur in mente atque conscientia; *De uera rel.* 2, 21: cuius essentia fruebatur.

30. *De immort. an.* 6, 11, BA, 5, p. 190:

Deinde quo magis est (ratio), eo quidquid sibi coniungitur facit ut sit . . .; *ibid.* 2, 18, BA, 5, p. 204: fatendum est . . . esse . . . in essentia certiore atque pleniore sapientem.; *De uera rel.* 17, 34, BA, 8, p. 68: ita diuina prouidentia . . . mutabili tamen creatureae uarie subuenit . . . ut a uitio unde mors incipit et ab ipsa morte, ad naturam suam et essentiam ea quae deficiunt, id est ad nihilum tendunt, reducat et firmet.

The expression *magis esse*, which expresses growth in being, has already been frequently quoted.

31. *De immort. an.* 10, 17, BA, 5, p. 202:

Haec autem quae intelliguntur eodem modo sese habentia, cum ea intuetur animus, satis ostendit se illis esse coniunctum . . .; cf. *De diu. quaest.* 83, q. 54, BA, 10, p. 154: Quod autem est omni anima melius, id deum dicimus; cui, quisquis eum intelligit, iunctus est . . . Cum igitur intelligit aliquid quod semper eodem modo sese habet, ipsum sine dubio intelligit. Haec autem est ipsa ueritas; cui quia intelligendo anima rationalis iungitur, et hoc bonum est animae, recte accipitur id esse quod dictum est: *Mihi autem adhaerere deo bonum est* (Ps. 72:28).

32. *De mor.* 1, 11, 18, BA, 1, p. 164:

At eum sequimur diligendo, consequimur uero non cum hoc omnino efficimur quod est ipse, sed ei proximi. . . .; ibid I, 12, 20, p. 168: Fit (animus humanus) similis quantum datum est, dum illustrandum illi atque illuminandum sese subiicit.; ibid 1, 13, 22, p. 170 sq.: Huic enim (ueritati) haeremus per sanctificationem. Sanctificati enim plena et integra caritate flagramus,qua sola efficitur ut a deo non auertemur, eique potius quam huic mundo conformemur. *Praedestinauit enim*, ut ait idem apostolus, *conformes nos fieri imaginis filii eius* (Rom. 8:29).

33. *De ord.* 1, 31, BA, 4, p. 418:

hinc nisi se auerterit, diuina non erit.; *De immort. an.* 10, 17, BA, 5, p. 202: ea quae intelligit animus cum se auertit a corpore, non sunt profecto corporea; et tamen sunt, maximeque sunt, nam eodem modo semper se habent.

34. *De immort. an.* 7, 12, BA, 5, p. 190:

si enim magis est (animus) ad rationem conuersus eique inhaerens, ideo quod inhaeret, incommutabili rei quae est ueritas, quae et maxime et primitus est; *De lib. arb.* 3, 16, 45, BA, 6, p. 410: Et tamen, quod meritum est conuerti ad eum ex quo es, ut ex ipso etiam melior sis, ex quo habes ut sis? *De mus.* 6, 11, 33, BA, 7, p. 430 sq: delectatione in rationis numeros restituta ad deum tota uita nostra conuertitur.

35. *De lib. arb.* 3, 7, 21, BA, 6, p. 362:

teque ita formari exoptabis, ut affectiones tuae non sint temporales; *De uera rel.* 41, 77, BA, 8, p. 138: Corrumpitur autem homo exterior aut profectu interioris, aut defectu suo. Sed profectu interioris ita corrumpitur, ut totus in melius reformatur, et restituatur in integrum in nouissima tuba, ut iam non corrumpatur neque corrumpat; *De uera rel.* 52, 101, BA, 8, p. 172: Haec est a temporalibus ad aeterna regressio, et ex uita ueteris hominis in nouum hominem reformatio.

We shall see a little later the development Augustine gives, in the last books of the *Confessions*, to this theme, which he had outlined in the *De libero arbitrio*, as we have pointed out earlier p. 36 ff.

36. *Conf.* 5, 1, 1, BA, 13, p. 462:

. . . ut exsurgat in te a lassitudine anima nostra innitens eis quae fecisti et transiens ad te, qui fecisti haec mirabiliter: et ibi refectio et uera fortitudo; *Conf.* 5, 3, 4, BA, 13, p. 468: . . . per impiam superbiam recedentes et deficientes a lumine tuo . . . et inuenientes quia tu fecisti eos, non ipsi se dant tibi, se ut serues quod fecisti . . . ut tu, deus, ignis edax consumas mortuas curas eorum recreans eos immortaliter. *Conf.* 5, 7, 13, BA, 13, p. 486: Aut quae procuratio salutis praeter manum tuam reficientem quae fecisti?

37. *De lib. arb.* 2, 16, 41, BA, 6, p. 294:

> quid igitur aliud agimus cum studemus esse sapientes, nisi ut quanta possumus alacritate ad id quod mente contingimus totam animam nostram quodammodo colligamus, et ponamus ibi, atque stabiliter infigamus; ut non iam priuato suo gaudeat quod implicauit rebus transeuntibus, sed exuta omnibus temporum et locorum affectionibus apprehendat id quod unum atque idem semper est; *Conf.* 1, 3, 3, BA, 13, p. 276: nec tu dissiparis, sed colligis nos; *Conf.* 10, 40, 65, BA, 14, p. 258: Neque in his omnibus quae percurro consulens te inuenio tutum locum animae meae nisi in te, quo colligantur sparsa mea nec a te quicquam recedat ex me; *Conf.* 11, 29, 39, BA, 14, p. 338: et a ueteribus diebus colligar sequens unum; *Conf.* 12, 16, 23, BA, 14, p. 378: colligas totum quod sum a dipersione et deformitate hac et conformes atque confirmes in aeternum.

38. *De beata uita* 1, 8, "Est autem aliquid, si manet, si constat, si semper tale est, ut est uirtus. . . ," see earlier pp. 16–17 and fn. 16; *De immort. an.* 2, 18, BA, 5, p. 204: "tunc est animus sapientissimus, cum ueritatem quae semper eodem modo est intuetur, eique immobilis inhaeret diuino amore coniunctus"; *De lib. arb.* 3, 8, 23: "quies autem habet constantiam, in qua maxime intelligitur quod dicitur est," see earlier p. 37 and n. 19.

39. *Conf.* 1, 1, 1, BA, 13, p. 272:

> inquietum est cor nostrum, donec requiescat in te; *Conf.* 1, 5, 5, BA, 13, p. 280: Quis mihi dabit adquiescere in te; *Conf.* 2, 10, 18, BA, 13, p. 360: Quies est apud te ualde et uita inperturbabilis; *Conf.* 4, 12, 18, BA, 13, p. 438; State cum eo et stabitis, requiescite in eo et quieti eritis.

40. *Conf.* 4, 12, 18, BA, 13, p. 438:

> Si placent animae, in deo amentur, quia et ipsae mutabiles sunt et in illo fixae stabiliuntur: alioquin irent et perirent; *Conf.* 11, 30, 40, BA, 14, p. 338: Et stabo atque solidabor in te, in forma mea, ueritate tua.

41. See earlier p. 36.

42. *De lib. arb.* 3, 7, 21. See earlier pp. 38–39 for the translation of this passage, and fn. 24.

43. *De diu. quaest.* 83, q. 35, BA, 10, p. 104: "fit ut sic amatum quod aeternum est, aeternitate animum afficiat."

44. *De lib. arb.* 3, 10, 30, BA, 6, p. 382 ff.:

> Quia enim rationalis creatura uerbo illo tanquam optimo cibo suo pascitur; humana autem anima rationalis est, quae mortalibus uinculis peccati poena tenebatur, ad hoc diminutionis redacta ut per coniecturas rerum uisibilium ad intelligenda inuisibilia niteretur: cibus rationalis creaturae factus est uisibilis, non commutatione naturae suae, sed habitu nostrae, ut uisibilia sectantes, ad se inuisibilem reuocaret.

Concerning the immutable *ratio*, the principle of being, cf. *De ord.* 2, 19, 50, a passage quoted p. 28 fn. 43 and the comment relating to this p. 15; *De immort. an.* 6, 11, passages quoted p. 18 and fns. 66 and 67; *De immort. an.* 7, 12, passage quoted p. 19 and fn. 70; *Conf.* 11, 8, 10, passage quoted p. 70 and fn. 16. The identification of the *ratio* with the Word is confirmed by the following text: *Epist.* 118, 3, 17, CSEL, 34, 2, p. 681:

> . . . sed non sicut illi (Epicurei et Stoici) errorum suorum ita Platonici uerae rationis personam implere potuerunt. Omnibus enim defuit diuinae humilitatis exemplum quod opportunissimo tempore per dominum nostrum Iesum Christum inlustratum est.

See the excellent commentary on this text made by A. Mandouze, *Saint Augustin: L'aventure de la raison et de la grâce*, p. 494 ff.:

> Christ having come, "true *reason*" (the word here is essential and we could be tempted to write it with a capital) has found its true holder. *Taken over, fully accepted as a responsibility*, it shows what it is capable of, without risking being diverted from its call. The *Platonicorum libri* indeed can give an idea of the *uera ratio:* it is the *libri ecclesiastici* — or *litterae ecclesiasticae* — that reveal, even to the most simple-minded, the only true holder and sole guarantor of Reason.

O. Du Roy, in *L'Intelligence de la foi dans la Trinité*, chap. 4, "From authority to Reason, the Intellect, and the Principle," p. 109 ff., has analyzed at length the texts concerning the *ratio*. He is of the opinion that it is with the Holy Ghost that Augustine would have identified this equivalent of the Plotinian *logos*.

45. The adaptation of *ipsum esse* to the Word is especially found in the texts in which Augustine compares the *Ego sum qui sum* of Ex. 3:14 with John 8:28; 8:58, as well as John 1:1 and 8:25 *(Ego sum principium et loquor uobis)*. See for example *Tract. in Ioh.* 39, 8, CC, 36, p. 349; concerning the Trinity ibid. 40, 3, CC, 36, p. 351; *Contra Maximin.* 1, 19, PL, 42, c. 757; ibid. 2, 26, 10, PL, 42, c. 811).

46. *Conf.* 1, 1, 1, BA, 13, p. 272: "fecisti nos ad te et inquietum est cor nostrum donec requiescat in te."

47. *Conf.* 1, 2, 2, BA, 13, p. 274 ff.:

> An quia sine te non esset quidquid est, fit ut quidquid est capiat te? Quoniam itaque et ego sum, quid peto, ut uenias in me, qui non essem, nisi esses in me?

48. *Conf.* 13, 1, 1, BA, 14, p. 424 ff.:

> Inuoco te, *deus meus, misericordia mea*, qui fecisti me . . . qui . . .institisti crebrescens multimodis uocibus, ut audirem de longinquo et conuerterer et uocantem me inuocarem te. Etenim, domine, deleuisti omnia mala merita mea, ne retribueres manibus meis, in quibus a te defeci, et praeuenisti omnia bona merita mea, ut retribueres manibus tuis quibus me fecisti, quia et priusquam essem tu eras, nec eram cui praestares ut essem, et tamen ecce sum ex bonitate tua praeueniente totum hoc, quod me fecisti et unde me fecisti.

49. Ibid., p. 426: "ut seruiam tibi et colam te, ut de te mihi bene sit, a quo mihi est, ut sim cui bene sit." As A. Solignac indicates, ibid., fn. 1, p. 426 ff.:

> *Bene esse* does not mean the undetermined existence, but rather the qualified existence of the man who confirms his destination to God through divine service and worship: *bene esse* is identical to the *sapienter uiuere, beate uiuere* of the following paragraphs.

See the next note.

50. *Conf.* 13, 2, 3, BA, 14, p. 428:

> ita etiam creato spiritui non id est uiuere quod sapienter uiuere: alioquin inconmutabiliter saperet. *Conf.* 13, 3, 4, BA, 14, p. 430: Neque enim eius informitas placeret tibi, si non lux fieret non existendo sed intuendo inluminantem lucem eique cohaerendo, ut et quod utcumque uiuit et quod beate uiuit non deberet nisi gratiae tuae, conuersa per conmutationem meliorem ad id quod neque in melius neque in deterius mutari potest. Quod tu solus es, quia solus simpliciter es, cui non est aliud uiuere, aliud beate uiuere, quia tua beatitudo es.

51. Ibid.: "Quod autem in primis conditionibus dixisti: *fiat lux, et facta est lux* (Gen. 1:3), non incongruenter hoc intellego in creatura spiritali, quia erat iam qualiscumque uita quam inluminares." The expression *utcumque esse* used by Augustine in the subsequent lines is quoted in the preceding footnote. Cf. *Conf.* 13, 5, 6, BA, 14, p. 432: "nisi conuerteretur ad eum, a quo erat qualiscumque uita, et inluminatione fieret speciosa uita."

52. *Conf.* 13, 4, 5, BA, 14, p. 432:

    cui non hoc est uiuere, quod beate uiuere,quia uiuit etiam fluitans in obscuritate sua; cui restat converti ad eum a quo facta est, et magis magisque uiuere apud fontem *uitae* et *in lumine* eius uidere *lumen* (cf. Ps. 35:10) et perfici et inlustrari et beari.

53. *Conf.* 13, 23, 33, BA, 14, p. 486.

54. *Conf.* 13, 32, 47, BA, 14, p. 516.

55. *Conf.* 13, 22, 32, BA, 14, p. 484: "Mente quidem renouatus et conspiciens intellectam ueritatem tuam. . . ."

56. *Conf.* 13, 32, 47, BA, 14, p. 516.

57. *Conf.* 13, 21, 31, BA, 14, p. 480 ff.

58. *Conf.* 13, 35, 50–38, 53, BA, p. 520 ff.

59. M. Blondel, *L'Etre et les êtres* (Paris: 1963), 3, "Becoming and Solidifying of Beings," p. 289:

    In order to light our way in this difficult passage towards access or occlusion, towards the possession or deprivation of being ἕξις or στέρησις with the meaning that we have recognized for these traditional words while studying this concrete logic that we have called normative, we shall make use to our advantage of a beautiful doctrine of Saint Augustine's and of unusually expressive phrases in the XIth book of the *Confessions*. What he says about time, in order to interpret it less as a physical reality than as a symbolic expression of our inner becoming and spiritual genesis, can be applied not only to the ontology of each mind, but to the entirety of beings, to this moral and religious cosmogony whose true name would finally be, from the Augustinian point of view, a Theogony with a dual outcome towards the City of God or towards incurable failure.

60. E. Gilson, *L'Esprit de la philosophie médiévale* (Paris: 1944), p. 137:

    Considered in its profound inspiration and even in the details of its technical structure, Saint Augustine's entire doctrine is dominated by one fact: the religious experience of his own conversion. In this way I believed myself to be able to write elsewhere, and I think that it is still true to say, that his philosophy is essentially a "metaphysics of conversion."

    Cf. by the same author, *Introduction à l'étude de Saint Augustin* (Paris: 1949), p. 316.

61. See p. 55 ff.

62. See J. Daniélou, *La Typologie millénariste de la semaine dans le christianisme primitif*, in *Vigiliae Christianae* (1949), 1 ff., and O. Rousseau, *La Typologie augustinienne de l'Hexaéméron et la théologie du temps*, in *Festgabe Joseph Lortz* (Baden-Baden: Verlag Bruno Grimm, 1958), vol. 2, p. 47 ff.

63. *Conf.* 11, 29, 39, BA, 14, p. 338:

    praeterita oblitus, non in ea qua futura et transitura sunt, sed *in ea quae ante sunt* non distentus, sed *extentus*. . . . Cf. *Philipp.* 3, 13.

64. That is why we shall resort to certain passages from this later work, to the extent to which they allow us to clear up the "metaphysics of conversion" offered in the last books of the *Confessions*.

65. Augustine interprets the expression *in principio* by basing himself on the Latin translation of John 8:25: *Ego sum principium et loquor uobis* (The Jerusalem Bible translates: "First what I tell you.") The principle of beings is identified at the same time with the Word and with the eternal *ratio*. *Conf.* 11, 8, 10, a passage quoted earlier p. 70 ff. and n. 16. Book 11, which comments on the *in principio* of Genesis, is dedicated to the relationship between eternity and time whose dissociation Augustine aspires to escape. He insists in contrast on the *stabilitas*, which characterizes the principle and in which the one who reverts to it participates. This *leitmotiv* from the first four books reappears here with force, accompanied in conclusion by the theme that is going to be developed in the last two books, that of the formative Word: see earlier p. 72, fns. 39 and 40. Cf. *Conf.* 11, 11, 13, BA, 14, p. 292:

> Quis tenebit illud (cor) et figet illud, ut paululum stet et paululum rapiat splendorem semper stantis aeternitatis et conparet cum temporibus nunquam stantibus. . . .

66. *Conf.* 13, 10, 11, BA, 14, p. 440 ff.:

> nisi dono tuo. . .mox ut facta est attolleretur nullo interuallo temporis in ea uocatione, qua dixisti: *fiat lux*, et fieret *lux* (Gen. 1:3). In nobis enim distinguitur tempore quod *tenebrae* (cf. Eph. 5:8) et *lux* efficimur: in illa uero dictum est quid esset, nisi inluminaretur, et ita dictum est, quasi prius faerit fluxa et tenebrosa, ut appareret causa qua factum est ut aliter esset, id est ut ad lumen indeficiens conuersa lux esset.

The following remark, made in connection with a similar passage from *De Genesi ad litteram* is also valid for this text of the *Confessions*, as are other comments from this article that we shall have the opportunity to quote again: J. Wytzes, *Bemerkungen zu dem neuplatonischen Einfluss in Augustins "de Genesi ad litteram,"* in *Zeitschrift für die neutestamentliche* Wissenschaft 39 (1941), 139:

> Jetzt der Text: dixit *deus fiat lux et facta est lux*. Nach dem Abwägen und Verwerfen verschiedener Möglichkeiten kommt Augustin 1, 2, 6 zu dem Schluss, dass auch hier von der *spiritualis materia* die Rede ist: ". . .*et facta est lux eam reuocante ad se creatore conuersio eius facta et illuminata intelligatur*." Wir sind hier noch auf demselben Gebiet. Vom Niederen aus gesehen redet der Neuplatoniker von ἐπιστρεφέσθαι oder ἐπιστρέφειν, intransitiv. Das Höhere, der Existenzgrund, ἐπιστρέφει in aktiver Bedeutung, eine Wirkung, die auch genannt wird, ἀνακαλείν, *reuocare*, vgl. .z. B. *Enn.* 6, 7, 23: "ἕλκον πρὸς αὐτὸ καὶ ἀνακα-λούμενον (das Eine) ἐκ πάσης πλάνης . . ."

67. *Conf.* 13, 14, 15, BA, 14, p. 450:

> Et adhuc tristis est, quia relabitur et fit abyssus, uel potius sentit se esse abyssum . . . Spera . . . donec transeat ira domini, cuius filii et nos fuimus *aliquando tenebrae* . . . *Mane astabo et uidebo salutare uultus mei*, deum meum, *qui uiuificabit et mortalia corpora nostra propter spiritum qui habitat in nobis*, quia super interius nostrum tenebrosum et fluidum misericorditer *superferebatur*. Cf. *Conf*, 13, 12, 13, BA, 14, p. 446: quia et apud nos in Christo suo *fecit deus caelum et terram*, spiritales et carnales ecclesiae suae, et *terra* nostra antequam acciperet formam doctrinae, *inuisibilis* erat et *incomposita* (Gen. 1:2), et ignorantiae tenebris tegebamur, quoniam *pro iniquitate erudisti hominem, et iudicia tua sicut multa abyssus* (cf. Ps. 54:6; 38; 12). Sed quia *spiritus* tuus *superferebatur super aquam* (Gen. 1:2), non reliquit miseriam nostram misericordia tua, et dixisti: *fiat lux* (Gen. 1:3) . . . et displicuerunt nobis tenebrae nostrae, et conuersi sumus ad te, *et facta est lux* (Gen. 1:3). Et ecce fuimus *aliquando tenebrae, nunc autem lux in domino* (Eph. 5:8).

68. *Conf.* 12, 16, 23, text quoted p. 119, at the end of n. 37.

69. *Conf.* 13, 8, 9, BA, 14, p. 436:

> Defluxit angelus, defluxit anima hominis et indicauerunt abyssum uniuersae spiritalis creaturae in profundo tenebroso, nisi dixisses ab initio: *fiat lux, et facta* esset *lux*. Cf. *Conf.* 7, 5, 7, BA, 13, p. 594: in multis quidem adhuc informis et praeter doctrinae normam fluitans; *Conf*. 13, 7, 8, BA, 14, p. 436: Cui dicam, quomodo dicam de pondere cupiditatis in abruptam abyssum et de subleuatione caritatis per spiritum tuum, qui *superferebatur super aquas?* . . . affectus sunt, amores sunt, inmunditia spiritus nostri defluens inferius amore curarum et sanctitas tui attollens nos superius amore securitatis . . .; *Conf.* 13, 20, 28, BA, 14, p. 474: A quo si non esset lapsus. Adam, non diffunderetur ex utero eius salsugo maris, genus humanum profunde curiosum et procellose tumidum et instabiliter fluidum . . . *Conf.* 13, 21, 30, BA, 14, p. 478: Operentur iam in terra ministri tui . . . sed operentur etiam sicut in arida discreta a gurgitibus abyssi et sint forma fidelibus . . .; *Conf.* 13, 23, 34, BA, 14, p. 490: abyssus saeculi; *Conf.* 13, 34, 49, BA, 14, p. 518: Ubi autem coepisti praedestinata temporaliter exequi, ut occulta manifestares et inconposita nostra conponeres — quoniam super nos erant peccata nostra et in profundum tenebrosum abieramus abs te, et *spiritus tuus bonus* (cf. Ps. 142:10) *superferebatur* ad subueniendum nobis in tempore oportuno . . .

70. *Conf.* 12, 6, 6, BA, 14, p. 352:

> Mutabilitas enim rerum mutabilium ipsa capax est formarum omnium, in quas mutantur res mutabiles. Et haec quid est? Numquid animus? Numquid corpus? Numquid species animi uel corporis? Si dici posset "nihil aliquid" et "est non est", hoc eam dicerem; et tamen iam utcumque erat, ut species caperet istas uisibiles et conpositas.

As A. Solignac, BA, 14, n. 23, p. 599 ff., brings to our attention:

> Just as Augustine owes Plotinus an exact idea of divine Being, he also owes him that of matter. Plotinus indeed gives, just like Augustine, mutability, especially generation and corruption, as evidence for matter (*Enn.* 2, 4, 6) . . . the Augustinian notion of matter does not correspond exactly to that of Aristotle's *first matter* which is thinkable and which exists only in correlation with a form. Through Plotinus, Augustine prefers to go back to the Platonic notion of χώρα . . . for Augustine, matter — just like time whose being is the tendency not to be (*Conf.* 11, 14, 17) — is a paradoxical reality, today we would say a *dialectical* one; neither a pure negation, nor a definite reality, but a *dynamic negativity*. In so far as it is *negativity*, it means a total absence of form, an absolute formlessness; in so far as it is a *dynamic* negativity, it is the principle of mutability, mutability itself and the ability to receive the forms.

71. *Conf.* 12, 28, 38, BA, 14, p. 410: fecisti omnia, non de te similitudinem tuam formam omnium, sed de nihilo dissimilitudinem informem. . . ."

72. *Conf.* 12, 17, 25, BA, 14, p. 382:

> uerum tamen quia non de ipsa substantia dei, sed ex nihilo cuncta facta sunt, quia non sunt idipsum quod deus, et inest quaedam mutabilitas omnibus . . . communem omnium rerum inuisibilium uisibiliumque materiem adhuc informem, sed certe formabilem, unde fieret caelum et terra, id est inuisibilis atque uisibilis iam utraque formata creatura, his nominibus enuntiatam, quibus appellaretur *terra unuisibilis et inconposita* et *tenebrae super abyssum* (Gen. 1, 2) ea distinctione, ut *terra inuisibilis et inconposita* intellegatur materies corporalis ante qualitatem formae, *tenebrae* autem *super abyssum* spiritalis materies ante cohibitionem quasi fluentis immoderationis et ante inluminationem sapientiae? Cf. 12, 17, 26, p. 382; 12, 19, 28, p. 386; 12, 21, 30 p. 390; 12, 22, 31, pp. 392–394.

Augustine insists on safeguarding the hierarchy between the spiritual created being and the material created being, even concerning their *materia informis*. *Conf.* 13, 2, 2, BA, 14, p.426: "spiritale informe praestantius, quam si omnino nihil esset, corporale autem informe praestantius, quam si omnino nihil esset." The difference is specified in *De Gen. ad lit.* 1, 1, CSEL, 28, 1, p. 4:

> spiritualis uidelicet uita, sicut esse potest in se, non conuersa ad creatorem, tali enim conuersione formatur ac perficitur, si enim non conuertatur informis est. Corporalis autem si possit intelligi per priuationem omnis corporeae qualitatis, quae apparet in materia formata.

Concerning the Plotinian origin of the notion of spiritual matter in *Enn.* 2, 4, 5, 19 ff., as well as the way in which Augustine uses it and transforms it, see J. Wytzes, *Bemerkungen zu dem neuplatonischen Einfluss in Augustins "de Genesi ad litteram,"* in *Zeitschrift für die neutestamentliche* Wissenschaft 39 (1941), 138 ff.

73. See earlier p. 20 ff.

74. See earlier p. 36 ff.

75. *Conf.* 13, 2, 2–3, BA, 14, p. 426:

> Dicant, quid te promeruerunt spiritalis corporalisque natura, quas *fecisti in sapientia tua* (Ps. 103:24), ut inde penderent etiam inchoata et informia quaequae in genere suo uel spiritali uel corporali euntia in immoderationem et in longinquam dissimilitudinem tuam. . . atque ita penderent in tuo uerbo informia, nisi per idem uerbum reuocarentur ad unitatem tuam et formarentur. . . Quid te promeruerit materies corporalis, ut esset saltem *inuisibilis* et *inconposita* (Gen. 1:2) . . . Aut quid te promeruerit inchoatio creaturae spiritalis, ut saltem tenebrosa fluitaret similis abysso, tui dissimilis, nisi per idem uerbum conuerteretur ad idem a quo facta est. . . ? Cf. *Conf.* 13, 3, 4, BA, 14, p. 430.

76. *Conf.* 13, 4, 5, BA, 14, p. 430.

77. See earlier pp. 37 and 41.

78. *Conf.* 12, 6, 6, end of the passage quoted in n. 70, p. 88:

> et tamen iam utcumque erat; *Conf.* 13, 3, 4, BA, 14, p. 430: Quod autem in primis conditionibus dixisti: *fiat lux, et facta est lux*, non incongruenter hoc intellego in creatura spiritali, quia iam erat qualiscumque uita quam inluminares . . . Neque eius informitas placeret tibi, si non lux fieret, non existendo sed intuendo inluminantem lucem eique cohaerendo, ut et quod utcumque uiuit et quod beate uiuit, non deberet nisi gratiae tua. . . ; *Conf.* 13, 5, 6, BA, 14, p. 432: nisi conuerteretur ad eum, a quo erat qualiscumque uita, et inluminatione fieret speciosa uita. Cf. *De Gen. ad litt.* 1, 4, CSEL, 28, I, p. 8 sq.: ut per id quod principium est, insinuet exordium creaturae exsistentis ab illo adhuc imperfecte; Ibid. 1, 5, CSEL, 28, I, p. 8 sq. Non enim habet informem uitam uerbum filius, cui non solum hoc est esse quod uiuere, sed etiam hoc est uiuere, quod est sapienter ac beate uiuere. Creatura uero quanquam spiritalis et intellectualis uel rationalis, quae uidetur esse illi uerbo propinquior, potest habere informem uitam: quia non sicut hoc est ei esse quod uiuere, ita hoc uiuere quod beate ac sapienter uiuere. Auersa enim a sapientia incommutabili stulte ac misere uiuit, quae informitas eius est. Formatur autem conuersa ad incommutabile lumen sapientiae, uerbum dei. A quo enim exstitit ut sit utcumque ac uiuat, ad illum conuertitur ut sapienter ac beate uiuat. Cf. *Conf.* 1, 6, 10, BA, 13, p. 290. Et quam multi iam dies nostri et patrum nostrorum per hodiernum tuum transierunt et ex illo acceperunt modos et utcumque extiterunt, et transibunt adhuc alii et accipient et utcumque existent.

79. Cf. *De Gen. ad litt.* 1, 4, CSEL, 28, 1, 0, 4:

> in qua conuersione et formatione, quia pro suo modo imitatur dei uerbum . . . non autem imitatur hanc uerbi formam, si auersa a creatore, informis et imperfecta remaneat.

80. *Conf.* 13, 2, 3, BA, 14, p. 424:

> nisi per idem uerbum conuerteretur ad idem a quo facta est, atque ab eo inluminata lux fieret, quamuis non aequaliter tamen conformis formae aequali tibi? *De Gen. ad litt.* 1, 4, CSEL, 28, I, p. 4: per id autem quod uerbum est, insinuet perfectionem creaturae reuocatae ad eum, ut formaretur inhaerendo creatori, et pro suo genere imitando formam sempiterne atque incommutabiliter inhaerentem patri, a quo statim hoc est quod ille.

81. A. Solignac, *Compl. Note* 27: *Conversion et formation*, BA, 14, p. 616:

> a) the *creatio* does not give the mind its full essence. . . . The mind exists on this first level in the form of the *utcumque*, of the indefinite, of the formless, of the imperfect. b) The *formatio*, which brings to it this full firmness, is made in an act which is at the same time *effecting* and *relational*, an act in which the created being conspires to its own making by confirming its essential relation to the creator and by thus becoming actually established in its destination. Therefore the *formatio* of the human mind is at the very same time part of man and part of God. It supposes, and requires, on behalf of man a *conuersio*, a return to his Principle; it comprises, on behalf of God, a *call* and an *enlightenment* which involve the *conuersio*. Forming thus implies *freedom*, better still freedom *pursued in its authentic sense* by accepting its essential reference to the creator, receiving from him in exchange the fullness of his being. The *formatio* thus comprises mainly, according to the exact comment by Dom Victor Warnach *(Erleuchtung und Einsprechung bei Augustinus)* in *Augustinus Magister*, 1, 1954, Etudes Augustiniennes, p. 447), a *personale Moment*, a decision by the free person. Paradoxically, from this viewpoint, it depends on the created mind to constitute itself as a mind at the very moment when it consents to receive from God the light which constitutes it as such. The *conuersio* is thus a counterpart of the *creatio:* it is a self-creation, or at least this self-creation is an essential and necessary stage in the dialectic of the relationship between man and God.

82. In the sense in which *bonitas* was already defined *De quant. an.* 33, 73, BA, 5, p. 378:

> Suscipe igitur atque insili quarto gradui, ex quo bonitas incipit, atque omnis uera laudatio. Hinc enim anima se non solum suo, si quam uniuersi partem agit, sed ipsi etiam uniuerso corpori audet praeponere, bonaque eius bona sua non putare, atque potentiae pulchritudinique suae comparata discernere atque contemnere. . .; *De Gen. ad. litt.* 8, 12, CSEL, 28, I, p. 249: tota eius actio bona est conuerti ad eum a quo factus est, et ab eo iustus, pius, sapiens, beatusque semper fieri. Ibid. 8, 12, p. 250: Semper ab illo fieri, semperque perfici debemus, inhaerentes ei, et in ea conuersione quae ad illum est permanentes, de quo dicitur: *Mihi autem adhaerere deo bonum est* (Ps. 72:28), et cui dicitur: *Fortitudinem meam ad te custodiam* (Ps. 58:10).

83. *Conf.* 12, 28, 38, BA, 14, p. 410:

> fecisti omnia, non de te similitudinem tuam formam omnium, sed de nihilo dissimilitudinem informem quae formaretur per similitudinem tuam recurrens in te unum pro captu ordinato, quantum cuique rerum in suo genere datum est, et fierent *omnia bona ualde* (Gen. 1, 31), siue maneant circa te, siue gradatim remotiore distantia per tempora et locos pulchras uariationes faciant aut patiantur.

Conclusion

When one follows the developments that Augustine gave the dialectic of *magis esse* and *minus esse* in different contexts, we are especially struck by the constancy of his explanation. He has adopted as his own, once and for all, the Platonic expression of this fundamental law of spiritual life, which decrees the growth or the reduction of the soul, according to whether the latter subsists on the internality of the mind or whether it turns away towards the world of externality. But we are also struck by the fact that Augustine did not merely lay this schema on the fundamental ideas coming from his faith. On the contrary, he has relived and reconsidered the spiritual experience expressed by this schema from the viewpoint of his faith, thus finding their deepest meeting point.

What strikes us in the way he has developed an ontology of Platonic origin is the synthetic unity of his thought rather than the alleged contradictions between this ontology and the tenets of Christian faith. This unity, it is true, does not develop in the way a rigid system does. On the contrary, it is structured in an organic and differentiated way, according to the elaborations called for by the new and different problems that face it. Therefore, the notion of being is grasped on different levels, and comprises variable values at the level of the created being, according to whether the emphasis is placed in a leading way on the ascending movement of anagogy or on the descent from the creative principle.

The sui generis characteristic of this "spiritual ontology" prohibits one from classifying it under the label of an "essentialism" or an "existentialism" as most of the critics have done in recent decades: some stigmatizing its "static essentialism," others exalting its "dynamic existentiality."[1] If they have surely discovered authentic aspects of Augustinian metaphysics, they have warped its real meaning because they did not see that these aspects are complementary. One must blame these critics for projecting on Augustine's thought definitions that were only elaborated later, in particular the famous distinction between essence and existence. This retrospective projection is even more awkward since these definitions were mostly elaborated under the effect of the impetus given to Western thought by Augustinian metaphysics. It seems to us that a study undertaken from the viewpoint of *magis esse* and *minus esse*, which is neither that of "essentialism"' nor of "existentialism," but that of an anagogical ontology, allows one to avoid this mistake, because it attempts to find Augustine's basic intention in this area.

The meaning of this theme revealed itself gradually, in different contexts, progressively as we were advancing in the analysis of the works called philosophical, and we saw that it gets its entire dimension in the *Confessions*, where it becomes the thread of a true metaphysics of creation. A study of the ontological implications contained in the later works would probably confirm our conclusions concerning the fundamental importance of this theme in Augustinian metaphysics: the research that we have already done in some of these works, and that we mentioned along the way, assure us of it.

However, if it is possible to assert without any hesitation that this Neo-Platonic theme allowed Augustine to delve deeper into certain of the most important implications of his faith, it is much more difficult to establish to what extent, in return, he "christianized" it. For, if it is easy to see it when it is a question of developments due to the influences of dogma, such as the eschatological transposition of the *beata uita* and the resurrection of the bodies conceived as a consequence of *magis esse*, the question is infinitely more delicate when it concerns the ontological constituting of the soul owing to conversion. Ever since its Greek sources have been known, it has become impossible to assert, as Blondel used to do, that it is a question of an exclusively Christian theme.[2] Will it be necessary then to say with J. Wytzes that we are only dealing with a "Christian variant of the πρόσοδος and ἐπιστροφή metaphysics,"[3] or to vouch with A. Solignac that Augustine gave a transposition of it that would make "the frameworks of Plotinian metaphysics burst"?[4]

The main arguments that A. Solignac offers concerning this have to do with the created being's freedom, and the personal call that God aims at him. This freedom, this call, would not exist in Plotinus. Without being able to go into the details that such a study would require, it is still necessary to recall, with J. Wytzes, the Plotinian origin of the "calling" that resounds all through the *Confessions*,[5] and, with C. de Vogel, that the Greek philosophers have known freedom and personality to an extent that is much larger than it is sometimes admitted.[6] Moreover, independently of any theory of freedom or of the person, the theme of *magis esse* implies, on behalf of the one who turns towards Being, the highest form of freedom and personality, or at the very least, on behalf of Being, the "call" to this highest form, which is the freedom of autonomy.[7]

While recognizing that there are specifically Christian elements in the way in which Augustine develops the "self-creation" theme, it is thus necessary to acknowledge that it is very difficult to differentiate between them in a sufficiently distinct way. Perhaps we would be able to see them more clearly by undertaking a broader comparison, that is to say by looking for the applications of this theme in other Church Fathers and by confronting them with the "self-constitution" as it was stated by the Neo-Platonic authors subsequent to Plotinus and Porphyry. The difficulty of such a comparison comes from the fact that, in this area, the doctrinal criteria are not the only ones questioned, since it is mainly a matter of the metaphysical translation of a spiritual experience. This is why it is delicate to hastily assert differences and superiorities that are constantly questioned.

Augustine himself did not hesitate to recognize fully his debt to the Platonic philosophers, concerning the conception of God and that of the soul that partakes of

Him. However, he believes he must exclude from the "fatherland" all those who did not find Christ, even those philosophers who saw it "from afar" and who helped him see it, but whose books did not allow him to rejoin it. Nevertheless, once the way, which is Christ, is found, the final salvation is achieved, according to the works that we studied, through a conversion of a Neo-Platonic nature to the Word, that is to say, through an *intellectus fidei* that is a *regressus in rationem*.[8]

This is why, when one attempts to penetrate the theme of *magis esse* and *minus esse* from its own viewpoint, which is that of the inner experience and meditation not only in Augustine but also in the *platonicorum libri* from which he borrowed it, one is led to think that such a metaphysical structure could only be established in order to translate an experience and a thought concerning salvation, or, if one prefers, deliverance. Thus, research in this area, in order to be truly "fruitful," must seek to discover the convergences of spiritual experience and meditation with an oecumenical approach. This approach is justified not only towards other "religions," but also towards Platonism; especially since, after having believed for centuries that certain themes were exclusively Christian, we have now discovered one of their sources in this "alien" thought.[9]

NOTES

1. Followed by many critics, the main representative of the essentialist interpretation is E. Gilson. Especially see *Le Thomisme* (Paris: Urin, 1948), p. 42 ff.; *God and Philosophy* (Yale: 1961), p. 60 ff. Concerning the existential interpretation, it is especially necessary to quote F. Körner, *Das Sein und der Mensch: Die existentielle Seinsentdeckung des jungen Augustin* (Freiburg-München: 1959). (The first chapter, pp. 1–27, gives a historical survey of the different interpretations of Augustinian ontology until the present time.) See concerning this the much less biased attitude of J. Chaix-Ruy, *Saint Augustin: Temps et histoire* (Paris: 1956) p. 120 ff., who is attempting to define the role of essence and that of existence in Augustinian metaphysics, by basing himself on the ontological status of the soul torn between "its distress of an ousted king," according to Pascal's expression, and the fact that it partakes "in a variable and until the end approximate way" (p. 124) of divine essence.

2. In the *Correspondance philosophique de M. Blondel et L. Laberthonnière*, published and presented by C. Tresmontant (Paris: 1961), especially see the letters of February 26, March 7, and March 10, 1921. In the introduction, p. 38, C. Tresmontant accepts as his own this opinion of Blondel's. Our criticism of Blondel only relates to his failure to recognize the Greek sources, for he is surely the modern philosopher who best understood the Augustinian expression of this theme, very close to his own research. What he considers to be "the essential point of Christian metaphysics" is "the question of the 'realizability' of divine life" in us (p. 282), or "the intussusception of man by God and of God by man, of 'He who is' by 'her who is not,' as the blessed Angela of Foligno used to call herself," (p. 284) or still that of the "solidification" of beings, as Blondel calls it, when dealing with the *Confessions*, in *L'Etre et les êtres*, p. 289 ff.:

As long as beings remain reduced to being scattered, dispersed, selfish, as long as people especially let themselves be scattered, divided up and as if torn by endless tugging for the pleasure of a vain curiosity or degrading passions, it would be of no use to win the universe, everything would be lost and dissipated: the kingdom of disorder, confusion, hatred, punishment, rising from the very depths of thought and will, rebellious to their light and to their inner impulse. On the contrary, faithful to the inner norms that support them and establish them in mutual order, subordinating them to the principle of truth and goodness, from which they originate and to which they tend, the beings — each one in what comes from him and all in what composes them in total harmony — organize, edify, confirm, and develop themselves as in the infinite solidity of the God who has called them to the dignity of being themselves beings in the Divine Being who has, in some way, become their cement, their reinforcement, their form, their indefectibility. See earlier, p. 86, n. 59.

3. J. Wytzes, *Bemerkungen zu dem neuplatonischen Einfluss in Augustins "de Genesi ad litteram,"* in *Zeitschrift für die neutestamentliche* Wissenschaft 39 (1940), 140:

   Als am Ende dieses Paragraphen (*De Gen. ad litt.* 1, 4, 9) Augustin noch einmal eine Zusammenfassung gibt vom Schaffen *in principio* als *exordium creaturae adhuc imperfectae* und das "dixit deus fiat" auf die *perfectionem creaturae reuocatae ad eum (deum)* bezieht, so handelt es sich um eine christliche Variante der πρόοδος-ἐπιστρόφη Spekulation und jetzt ist es klar, warum am Anfang des Schöpfungsberichtes das *dixit deus fiat* nach Augustin unangebracht war, da zuerst das Entstehen des Ungeformten stattfindet (siehe zu *in principio* usw.) und nacher die Formung durch Zuwendung, angedeutet durch *dixit deus fiat*.

4. A. Solignac, Complementary Footnote 13, *Conversion et formation*, BA, 14, p. 614 ff.:

   By interpreting the Scripture in this way, all Augustine does is apply Plotinian metaphysics in its dual rhythm of procession and ascension. The hypostases inferior to the One are differentiated and receive their being by the procession movement which ontologically separates them from the superior hypostasis, but they only receive the fullness of their essence and action through a *conversion*, a *return* movement towards this generative principle. Thus it is at first with Intelligence: a superabundance of the One, it is different from him; its deviation and its stopping in this differentiation movement establish it as being (τὸ ὄν); its conversion and its gaze towards the One establish it as *Intelligence* (τὸν νοῦν): it is thus by the ἐπιστροφή that it truly becomes what it is (*Enn.* 5, 2, 1, 9–13). . . . The same exists for the soul and more particularly the individual soul. . . . Thus Augustine received from Plotinus the doctrine of the conversion and enlightenment of the soul; he will explicitly recognize it in the *City of God* (10, 2). However, here again Christian revelation makes the framework of Plotinian metaphysics come apart. It is not a question in Plotinus of the Word's call to the created being so that it may turn towards it: there is no *uocatio* in Plotinus, but at the very most a natural bond from the soul to Intelligence and to the One. On the contrary, for Augustine, the relation of the soul to the Word is set from the start in terms of a *personal relationship:* the Word speaks to the soul, and the soul answers by turning towards him; the creation of the soul is made by a spoken word, which gives it being in virtue of a free divine will, but this word is immediately developed into a precise call, which the soul is invited to answer. A metaphysical dialogue is thus established between the creator and his created being: the creative Freedom is answered by the created freedom.

5. See earlier p. 75 and n. 66.

6. C. De Vogel, *The Concept of Personality in Greek and Christian Thought*, in *Studies in Philosophy and in the History of Philosophy* (Washington, D.C.: 1963), 2, 20 ff. Concerning Plotinus see p. 46 ff.

7. A thorough analysis of the implications of the conversion constitutive of being is found in J. Trouillard's introduction to *Proclos, Éléments de théologie* (Paris: 1965), p. 51 ff.: "Now

any being that enjoys sufficient internality to take upon itself its causes and spontaneously give itself its constituent characteristics in cooperation with these causes is "*self-constituting*" (αὐθυπθόστατος). . . . As Dodds writes, self-constituting is implied by autonomy (αὐτάρχεια), but does not exclude the derivation from higher principles. It assumes it, on the contrary, since everything that proceeds and becomes converted (even to itself) is two-fold and must thus find its center in the strict simplicity of the Goodness that is anterior to any autonomy and to any procession and inner conversion. Self-constituting is not self-existence. The self-constituting being creates itself . . . it internalizes procession and conversion. *Instead of being a simple fragment of the cycle, it plays it in its entirety*, bringing together the end and the origin and setting itself in Goodness. . . . Self-constituting is based on a "substantial conversion" (οὐσιώδης ἐλιστροφή) towards oneself. The self-constituting being is the one which, according to Plotinus' word, "makes its own center coincide with the universal center." (*Enn.* 6, 9, 8, 19–20)

8. The ambiguity of Augustinian thought relating to this has been picked up by O. Du Roy, *L'Intelligence de la foi en la Trinité*, p. 105:

> Knowing where to go is thus possible, to a certain extent, for man left to himself. Which way to go, that is what Christ reveals to us by his Incarnation. He is a sure way because he is the road and the goal. Knowing where to go is getting to know God, the immutable Truth, who speaks at the acme of understanding. Faith is only a preparation. But can one see the problem that this creates? If the supreme mode of knowledge could be reached to some extent by the pagan philosophers without the faith, if then supreme enlightenment is not intrinsically transformed by faith, if it is only the degree and the stability which differ, then the revealed God, the God Trinity, can be known without the economy of revelation. What will then be the *intellectus fidei*, since the *intellectus* is a step of enlightening nature and the *fides* is a moral step and between the two this gap is opened, felt by Augustine at the time of his conversion, that has produced, and very rightly so, the comment that this first stage of his conversion was the experience of the "ineffectual light"? It is understood that, with faith not radically (nor explicitly, nor consciously at least) modifying the movement proper to the *intellectus*, there is established between the two terms a very dense dialectic between impulse and regulation, boldness and discipline, mystical ascent and humble return to the ecclesial norm. This dialectic is the entire history of Augustine's thought. . . .

9. It is Blondel himself who suggests to us the relation that must be established between the "metaphysical and moral" aspect of the theme that we have studied and a truth revealed in the Gospel, in a paragraph on the "solidification of beings" from which we have already quoted passages. M. Blondel, *L'Etre et les êtres*, p. 288 ff.:

> We have probably already shown how, under the divine initiative, the cooperation of personal beings with their own orientation comprises an option to make, owing to the stimulation of effective assistance. It is necessary, however, to go beyond that and to follow the execution and the consequences of this collaboration, and that being so in both directions where the option of secondary causes and personal beings can guide and determine their destiny. It is legitimate to seek, even for the metaphysical and moral order, the meaning of a spoken word, which only acquires, it is true, its full implications in a superior order, but which bases its truth and its severity on the most inner decision of thought and will: "he who does not gather with me scatters" (Matt. 12:30; Luke 11:23) and "from him who has not, even what he has will be taken away" (Matt. 13:12; 25:29; Mark 4:25; Luke 8:18; 19:26; John 15:2). If it is added that for those who have, infinitely more still will be given, it is then necessary to explain how the riches can be naturally acquired or lost in order to allow either this increase, or this strange withdrawal, which strips being without suppressing it.

See earlier p. 86, fn. 59 and pp. 93–94, n. 2.

APPENDIX

The Augustinian Exegesis of *"Ego sum qui sum"* and the "Metaphysics of Exodus"

Discovering "He Who Is"

Immutability, an Innate Notion

In the *De beata uita* and in the *Confessions*, Augustine tells how he won access to "He who is," thanks to the conversion of his gaze. At first he had adhered to the Manichean doctrine of the two substances. Then, while opting for a single ultimate principle, he had imagined it as being corporeal and changing (*Conf.* 4, 16, 31). Therefore, when Ambrose's preaching began to open his eyes about this, he did not succeed in convicting the Manichean doctrine of falsehood in its very root, because he was unable to conceive a purely spiritual reality (*Conf.* 5, 10, 20). The first outcome of his efforts to undeceive himself was the perception of divine immutability:

> With all my heart, I believed you to be incorruptible, inviolable and immutable, because without knowing whence nor how this certainty was coming to me, I still saw clearly that what can be corrupted is less good than that which is incorruptible, that what is inviolable is indubitably above that which can sustain violence, that what is immutable is better than that which can change" (*Conf.* 5, 14, 25).

"Without knowing whence nor how"; Augustine wants us to understand that his certainty is that of an innate notion, a vestige of the original inward light and something that allows one to attain truth in a direct way (*Conf.* 7, 1, 1). This notion, which means divine transcendence in contrast with the world here below, subject to change and corruption, will prove to be fundamental in his work from the dual point of view of the "true philosophy" and scriptural exegesis. But at this stage of the journey that is going to lead him to God-Being, Augustine does not yet manage to understand that immutability implies incorporeity. In spite of his efforts to stretch his mind in this direction, he remains a prisoner of the phantasms of the imaginary realm, which, appearing as kingdoms of light, depict for him a corporeal God (*Conf.* 7, 6, 10).

The Inward Look, the Only Access to Incorporeal Being

Up until the time that the Immutable began to reveal to him its true nature, Augustine had known nothing, according to him, except with this knowledge he designates as external, terrestrial, and carnal, because it has as its object the realities here below and shows itself incapable of transcending them, even when it is endowed with superior qualities: "I did not know this other reality . . . the one that truly is . . . . I did not know that God is spirit." (*Conf.* 3, 6, 11). That is why, far from helping him in his quest, his philosophical and scientific cognitions were only leading him astray, for he was using them to project on the "Wholly Other" categories that are only useful for knowing what is here below.

Augustine repeats it constantly: it is his conception of reality that was wrong, an error described by the Platonic myth of the cave. "For I had my back against the light and my face turned towards the lit objects, therefore my face was not lit" (*Conf.* 4, 16, 30). It is the books "by Plato" or "by Platonic authors" that will teach him to convert his eyes towards incorporeal Being. He will then be able to penetrate the meaning of Ambrose's assertions concerning the spirituality of God and that of the soul, by acquiring, or rather by recovering a cognitive faculty giving access to this "other reality, the one which truly is." It is a question of the spiritual understanding *(intellectus mentis)* or inward look *(interior aspectus)*, which corresponds to the *voûs* of the Platonic tradition and which Augustine, according to patristic practice, considers identical to the Biblical knowledge by the "heart."[1] He recounted this experience in a famous passage of the *Confessions* (7, 10, 16), which happens to be one of his most important "commentaries" on the *Exodus* verse 3:14, not only on account of the biographical aspect of this passage, but because Augustine has given shape there to his discovery of God-Being. This account was written indeed ten years after the event, when the Catechumen had become a Bishop. One recognizes there the will to reconcile in an orthodox way the truths contained in the "Platonists' books" with Christian doctrine, but also the care for summing up the ontology that Augustine had worked out from the one these books contain. We shall only quote here the heart of the text:

> . . . you have lifted me up to show me that it is, the reality I would see, but that as for me I was not yet the one who would see it. You struck the weak light in my eyes with the violence of your brightness: I shook with love and awe, and I discovered that I was far from you, in the region of unlikeness, and it seemed to me that I heard your voice saying to me from above: "I am the sustenance of the great ones: grow and you will eat me. You will not change me into you as for the nourishment of your flesh, but it is you who will be changed into me." And I got to know that on account of his iniquity you chastised man, and made my soul dry up like a spider's web. [Ps. 38:12].[2] And I said "Isn't truth then anything since it does not extend into finite or infinite space?" And from far you shouted to me: "I am who I am" (Ex. 3:14). I heard that as one hears inside one's heart, and there remained no more reason for me to doubt: I would have rather questioned my own life than the existence of the truth one sees "by understanding it through the instrumentality of the created beings" (Rom 1:20).

One may ask what significance should be attributed to this text. Must we assume that its author received the enlightenment of Being under the impact of the name revealed to Moses? As a matter of fact, it does not seem necessary to understand in too literal a sense the use of the Biblical verse made here by Augustine. He himself tells us in confidence that it is owing to the warning given by the "Platonists' books," read in 386 — the year that was also that of his conversion to Christianity — that he found a way to inner meditation that finally allowed him access to incorporeal Being (*Conf.* 7, 20, 26). He worked out the consequences of this discovery in his early works before encountering the text of Exodus 3:14 or at least before paying it any particular attention. Indeed, he begins to quote it and comment on it only with the *De uera religione*, written around 391.

One understands the reasons that have pushed Augustine to quote the revealed text in that passage of his autobiographical account, even if it isn't consistent with the strict literal and chronological truth. The answer given to man's anguished quest (for this autobiography is meant to be, in what it contains that is typical, that of every man[3]), expressed in the revealed form in the Exodus verse, is thus based on the authority of the Scripture. This allows Augustine to bring out the dramatic aspect of this quest and at the same time the intervention of grace that he believes to have been at work when, while reading the "Platonists' books," he won access to the knowledge of God-Being, the meeting point between the "true philosophy" of the Platonists and the Revelation. Far from denying the objective value of these lines from the *Confessions*, we are led to ascertain that they thematize the experience lived by Augustine. After the failure of his first attempts at conversion and after the temptation of skepticism, the discovery of God-Being was one of the most important stages of his return journey. This experience was combined with the thought Augustine gave, quite a few years later, to the meaning of his conversion and its different stages. In the lines that follow, we shall take note of the aspects of this thematization that concern our subject most directly.

He who discovers Being discovers simultaneously his own unlikeness: that unlikeness resulting from the fall, and not simply that which characterizes what is created, as such. For true knowledge of the latter results as well from the discovery of "He who is," and the ontological value of the created, intermediary between Being and nothingness, is defined in a passage that follows the text quoted above. But the specific experience of the knowledge of oneself as unlike (i.e., as ontologically separated from the Principle by the alienation due to sin) takes place on another level, inseparably metaphysical and moral.[4] This is why the discovery of God-Being still only constitutes an imperfect and distant knowledge. In the "region of unlikeness," it is possible for Augustine to see that Being exists *(ut uiderem esse quod uiderem)*, but that he cannot yet truly see it *(nondum me esse qui uiderem)*, nor adhere to it in the union of love *(me nondum esse qui cohaererem)* (*Conf.* 7, 17, 23). In relation to the reality that "is," he "is not yet." The unlikeness of sin constitutes a state of "nonbeing," or, as it is here, of "not yet being," which metaphysically corresponds to the drying up of the soul called to mind by the Scripture, or more exactly by the translation that Augustine had at his disposal. It will only be possible to attain the union of knowledge and love with the reality that "is," if one is transformed into it. Thanks to the analogy of food, familiar in his work since the *De beata uita*, Augustine establishes the connection between the philosophical theme of participation, most often expressed by the growth in being, and the Biblical and Christian theme of the assimilation to God. The conversion outlined would remain ineffectual, and the knowledge of God-Being would remain distant *(de longe)*, if they did not lead to ontological assimilation. That is why this theme will play an important part in the Augustinian exegesis of Exodus 3:14. But, in this autobiographical text, the author still only indicates it as a promise.

Preludes to the Exegesis of Exodus 3:14

The Definitions of God-Being

We shall start by examining some of the definitions of God-Being that Augustine formulated in the works preceding the *De uera religione*, for they serve as a prelude to those we shall find in the passages in which he quotes and comments upon the Exodus verse. We shall be satisfied with choosing the most typical examples, without following step by step the development of the Augustinian ontology all through the early works, as we have done in the previous study.[5]

What is "being" *to us?* Such is the intermediary question through which, in the philosophical dialogues, Augustine attempts to make his disciples understand what Being is *in itself*. Having defined it, by examining vice, which results from ignorance, and virtue based on knowledge, "that which remains, lasts and always stays the same" (*De beata uita* 2.8), he endeavors to make them understand that God is the reality that corresponds to this definition: "Do you think that God is eternal and always remains?" (*De beata uita* 2.11).

Augustine does not insist further during this first attempt, surely remembering the difficulties he experienced himself before being able to grasp this truth. He prefers to make them understand first that "being" for man means partaking of God. In the dialogues that follow the *De beata uita*, it is at the end of different developments answering the present problem that the definition of God-Being is proposed, when the field has been sufficiently cleared so that the interlocutor may be able to grasp it, not through simple reasoning, but because his mind's eye *(intellectus mentis, rationis aspectus)* has been opened: it is a question of an intellectual intuition (*Sol.* 1, 6, 12–13).

> But, I ask you, if you only find above our reason eternal and immutable Being, will you be reluctant to call it God? . . . If then . . . reason perceives by itself something eternal and immutable, will you be reluctant to call it God? (*De lib. arb.* 2, 6, 14).

According to the point of view that Augustine chooses, the supreme reality is envisaged as "the truth . . . which is in the highest degree" because it is "always in the same way," or as the entirety of "these truths," which "are in the highest degree" . . . "always in the same way" (*De immort. an.* 7.12 and 11.18), or as this equivalent of the

Plotinian *voûs*, "the *ratio*, in which we notice the greatest immutability," which "is in the highest degree" (*De immort. an.* 6.11), or still as "this immutable form, which always remains," "this form, which is always the same" (*De lib. arb.* 2, 17, 45–46). Considered from its specifically ontological point of view, the supreme reality is called "that which truly is" (*Sol.* 1, 1, 5), "that which" or even "He who is in a supreme way" (*De lib. arb.* 3, 20–21). It is also called "essence" or "substance" (*De immort. an.* 12, 19), and, in the later dialogues, there appears the expression *ipsum esse* or *idipsum esse*, which Augustine will abundantly use in his exegesis of *Exodus* 3:14 (*De immort. an.* 7, 12; *De lib. arb.* 3, 20–21; *De mor. Eccl.* 1, 14, 24).

The Wisdom Constitutive of Being

In the dialogues, the soul's life is defined as being *(esse)* or nonbeing *(non esse)* according to whether it turns towards God-Being or, on the contrary, towards the nothingness of the outside world. The wise man is he who ontologically subsists on truth: this is what Augustine is attempting to make his disciples understand beginning with the *De beata uita* (2, 8), according to a method that will be specified in the *De ordine*. It is there that one finds the definition of the order of the liberal sciences, which must be practised by the one who wants to go beyond the level of simple faith in order to come to the understanding of the revealed truths, and, having reached the top, to contemplate God in his eternity and to partake of "the one who truly is" (*De ordine* 2, 2, 6). It is thus that we achieve our true end: going from *non esse* or *nondum esse* to *perfecte esse* thanks to the conversion of wisdom. But this ordination to being, inscribed in us, merely tortures the soul with its uncomprehended and unachieved finality, if it clings to passing possessions that carry it along towards a nothingness in which it can never be completely annihilated. It is the tearing asunder of this contradiction, the misunderstood requirement of being, that is felt by the wretched man who desires to commit suicide but who even more fears being nothing:

> Consider therefore the greatness of this asset, which is true Being, desired by the wretched as much as the blessed ones. If you consider that well, you will see that you are wretched to the extent to which you remain distant from what is in a supreme way; you will understand how you were able to believe that it is better not to be rather than to be wretched: it is because you were not seeing what is in a supreme way. You will finally perceive why you want to be nevertheless: it is because you are thanks to the one who is in a supreme way" (*De lib. arb.* 3, 7, 20).

This theme of being in God will play a capital part in the Augustinian exegesis of *Exodus*. Too often, in this connection, critics were only interested in the definition of *Ego sum qui sum*, without seeing its linkage to wisdom constitutive of being or without giving it their attention. Now if the Immutable is not envisaged from the point of view of a metaphysics of conversion, the Augustinian definition of God-Being is cut down, for Immutable Being is only reached at the conclusion of a return that transforms the soul to its likeness, in virtue of the principle according to which the like is only known by the like. It is why, like that of its Platonic models, this ontology is essentially an ontology of spiritual life.

The Exegesis of Exodus 3:14

The Difference between Believing and Understanding

After this study of the preparations, we are going to tackle the exegesis of *Ego sum qui sum* as it is presented in about fifty passages, of different lengths, distributed over Augustine's entire opus beginning with the *De uera religione*. In these texts, which we shall call, for reasons of convenience, "commentaries" on Exodus 3:14, Augustine often uses this verse to clear up the meaning of other passages from the Scripture, and vice versa, following a method of scriptural groupings that was familiar to him.[6] Thus, from this first "commentary" on, *Ego sum qui sum* is compared with Romans 1:20 and more generally with the context of this last verse, Romans 1:18–25.[7] In this text Augustine reads the condemnation of the Neo-Platonic philosophers who had come to know the true God, but who ended up worshipping idols, for want of having found the only true mediator who is Christ. Augustine's goal in the *De uera religione*, meant for his friend Romanianus, still a Manichean, is to show that the "true philosophy" has as a preliminary condition the acceptance of the Christian faith, otherwise it loses its true nature. As a matter of fact, philosophy loses almost none of the privileges Augustine had recognized it to possess in the early dialogues; even if he insists more on the primacy of faith — a primacy *de facto* and not *de iure* — nevertheless reflection or *ratiocinatio* still plays an essential part. Indeed, the full development of the new man is seen in the light of the *intellectus*, faith having as its mission the preparation of man for the *ratio*, which will lead him to knowledge (*De uera rel.* 24, 45). It is thus that the impairment of the *anima rationalis*, a consequence of the sin that pushed it to turn away from the immutable inner truth towards the changing outside world (*De uera rel.* 20, 38), will be rectified. This *ratio* is none other than "the light that enlightens every man coming into this world" (John 1:9; *De uera rel.* 42, 79). That is why, finishing off the teaching of faith and morals, which give us his life, his death, and his resurrection, the doctrine of Christ is a *disciplina rationalis* (*De uera rel.* 17, 33). It is in the gnosis of the *ratio* that the righting of the three major concupiscences of fallen man, sensuality, pride, and *curiositas*, takes place. In these new developments, the theme of the *regressus in rationem* described in the *De ordine* (2, 11, 31) is recognized.

It is at the conclusion of this return, that is to say, during the third righting, which transforms the *curiositas*, the longing to acquire cognitions that please the imagination, into an authentic pursuit of the truth that the mind reaches "He who is." The criterion allowing the recognition that this concerns true Being and not the imaginary representation of the Manicheans is the *intelligere* insofar as it is differentiated from simple faith. It is a question of the clearest and surest intuition, the one "that allows one to see with certainty what difference exists between believing and understanding."

The word *intelligere* is the leitmotiv of this "commentary," for "what eternity is, I only perceive by understanding it." This entirely Plotinian definition of eternity is of the same kind as those we have encountered in the different definitions of God-Being that have been previously examined:

> Now, in the eternal, nothing passes on and nothing is to come, for that which passes on stops being and that which is to come has not yet started being; eternity itself does nothing else than be; it is impossible to say for it that it has been, as it is said of something which no longer is, nor that it will be, as it is said of something which is not yet. That is why it alone succeeded in saying quite truthfully to the human mind: "I am who I am"; and that is why it has been possible to say for it quite truthfully: "He who is has sent me to you" (*De uera rel.* 49, 97).

We find out here that Augustine is defining "He who is" and the knowledge that gives access to him, as he was defining earlier supreme *esse* and its epistemological conditions. It is also necessary to note that it is from the point of view of the return to the *ratio* that he correlates the Exodus 3:14 verse with that of Romans 1:20. The Paulinian verse proves to Augustine, according to the patristic tradition, the correlation between the tangible world and the intelligible world, as well as the possibility of going up again from the first to the second.[8] Romans 1:20 thus is not interpreted here in the strictly rational sense of a proof of God's existence, as will be done later by the Vatican Council, following the point of view of Saint Thomas Aquinas.[9] That is to say, for Augustine, the understanding that perceives the *inuisibilia dei* is that of the man who, within the viewpoint of the Christian religion, allowing philosophy to find and to achieve its authentic finality, turns towards what is true with all the powers of his soul. That is why this understanding is able to transform the old man into a new man, that is to constitute him in true Being.

The "proof" that relies on the tangible world to lead to knowledge of the *inuisibilia dei* is used, in the *De uera religione*, in different forms, which are varied aspects of the return to the *ratio* (for example, the evidence through doubting, *De uera rel.* 29, 73). That is why this kind of proof always appeals finally to the internality of the *mens* (*De uera rel.* 29, 72).

The Ontological Themes:

1. *The Dialectic of Being and Nothingness*

After having seen in the *De uera religione* that Augustine places the exegesis of Exodus 3:14, from the point of view of the *intellectus* set against simple faith, at the conclusion of the inner conversion, which is a return to the *ratio*, it seems useless and tedious to expound each time the text of the "commentaries" on this verse is contained in his opus: a list of them, arranged as far as possible in chronological order, will be found at the end of this Appendix.[10] Rather, we shall attempt to throw light on the great themes developed by Augustine in these "commentaries." Indeed, whether they are long or brief, whether they take a more philosophical, oratorical, or lyrical turn according to whether they are found in theological, catechistic, exegetic, or pastoral works, does not change in any way the meaning Augustine, from the *De uera religione* up to his last writings, reads into the Name revealed to Moses. In it he sees, as he says in the *De ciuitate dei*, a work of his middle years, the essence of the meeting between the Revelation and Plato's thought:

> Here is what, more than all the rest, would almost prompt me to assert that Plato was not unaware of these books: when Moses asks to know the name of the one who was sending him to the Hebrew people to bring them out of Egypt, he received from God, through an angel's mouth, the following answer: "I am who I am and you will say to the children of Israel: he who is has sent me to you"; which means that, compared to the one who truly is, because he is immutable, the changing created things are not; it is exactly what Plato asserted forcefully and taught without getting tired of it; and I do not know if such an assertion can be found in the books prior to Plato, except in the one in which it is said: "I am who I am and you will say to them: he who is has sent me to you" (*De ciu. dei* 8, 12).

Indeed, if Augustine reads in this verse the Revelation of God as *ipsum esse*, it is to the immutability attribute that he turns in order to interpret its meaning as well as to the equivalents of this attribute: eternity, identity with oneself, and less often in the "commentaries" on Exodus 3:14, simplicity.

We have pointed out earlier, while quoting Augustine's own testimony in the *Confessions*, that the Platonists' books have initiated him to the spiritual sense of the notion of immutability by teaching him the method of the return to the self. That is why, instead of seeing there a purely speculative — or "essentialist" according to the meaning Gilson gives this word[11] — definition, it is necessary to interpret in it a dialectic of anagogy, which contrasts, in order to lead us to it, Being with what "is" not, the Immutable with that which changes, the Eternal with that which passes:

> If, pulling myself away from these days which pass, I contemplate things from up above, if I compare what is transitory to what is eternal, I see what truly is" (*En. in Ps.* 38, 6).

> . . . the other realities that we call essences or substances comprise accidents, which more or less transform them. But to God, nothing like that can happen, in such a way that the only substance or essence that is immutable is that of God; and it is for him precisely that this expression is the most suitable and the most exact, Being itself *(ipsum esse)* from which essence derives its name. For that which changes does not hold Being itself; something liable to change, even if it does not change, can no longer be what it used to be. Only that which does not change and can absolutely not change deserves without any reservation the name Being (*De Trin.* 5, 2, 3).

These definitions, more or less developed, that are found in almost all of the Augustinian "commentaries" on Exodus 3:14, always aim at showing the contrast between the Immutable and change, which is a sign of the nonbeing of the world here below and of our own nothingness, as long as the conversion to "He who is" has not founded us in Being. The way in which Augustine expresses, in his "commentaries" on Exodus 3:14, the triple dialectic of Being and nonbeing, of the Immutable and change, of the Eternal and the temporal, indeed shows that these notions correspond for him to a fundamental apperception. He is attempting to awaken the knowledge solicited by the desire for being and for eternity implanted deep within each one of us, even if we are unaware of it or even if we deny it. That is why he constantly calls to mind the painful experience of the time of the fall, when we disintegrate, in order to lead us towards the only true present. This anagogical viewpoint always goes, whether it is explicity formulated or not, with the speculative definitions of "He who is":

> Now the psalmist. . . used the present in order to make us understand that God's substance is absolutely immutable, that one cannot say that it was nor that it will be, but only that it is. Whence the spoken words: "I am who I am," and: "He who is has sent me to you," and again: "You will change them and they will change, but you, you are always the same and your years will not pass away" (Ps. 101:27–28). Here is this eternity, which has become our refuge so that in it and in order to remain there we flee from the mutability of time here below (*En. in Ps.* 89, 15).

2. *Immutability and Eternity*

Immutability is the distinctive mark of divine transcendence. We have pointed out elsewhere that at the time when Augustine was attempting to define the soul's structure in order to demonstrate its immortality, he not only tended to recognize in it this partaking of immutability that is the knowledge of the principles of science and the arts, but also he considered the soul as a kind of immobile motor, while recognizing the aporia of a certain change in it (*De immort. an.* 3, 3–4). But later on he worked out his explanation differently and set aside this attribute exclusively for God, paying attention on the contrary to what there is in the soul that is changing as long as it is not "made eternal" through its return to "He who is" (*En. in Ps.* 134, 6).[12]

Immutability characterizes what is trancendental, Truth or *ratio*, by the same right as Being; we have already seen it in the texts that serve as prelude to the "commentaries" on Exodus 3:14. This attribute characterizes also what is Good. However, neither the aspect of Good nor that of Truth is first in the Augustinian commentaries on Exodus 3:14, even though that of what is Good is sometimes considerably developed there with regard to scriptural verses glorifying divine goodness (especially in the *En. in Ps.* 134, 4–6). It is the immutability of Being that is especially brought to light, as well as its consequence, ontological causality.

If Augustine does not get tired of repeating that God "is" because he is immutable, he is not reluctant either to assert that immutability follows from absolute Being: "Since God is the supreme essence, that is to say, he is in a supreme way, and for this reason he is immutable . . ." (*De ciu. dei* 12, 2). The first assertion corresponds to the way in which we have access to the knowledge of Being by means of this innate notion. The second corresponds more to a "deduction" of the attributes proceeding from Being, in as much as this expression may be used concerning Augustinian thought.

Indeed the question is raised: one could consider immutability in Augustine to be the reason for eternity, because he sometimes defines, indirectly, the second by means of the first: "We are distant from eternity to the extent to which we are changing" (*De Trin.* 4, 18, 24). But one must take care not to set these expressions hierarchically, more especially as opposite assertions are found in him: ". . . just as God is eternal, his wisdom is eternal, and for this reason immutable, as he himself is" (*De Trin.* 15, 20, 38). In the "commentaries" on Exodus 3:14, the eternity attribute often accompanies that of immutability, but often also it is used alone in order to mean the transcendence of *ipsum esse*. It has a sui generis wealth, which completes the notion of stability with that of a true present to which man has access by surmounting the "distension" of time and of the fall: eternity is God's "today" (*Conf.* 11, 13, 16; cf. *En. in Ps.* 121, 6; *In Io. Ep.* 2, 5; *En. in Ps.* 101, S. 2). This attribute thereby makes up one of the elements of the *simplex multiplicitas* and *multiplex simplicitas* praised by Karl Barth.[13]

3. *Simplicity and Propriety*

Whereas according to Gilson it is immutability which above all characterizes Augustine's God,[14] for M. Schmaus it is simplicity which is the reason for immutability.[15] It seems to us that these attributes correspond to problems that are not exactly the same, but whose answers mutually complete each other.

The notion of immutability is first in the discovery of God-Being. It is that which allows the *ratio* or the *mens*, purified, to have access to knowledge of "He who is" (Cf. *De ciu. dei* 8, 6). That is why it is so constantly found in the Augustinian "commentaries" on Exodus 3:14.

The notion of simplicity is that which is first in the order of reasons. It answers two fundamental problems for Augustine: that of the identity of the attributes in God, and that of the unity of the Persons in the Trinity. This attribute will take on increasing importance in his thought. It is asserted in certain relatively late "commentaries" on Exodus 3:14. In them, simplicity is defined by the identity of divine Being with its attributes, that is why it is not properly speaking a substance but rather an essence (*De Trin.* 7, 5, 10).

> He did not say: I am the Lord God, almighty, merciful, righteous; if he had said it, he would have told the truth in any case; but, doing away with all the attributes that could have been useful for naming him and designating him as God, he answered that he was called Being itself, and as if it were his name: "You will tell them this: He who is has sent me to you" (*En. in Ps.* 134, 6).

One also finds in the "commentaries" this other way, familiar to Augustine, of defining divine simplicity by the identity of being and having, which Gilson has pointed out represents one of the origins of the medieval distinction between essence and existence (*In Io. Eu.* 99, 4. Cf. *De ciu. dei* 11, 10, 1 and *De Trin.* 15, 17, 28).[16] It is thanks to Augustine's theory of the convergence of God's attributes to a single center (Being) that considerable progress was made in the theology of divine names.[17] If there is in God an identity between being and his attributes, it is because he is by himself the reason for his being, *in se habens ut sit* (*De Gen. ad litt.* 5, 16). Such is finally the ultimate foundation of the difference between God and the created being. God is what he has, he is by himself; the created being is not what it has, it only has a borrowed being. That is why the Scripture itself, according to Augustine, informs us that he alone deserves the name being in the proper sense of the word.

> . . . the assertions peculiar to God, of which no created being gives an example, are rare in the Holy Scripture. Let us take these words spoken to Moses: "I am who I am" or "He who is has sent me to you." Whereas the body and the mind are in a certain way, the Scripture would not have used this expression, if it had not wanted it to be understood in the proper sense (*De Trin.* 1, 1, 2).

4. *"To Be, You Also" or "to Return to Nonbeing"?*[18]

The ontological reality of the created being can only be grasped in a dialectic way, in its contrast with true Being, on the one hand, in its relation with it, on the other.

> Indeed, it is such that in comparison with it the created things are not. If they are not compared to it, they are, because they proceed from it; compared to it, they are not, because to truly be is to be immutable, something it alone is. For it is "is," as the good of goods is "good" (*En. in Ps.* 134, 6).

Therefore, if in Augustine there is no possible equivocation between God's being and that of the created beings,[19] there also isn't any real duality between them in this monism of Being inspired by Plotinus, but also by Porphyry, especially with regard to the nonbeing of evil.[20] It has been pointed out earlier: it is only after the discovery of "He who is," whose reality henceforth is more certain for Augustine than that of his own existence, that he is able to establish the relative reality of the created world (p. 99). Even then, he experiences somewhat of a difficulty in defining it.

> Thus, I say "the number of my days that is" and not that is not, or rather, a reality whose comprehension presents difficulties and obstacles that embarrass me: that is and that is not; for we cannot say that what is not stable is, nor that what comes and passes is not (*En. in Ps.* 38, 6).

This epistemological difficulty results from the nature of the created being: the latter escapes the grips of our knowledge to the extent to which it is nonbeing, but to the extent in which it partakes of God it is, and it is good, adhering to the rank that falls to it by right in the hierarchy of essences (*De ciu. dei* 12, 1, 2). Among them, the spiritual created being enjoys a unique privilege, for its end is not simply to serve the universal order, as others do, but to unite with God in a participation of knowledge and love. The possibility of this participation is implied in the divine Name, for the one who knows how to understand its meaning.

> For if I am what I am, if I am Being in itself, this means that I shall never be missed by men *(sic sum ipsum esse ut nolim hominibus deesse)* (*Sermon* 7, 7).

In the "commentaries" of Exodus 3:14 the theme of *magis esse*, i.e., of constitution in being, is no longer the object of new research or new developments on the part of Augustine, as it was in the *Philosophical Dialogues* and in the *De uera religione*. However, with the definition of "He who is" as immutable Being, it forms one of the leitmotives of these "commentaries." In which way can man attain it? The essential condition is adherence to Christ the mediator: man can only be deified if he recognizes God made man. "So that you may partake of the 'identical' one, he has first participated in your nature..." (*En. in Ps.* 121, 6).

If the little ones, the *paruuli*, can be satisfied with clinging to the cross of Christ while waiting to know in the hereafter the revelation of "He who is," it is from the point of view of the *intellectus* that the meaning of the divine Name is perceived and that, through anticipation, eternal life is ushered in. The thought effort, the strain of the contemplative gaze required by the conversion to true Being can from here below, even if it is in rare moments, allow us to transcend the time of the fall, that is to say, to transcend that which in us is changing and successive (*Denis Sermon* 2, 3; *En. in Ps.* 130, 12). The "distension" of this time scatters us and makes us come undone, in such a way that our life, considered from its existential point of view, is only a race towards death, just as the existence of things is nothing but a race towards nothingness.

> Think God, you will find "is".... In order to be, you too, transcend time.... When he attains it, at the end of a long contemplation effort, he participates, in the flash of an instant, in the eternal stability of Being... (*In Io. Eu.* 39, 8–10).

> Think if you can "I am who I am." Do not let yourself be tossed about by your feelings, do not let yourself be troubled by thoughts connected with the temporal world and your desires. Remain firmly attached to Being, remain firmly attached to Being itself. Where are you going? Remain in order to be able, you too, to be. But when shall we hold back the inconstant thought, when shall we cling to that which remains? When shall we be able to do it? (*Denis Sermon* 2, 5).

He who succeeds at it discovers, at the same time divine transcendence, and in contrast with it, his "total" unlikeness, for it results from his sin, which separates him from God:

> For he who has been able to have access to an understanding worthy of that which is, and who truly is, because he has been touched by a flashing ray emanating from the true Essence, that one sees himself completely below, very far and totally dissimilar... (*Sermon* 7, 5. Cf. *Conf.* 7, 10, 16 quoted p. 3).

Therefore, the nothingness theme always accompanies as a counterpoint that of Being, whether the soul turns away from it "in order for it also to be," or whether, on the contrary, for its misfortune, it chooses it. "He who goes away from Being goes towards nonbeing: (*En. in Ps.* 38, 22).

Augustine will not be reluctant, in the *Enarratio in Psalmum* 38 from which the sentence above was drawn, to apply the "nihilation" theme to the torments of hell. We shall see it concerning his ontological interpretation of the Scripture. Let us observe for now that, in his "commentaries" on *Ego sum qui sum*, the emphasis in general is placed on the eschatological aspect of participation. Indeed, beginning with the *De uera religione*, Augustine, for reasons of orthodoxy, has given up the idea of considering that the partaking of immortality based on the contemplation of wisdom can reach its end already in this life, as he used to assert, for the *pauci*, in the *De ordine* (1, 8, 24 and 2, 9, 26). But he still considers that the ontic reality of bliss begins to be constituted here below.[21]

At the conclusion of this analysis, we find out that the themes used by Augustine in the "commentaries" on Exodus 3:14 are those he has prepared beginning with the *De beata uita* in order to achieve the purpose of the *intellectus fidei* defined in the *Contra academicos* (3, 20, 44). These excerpts, relatively brief, express in general a solution Augustine already possessed, and that he repeats in various forms, according to the context of the time. In them one would look in vain for developments comparable to those of the *De immortalitate animae* and of the *De libero arbitrio*, for example, in which he strives to specify the ontological constitution of the soul; of the *De uera religione*, in which he interprets the doctrine of the resurrection of the bodies in the Neo-Platonic language of "being more"; of the last books of the *Confessions* and of the *De Genesi ad litteram*, in which he works out a Christian theogony by using the metaphysics of ἐπιστροφή.[22] Nothing similar is found in his "commentaries" on *Ego sum qui sum*, an exception possibly being made for some of them, for example in the *De Trinitate*, which bring definitions of divine simplicity and of *essentia* (*De Trin.* 5, 1, 1–2; 5, 2, 3; 7, 4, 9–5, 10). In this case, the theological pursuit that is found there is not typical of the fragment in question, but of the broader context in which the divine Name is called to mind.

The texts in which Augustine has used or commented on the Exodus 3:14 verse thus hardly bring any new elements relating to the study of the problems of being. In them, a reminder of already-familiar themes is especially found, often in an eloquent and beautiful form, which make them models of Christian anagogy, in genres as different as theological works, scriptural exegesis, and sermons. These texts represent however something sui generis in the development of Augustinian thought. If the ontological themes there are not new, the way in which Augustine uses them in his interpretation of the Bible combines with the *exercitatio scripturarum*, which replaces the *disciplina scientiarum* or rather absorbs it. It is this aspect of the "commentaries" on Exodus 3:14 that we shall now examine.

The "Metaphysics of Exodus"

The Ontological Interpretation of the Scripture

We know that the ontological interpretation of Exodus 3:14 has nothing original in itself and that it fits in the tradition of the Greek and Latin Fathers, the predecessors and contemporaries of Augustine who, after Philo of Alexandria, read in this text the meaning given to it by the translation of the Seventy: ἐγώ εἰμι ὁ ὤν. But the new fact, in Augustine, is the unequalled use he makes of this verse, in the abundance of his "commentaries" as much as in that of the scriptural parallels that he suggests for it.[23] It is in this that his originality lies, and it is this that has given a strong stimulus to the ontological speculation of medieval philosophy: as a proof, found among so many others, the "commentaries" on the same verse by Thomas Aquinas, which, partly through the instrumentality of Peter Lombard, are based on the very text of those by Augustine.

Thus, it is necessary for us to examine how Augustine read a certain number of Biblical texts in the light of the spiritual ontology that he developed in his philosophical works, into a pursuit of understanding faith which makes him discover correspondences between these texts and the way in which, with the Christian tradition, he interprets the revelation made to Moses.

If Augustine follows an already established tradition, to study it more thoroughly or to develop it, by comparing *Ego sum qui sum* with certain scriptural verses, such as Romans 1:20, he is the first among the Latin Fathers to have explicitly related the name revealed to Moses to Saint John's ἐγώ ἐιμι: "If you do not believe that 'I am,' you will die in your sins." (John 8:24, in *In Io. Eu.* 8, 11); "When you will lift up the Son of Man, then you will know that 'I am'" (John 8:28, in *In Io. Eu.* 40, 2–3); "Before Abraham was, 'I am'" (John 8:58, in *In Io. Epist.* 2, 5, and *In Io. Eu.* 43, 17–18). To our knowledge, this parallel is not found in the Greek Fathers before Saint John Chrysostom, who drew it very briefly, concerning John 8:58 (*Comm. on Saint John, Homelia* 55, 2, P.G. 59, c. 303), at about the same time as Augustine, around A.D. 391. It seems that, here and there, the preoccupation with answering the Aryans, who denied the divinity of the Son, contributed to the creation of this interpretation.[24] But it seems to us that this explanation must be inserted into an entire group of more complex factors, which little by little led the Fathers to develop an ontological reading of the Scripture and to discover correspondences concerning this between the Old and the New Testament.[25]

> And the Lord: "Amen, amen, I tell you, before Abraham was created, 'I am.' Feel the weight of these words and grasp this mystery." "Before Abraham was created": understand that "was created" is suitable for the human created being, but "I am" for the divine substance. "Was created," for Abraham is a created being. He did not say: Before Abraham was, I was, but: "Before Abraham was created" (and without me he would not have been created), "I am." He did not say either: "Before Abraham was created, I was created." For "in the beginning God created the heavens and the earth" [Gen. 1:1]; for "in the beginning was the Word"; [John 1:1]. "Before Abraham was created, I am." Recognize the Creator, distinguish the created being (*In Io. Eu.* 43, 17).[26]

Esse, which characterizes the Trinity, is attributed in its own right to the Word.

> "In the beginning was the Word" [John 1:1]. He is the identical one, he is like himself, he is always the same, he cannot change, that is to say: he is. It is the name he revealed to his servant Moses: "I am who I am," and "He who is has sent me" (*In Io. Eu.* 2, 2).

Such is the knowledge Augustine recognizes as that of the Platonic philosophers, according to his interpretation of Romans 1:20 and of the context of this verse.

> Thus, those of whom it is said "that they knew God" [Rom. 1:21] saw what John said: that all things were made through God's Word [John 1:3]. For that is equally found in the philosophers' books; and also that God has an only Son, through whom all things are. They succeeded in seeing what is, but they saw it from afar" (*In Io. Eu.* 2, 4).

Nevertheless, if the Platonic philosophers knew "what is," Augustine henceforth takes care to show that the assertion of immutability obtains its authority, in the first place, from the Scripture. The main texts that he usually quotes concerning this in the "commentaries" on Exodus 3:14 are found grouped in the following passage.

> It is necessary to base these truths that our faith possesses, in whatever way reason may have examined them closely, on the evidence found in the Holy Scripture; thus, those who, endowed with a lesser intelligence, cannot grasp them, will believe in them because of the divine authority and thereby will deserve to understand them. As for those who understand these truths but have little knowledge of the sacred books, let them not think that I have pulled them more out of my mind than out of these books. That God is immutable, that is written in the Psalms: "You will change them and they will change; but you, you are always the same" [Ps. 101:27]. And in the Book of Wisdom it is said of Wisdom itself: "Dwelling in itself, it renews all things" [Wisd. of Sol. 7:27]. Whence comes what the apostle Paul asserts: "To the invisible, incorruptible, only God" [1 Tim. 1:17], and the apostle James: "Every excellent endowment, every perfect gift is from above and comes down from the Father of lights, in whom there is no change nor the shadow of a change" [James 1:17]. Likewise, the Son expresses in a concise way that what God begot is still himself when he says: "I and the Father are one" (John 10:30) (*De nat. boni* 24, 24).[27]

If Augustine deliberately recognizes in the Scripture the repeated assertion of divine immutability and eternity, the Latin translation he uses leads him to find there the more abstract one of the "identical one," as well as the word "participation."

> . . . one must not understand in a carnal way "Jerusalem, which is built as a city and which partakes of the identical one" [Ps. 121:3] (*En. in Ps.* 121, 5–6).

This mistranslation gives us a very beautiful exegesis, which compares the *idipsum* not only with Exodus 3:14, but also with verses 27 and 28 of Psalm 101, often quoted in the "commentaries": "You will change them, and they will change, but you, you are the identical one." Elsewhere Augustine compares these two texts with the assertion of being, found in *Psalm* 89, verse 5.

> "You are from the beginning to the end of all ages. . . . " Now the remarkable fact is that the psalmist did not say: you were since the beginning of all ages, and you will be until the end of all ages, but he used the present in order to make us understand that God's substance is absolutely immutable, that one cannot say that it was nor that it will be, but only that it is. Whence the spoken words: "I am who I am," and "He who is has

> sent me to you," and again "You will change them and they will change but you, you are always the same and your years will not pass away." Here is this eternity, which has become our refuge so that in it and in order to remain there we flee from the mutability of time here below" (*En. in Ps.* 89, 2–5).

Let us point out also the parallel between Exodus 3:14 and Isaiah 46:4: "I am, and even to your old age I am" (*En. in Ps.* 112, 1–2) and the one in Malachi 3:6; "I am the Lord and I do not change," that the Aryan bishop Maximinus contrasts with Augustine in order to show the immutability of the Father in opposition to the Son's nature, which would be subject to change. To answer him, Augustine compares Psalm 101, verses 26 to 28, with these two texts, and recalls that Saint Paul, in the Epistle to the Hebrews 1, 10–11, applies this passage to the Son (*Contra Maxim.* 1, 19 and 2, 26). We learn here of one of the repercussions of the anti-Aryan controversy led by Augustine on the development of his "metaphysics of Exodus."

If this metaphysics is characterized by putting the definition of immutable Being in relation to a series of important scriptural texts, this aspect is completed, as we saw earlier, by the assertion that the created being is nonbeing: it is the dialectic of Being and nothingness that Augustine finds in Moses and in Plato:

> . . . when Moses asks to know the name of the one who was sending him to the Hebrew people to bring them out of Egypt, he received from God, through an angel's mouth, the following answer: "I am who I am and you will say to the children of Israel: he who is has sent me to you"; which means that, compared to the one who truly is, because he is immutable, the changing created things are not . . . " (*De ciu. dei* 8, 12).

This truth, which complements knowledge of the one with the name "He who is," is found by Augustine in an explicit way in other scriptural texts that aim at making man conscious of his own nothingness.

> "Man is like nothingness" (Ps. 143:3); and yet you showed yourself to him and you value him. . . . But all these fleeting, changing, terrestrial things, all that passes, if it is compared to the Truth that said: "I am who I am," all that is called nothingness. All that vanishes in time like smoke in the air. And what could be added to what the apostle James said to bring back the proud ones to humbleness: "What, he said, is your life? A mist that appears for a little time and then vanishes" (James 4:15) (*En. in Ps.* 143, 11; cf. *En. in Ps.* 38, 6–10 and 22).

Augustine also finds in the Scripture the assertion of this other Platonic theme that complements those we have just mentioned: the conversion constitutive of being and its opposite, nihilation. We have already pointed out this "partaking of the identical one" that, on the strength of the translation he uses, Augustine reads in verse 3 of Psalm 121. He is also misled by the translation of Psalm 38, verse 5: "the number of my days which is," instead of "what is the measure of my days" (*Jer. Bible*). The philologically inaccurate way in which he understood some of the verses of this Psalm is the reason for having one of his very beautiful "commentaries" on *Ego sum qui sum.*

"Lord, let me know my end, and the number of my days, this number which is". . . . Let me know the number of my days, but the number which is.—What then? The number of these days in the midst of which you exist is not?—By looking closer at this, it becomes clearly apparent that it is not; if I cling to it, it is as if it were; but if I transcend it, it is not. If, pulling myself away from these days that pass, I contemplate things above, if I compare what is transitory to what is eternal, I see what truly is: can one imagine something that is more than this "is"? Shall I dare to say of my days that they are? Shall I say that these days are, and shall I unthinkingly apply this word that is so great to the flow of the ephemeral things here below? For I who pass, I am not, so to speak, so that I am deprived of him who said: "I am who I am." Will a number of days exist then?—Yes, and it truly is, it is without end. . . . I am looking for this simple "is," this true "is," this authentic "is," this "is" whose seat is celestial Jerusalem, my Lord's bride-to-be, in which there will be neither death nor decline, in which there will not be a day that passes, but a day that remains, in which today is not preceded by yesterday nor driven away by tomorrow. This is, I said, the day to which these words refer: "let me know the number of my days which is' " (*En. in Ps.* 38, 6).

That the partaking of being is a common theme for the Greeks and the Christians, Augustine finds the sure proof in Saint Paul:

. . . moreover (the deity) is not far from each one of us. It is in him indeed that we have life, movement, and being. As, furthermore, some of your people have said: "For we are also his offspring" (Acts 17, 27–28).[28]

Just as Augustine finds the partaking of being asserted by the Scripture, he finds there the assertion of its opposite: nonbeing affecting the one who turns away from God.

"The way of the sinners will be annihilated" (*En. in Ps.* 1, 6).

How should this annihilation be understood? We find in the *Enarratio in Psalmum* 38 an echo of the problem Augustine tried to work out in the *De immortalitate animae* and in the *De libero arbitrio*: if it is by turning towards God-Being that the soul is constituted in him, if it "is less" by turning away from him, how is it that in an extreme case it is not completely annihilated? Augustine had given a metaphysical answer to this problem, from the point of view of the *intellectus fidei*, by distinguishing in the soul two levels of participation: the first, indestructible, that of simple existence, the second, which can be acquired or lost, that of true Being.[29] In the exegesis of Psalm 38, Augustine is satisfied with bringing a scriptural argument to the question that seems to be raised by Idithun's complaint: "and I shall be no more."[30]

But a question is raised: how will he be no more? He has not yet gone towards rest; may God let him get there; certainly Idithun will depart and he will go towards rest. But let us take someone else, not Idithun, not a man already turned towards the hereafter: a miser, a usurper, unjust, proud, vain, full of haughtiness, holding in contempt the poor man sitting at his door, can it be said about this man: he will not be? Thus what does this mean: "I shall not be"? If the wicked rich man were not, then who was the victim of the flames, who desired passionately that the poor Lazarus moisten his tongue with a drop of water, and who then was saying "Father Abraham, send me Lazarus" (Luke 16:24)? (*En. in Ps.* 38, 22).

We have seen that in the "commentaries" Augustine defines sin as choosing nothingness and the sinner's life as walking towards nothingness, but this *Enarratio* contains one of the passages in which the eschatological application of the theme is the most clearly shown, since the torments of hell themselves are described as a kind of nihilation without end:

> Why then did Idithun say: "I shall not be," if it weren't because he knows what it is to be and not to be? . . . For being remains, things here below are changing, mortal, fragile, and the eternal torments themselves are only perpetual deterioration, an infinity of finitude. . . . "Forgive me so that I may be refreshed before I depart, and I shall be no more." For if you do not forgive me, I shall go far from you for all eternity; far from whom? From the one who said: "I am who I am"; from the one who said: "Say to the children of Israel: he who is has sent me to you." For the one who goes contrary to what truly is goes to nonbeing (*En. in Ps.* 38, 22).

Let us finally point out that Augustine corroborates the theme of knowledge consitutive of being with a text by Saint John.

> For this contemplation is promised to us as the end of all our actions and as the fulfilment of our joys in eternity. "We are God's children, and what we shall be does not yet appear. We know that, when he appears, we shall be like him, for we shall see him as he is' [1 John 3:2]. For what he revealed to his servant Moses: "I am who I am. You will say to the children of Israel: He who is has sent me to you," this, we shall behold it when we shall live in eternity. For he spoke thus: "eternal life is that they know you, you the only true God, and Jesus Christ whom you have sent" (John 17:3) (*De Trin.* 1, 8, 17).

Then the "region of unlikeness" that man discovers in himself when he discovers "He who is" will be annihilated, and the final conversion will permanently consecrate the victory of Being over nothingness.[31]

The God of Abraham, Isaac and Jacob

Before concluding our discussion of the "metaphysics of Exodus," as it is characterized in the passages that comment on the Exodus verse 3:14, it is absolutely necessary to draw attention to the scriptural text that is compared the most often with this verse, beginning with the time Augustine discovered its complementary connection with the former, that is to say since the *Enarratio in Psalmum* 121, 6. This complementary text is the Exodus verse 3:15: "I am the God of Abraham, the God of Isaac, and the God of Jacob." Augustine will end by granting such an importance to this second verse that he will not hesitate to assert in *Sermon* 7 (1, 5, 7) that it creates, with the first, "a sort of manuscript containing the sum of the divine mysteries," the first expressing what God is in himself, the second the economy of salvation. Thus, if the wisdom name is inaccessible to the *paruuli*, these "little ones" that we are all at one time or another, they can always resort to the "consolation name" (*En. in Ps.* 101, S. 2, 10). It is the same dialectic between the name God has in himself and the one he has for us

(*Sermon* 7, 1, 5, 7); the name we cannot understand and the one we can understand (*En. in Ps.* 143, 4–6); the eternal name and the temporal name, whose function is to lead us from time to eternity, to "make us eternal" (*En. in Ps.* 101, S. 2, 10; *En. in Ps.* 134, 4–6).

> As Moses saw himself so inferior to what he was hearing from the one he could not see and so powerless to know him, he, who was completely burning with the desire to see him, said to God with whom he was speaking: "Show yourself to me" [Ex. 33:18]. Because to discover himself so unlike facing the transcendent Essence made him despair, but God, seeing his fear, lifted up again the one who was despairing, as if he were saying to him: "Because I said 'I am who I am' and 'He who is has sent me to you,' you understood what Being is and you despair of attaining it. But be hopeful again: 'I am the God of Abraham, the God of Isaac and the God of Jacob.' For if I am what I am, if I am Being in itself, this means that I shall never be missed by men." Therefore, in whatever way we may seek God and examine closely what is, actually he is "not far from us. For it is in him that we have life, movement, and being" (Acts 17:27–29).
>
> Thus, let us praise his Essence ineffably and let us love his mercy (*Sermon* 7, 7).

If the approach necessary for partaking of the God of Exodus and for being "made eternal" is faith, the ultimate finality remains the vision of "what is" (in the hereafter for the "little ones," but already begun here below for the great spirits). There is no opposition, rather a progression in knowledge from the God of Abraham, Isaac, and Jacob to that of the philosophers: those who philosophize without faith remain, it is true, "in the distance," but the vision of the "great ones" is none other than their intuition of Being.

> It would thus be better not to see with the mind what is, and yet not to stray from the cross of Christ than to see with the mind what is and to despise the cross of Christ. On the other hand, if this is possible, it is still better, and even excellent, to see where it is necessary to go while holding on to the one who carries us to our goal. That, the great minds succeeded in doing, high mountains completely illuminated by the sun of justice: they succeeded in doing it and they saw what is. It is by seeing it that Saint John said: "In the beginning was the Word, and the Word was with God, and the Word was God" (John 1:1) (*In Io. Eu.* 2, 4).

Translation or Treason?

Such are the main correlations Augustine finds, or sometimes, trusting faulty translations, thinks he has found with the main themes of his spiritual ontology. It has been pointed out that as a general rule these themes are not developed in the brief excerpts represented by the Augustinian "commentaries" on Exodus 3:14 as they are in the writings Augustine intended for the thorough study of this or that aspect of his ontology. And especially these "commentaries" do not give some of the most profound implications of this ontology and of the *intellectus fidei* it proposes. We mean to refer to those found in the last books of the *Confessions* and in the *De Genesi ad litteram* in which Augustine sets up a true Christian theogony.[32] What we have called here, repeating Gilson's expression, a "metaphysics of Exodus," thus does not reflect the entire Augustinian ontology in all its breadth. Or it would be necessary to give this suggestive expression a much more comprehensive meaning, which would relate at the same time to the mystery of creation, to that of the original fall, and to their mysterious analogies, more clearly seen from the viewpoint of the final return, which makes the metaphysics of Exodus coincide with the metaphysics of conversion.

The main interest of such an analysis, which should be combined with a broader study, is, in our view, to have shown that Augustine developed into a true ontological reading of the Scripture what his predecessors had initiated in an incomplete way. Must we, with Gilson and most of the modern exegetes, blame him for having inserted into the Scripture notions of a Platonic origin that would be foreign to the revealed text? Shouldn't we rather be grateful to him for having expressed the main themes of this revelation in a language that was accessible to the people of his culture? For the problem that faces us concerning this appears to be that of the interpenetration of two spiritualities and of two cultures more than that of reason and Revelation, philosophy and faith. If the "Platonists' books" had only offered Augustine a theoretical speculation on immutable Being, they would not have succeeded in helping him penetrate the deep meaning of the revealed truths. It is because the teaching passed on by these books aims at the deliverance of the soul that they allowed the Christian neophyte imbued with Hellenic culture to elaborate this ontology of spiritual life that we might hazard to call a soteriological ontology.

NOTES

1. See A. Maxsein, *Philosophia cordis*, in *Augustinus Magister*, 1, p. 368 ff.

2. This concerns the Latin translation available to Augustine. Cf. Dhorme, 2, p. 977: "Through sanctions against the transgression you chastise man and, like the moth, you gnaw the object of your desire. . . ."

3. See J. J. O'Meara, *The Young Augustine: the Growth of Augustine's Mind up to his Conversion* (London: 1954), p. 13.

4. Cf. *Sermo* 7, 7, CC 41, p. 75.

5. See the main part of the text.

6. See concerning this A.-M. La Bonnardière, *Recherches de chronologie augustinienne* (Paris: Etudes Augustiniennes, 1965), p. 29 ff. and *Biblia Augustiniana, Le Livre de la Sagesse* (Paris: Etudes Augustiniennes, 1970), p. 109 ff.

7. See concerning this G. Madec, *Connaissance de Dieu et Action de grâces: Essai sur les citations de l' "Ep. aux Romains" 1, 18–25 dans l'oeuvre de Saint Augustin*, in *Recherches Augustiniennes*, 2 (Paris: 1962), 273 ff.

8. See M. Harl, *Origène et la fonction révélatrice du Verbe incarné* (Paris: Seuil, 1958), p. 141 ff.

9. See *Concilium Vaticanum, Sessio 3 Constitutio apostolica de fide catholica* (Denzinger nos. 1785 and 1795) and *Iusiurandum contra errores modernismi* (Denzinger no. 2145). Cf. our article on "La 'Métaphysique de l'Exode' selon Thomas d'Aquin," in Dieu et l'Être. Exégèses d'Exode 3, 14 et de Coran 20, 11–24 (Paris: Etudes Augustiniennes, 1978), p. 254.

10. See p. 117, the list of Augustinian "commentaries" on Exodus 3:14.

11. E. Gilson, *L'Être et l'Essence* (Paris: Vrin, 1948), p. 35.

12. See E. Fortin, *Christianisme et culture philosophique au cinquième siècle* (Paris: Etudes Augustiniennes, 1959), p. 101 ff.

13. See "La 'Métaphysique de l'Exode' selon Thomas d'Aquin," p. 255.

14. E. Gilson, *Philosophie et Incarnation Saint Augustin* (Montréal: 1947), p. 12 ff.; *Le Thomisme* (Paris: VRIN selon 19485), p. 73 ff., *Introduction à la philosophie chrétienne* (Paris: 1960), p. 105.

15. M. Schmaus, *De psychologische Trinitätslehre des heiligen Augustins* (Münster: 1927), p. 85 ff.

16. E. Gilson, *Introduction à l'étude de Saint Augustin* (Paris: 1943), p. 286 ff.

17. See C. De Moré-Pontgibaud, *Du fini à l'infini* (Paris: Aubier, 1957), p. 15 ff.

18. *En. in Ps.* 38, 22 and *In. Io. Eu. Tr.* 39, 8.

19. See J. Chaix-Ruy, *Saint Augustin, temps et histoire* (Paris: 1956), p. 121.

20. See O. Du Roy, *L'Intelligence de la foi en la Trinité*, p. 193 ff.

21. See R. Holte, *Béatitude et sagesse* (Paris: 1962), p. 220.

22. See earlier in the text 1, 5, p. 28 ff.; 2, 2, p. 52 ff.; 3, 2, p. 84 ff.; 4, 3, p. 106 ff.

23. See C. De Moré-Pontgibaud, *Du fini à l'infini*, p. 15 ff.

24. See J. Quasten, *Initiation aux Pères de l'Église*, vol. 3 (Paris: Cerf, 1963), p. 615 ff.

25. Saint John's **ἐγώ εἰμι** is a reminder of Isaiah 43:10:

    Become witnesses for me, and I, I am a witness, said the Lord God, and the son whom I have chosen, that you may know, that you may believe, and that you may understand that I am (ὅτι ἐγώ εἰμι). Before me there was no other God, after me there shall not be any. I am God, and besides me there is no savior. I declared, I saved, I proclaimed... It is I, I am God and there is none who can deliver from my hand. Cf. Deut. 32:39: See, see that I am (ὅτι ἐγώ εἰμι) and there is no God beside me. I kill and I make alive, I shall strike and I shall heal, and there is none that can deliver out of my hand.

26. We shall notice that in *In Io. Epist. Tr.* 2, 5, John 8:58 is compared to John 1:3: "All things were created through him," to Ps. 101:28 and to Ps. 2:7: "Today I have begotten you," Augustine frequently attributes these texts to the Son.

27. Verses 26 to 28 of Psalm 101 make up one of the main harmonics of Exodus 3:14. Cf. *En. in Ps.* 101, S. 2, 10; *En. in Ps.* 121, 5–6; *En. in Ps.* 38, 6; *En. in Ps.* 80, 2–5 and 15; *Contra Maximin.* 2, 26. In *De Trin.* 1, 1, 2; 1 Tim 6:16; James 1:17 and Ps. 101:27–28 are grouped with Ex. 3:14.

28. Cf. *Conf.* 7, 9, 15. P. Courcelle, in *Recherches sur les Confessions de Saint Augustin* (Paris: 1950), p. 31, points out that this parallel is due to Saint Ambrose (*De Isaac*, 1, 78; *Enn.* 1, 6, 9). P. Henry in *Plotin et l'Occident*, points out concerning this another text by Plotinus, very close to that of Saint Paul, *Enn.* 6, 9, 9, 7–11. Also see P. Courcelle, *Un vers d'Épiménide dans le "Discours sur l'Aréopage" in Rev. des Études Grecques* 76 (1963), 404 ff. and G. Folliet, *Les Citations des Actes 17, 28 et Tite 1, 12* in *Rev. Ét. Augustin.*, 2 (1965), 293 ff. Among the Augustinian "commentaries" on Exodus 3:14 we find again the Paulinian quotation in *De Gen. ad litt.* 6, 16 and *De ciu. Dei* 8, 10, in which Augustine characterizes this text as expressing "this great truth that very few are capable of understanding."

29. *De lib. arb.* 3, 7, 21.

30. Ps. 38:14. Trans. Jersualem Bible: "Turn your eyes away that I may breathe before I disappear." ("Remitte mihi ut refrigerer priusquam eam, et amplius iam non ero.")

31. Cf. *De uera rel.* 12, 25: "uincit enim essentia nihilum," and sic "absorbetur mors in uictoriam" (1 Cor. 15:54).

32. See note 59, chap. 4, p. 86.

List of Augustinian Commentaries on Exodus 3:14

We owe this list to the Benedictines of Beuron, through the intervention of A.-M. La Bonnardière.

1. *De uera rel.* 49, 97.
2. *De fide et symb.* 4, 6.
3. *En. in Ps.* 1, 6.
4. *En. in Ps.* 9, 11.
5. *De doctr. christ.* I, 32, 35.
6. *Conf.* 7, 10, 16.
7. *Conf.* 13, 31, 46.
8. *Contra Felicem* 2, 18.
9. *De natura boni* 19, 19 and 24, 24.
10. *De Trin.* 1, 8, 17.
11. *En. in Ps.* 121, 5.
12. *In Io. Eu. Tr.* 2, 2–4.
13. *En in Ps.* 127, 5.
14. *En. in Ps.* 130, 12.
15. *In Io. Ep. Tr.* 2, 2–4.
16. *En. in Ps.* 101, S. 2, 10.
17. *De Gen. ad litt.* 5, 16.
18. *Sermon* 7, 1, 5.
19. *Sermon* 6, 1, 2, 4, 5.
20. *En. in Ps.* 103, S. 1, 3.
21. *En. in Ps.* 80, 14–15.
22. *En. in Ps.* 143, 11.
23. *En. in Ps.* 134, 4–6.
24. *En. in Ps.* 49, 14.
25. *En. in Ps.* 38, 6–10 and 22.
26. *De perf. iust. hom.* 14, 30.
27. *De Trin.* 5, 1, 1–2; 5, 2–3.
28. *De Trin.* 7, 4, 9–7, 5, 10.
29. *De ciu. dei* 8, 8–12.
30. *En. in Ps.* 82, 14.
31. *En. in Ps.* 89, 2–5 and 15.
32. *De ciu. dei* 12, 1–2.
33. *In Io. Eu. Tr.* 38, 8–11.
34. *In Io. Eu. Tr.* 39, 7–8.
35. *In Io. Eu. Tr.* 40, 2–3.
36. *In Io. Eu. Tr.* 43, 17–18.
37. *En. in Ps.* 104, 3–4.
38. *De Trin.* 1, 1, 2–3.
39. *En. in Ps.* 112, 1–2.
40. *Sermon* 156, 6.
41. *Sermon* 341, 8, 10.
42. *In Io. Eu. Tr.* 99, 4–5.
43. *Contra Maxim.* 1, 19.
44. *Contra Maxim.* 2, 26 (10, 11, 14).
45. *Denis Sermon* 2, 5.
46. *Caillau and Saint-Yves Sermon* 1, 57, 1–2.
47. *Sermonum fragmenta*, P.L. 39, c. 1725–26.

BIBLIOGRAPHY

Blondel, M. *Correspondance philosophique de M. Blondel et L. Laberthonnière.* Paris: Seuil published and presented by C. Tresmontant, 1961.

Blondel, M. *L'Etre et les êtres.* Paris: P.U.F., 1962.

Burnaby, J. *Amor Dei: A Study of the Religion of St. Augustine.* London: 1942.

Chaix-Ruy, J. *Saint Augustin: Temps et histoire.* Paris: Etudes Augustiniennes, 1956.

Gilson, E. *Introduction à l'étude de Saint Augustin.* Paris: Vrin, 1943.

Gilson, E. *L'Esprit de la philosophie médiévale.* Paris: Vrin, 1942.

Holte, R. *Béatitude et sagesse: Saint Augustin et le problème de la fin de l'homme dans la philosophie ancienne.* Paris: Etudes Augustiniennes, 1962.

Körner, F. *Das Sein und der Mensch: Die existentielle Seinsentdeckung des jungen Augustin.* Freiburg-München: Karl Alber, 1959.

Lorenz, R. *"Fruitio dei" bei Augustin,* in *Zeitschrift für Kirchengeschichte* 63 (1950), 75–132.

Madec, G. *Connaissance de Dieu et action de grâces: Essai sur les citations de l'Epître aux Romains, 1, 18–25, dans l'oeuvre de Saint Augustin,* in *Recherches Augustiniennes,* 2 (1963), 273–309.

Mandouze, A. *Saint Augustin: L'aventure de la raison et de la grâce.* Paris: Etudes Augustiniennes, 1968.

Marrou, H. *Saint Augustin et la fin de la culture antique,* 1–2. Paris: De Boccard, 1938–1949.

O'Connell, R. J. *The Plotinian Fall of the Soul in St. Augustine,* in *Traditio* 19 (1963), 1–35.

O'Connell, R. J. *The Riddle of Augustine's "Confessions": A Plotinian Key,* in *International Philosophical Quarterly* 4 (1964), 327–72.

Roy, O. Du. *L'Intelligence de la foi en la Trinité selon Saint Augustin: Genèse de sa théologie trinitaire jusqu'en 391.* Paris: Etudes Augustiniennes, 1966.

Theiler, W. *Porphyrios und Augustin.* Halle: M. Migmeyer, 1933, reedited in *Forschungen zum Neuplatonismus* (Berlin: 1966), 160–251.

Solignac, A. *L'Existentialisme de Saint Augustin,* in *Nouvelle Revue Théologique,* 70 (1948), 3–19.

Trouillard, J. *Proclos, éléments de théologie. Traduction, introduction et notes.* Paris: Aubier Montaigne, 1965.

Wytzes, J. *Bemerkungen zu dem neuplatonischen Einfluss in Augustins "de Genesi ad litteram,"* in *Zeitschrift für die neutestamentliche Wissenschaft* 39 (1940), (1941), 137–151.

Index